Review of Scottish Culture 2

To Dr I F Grant

Founder of the Highland Folk Museum

Review of Scottish Culture 2

Edited by
ALEXANDER FENTON
with
Hugh Cheape and Rosalind K Marshall

JOHN DONALD PUBLISHERS LTD
and
THE NATIONAL MUSEUMS OF SCOTLAND
EDINBURGH

Address for Reviews, Correspondence, etc:
Editors, ROSC, National Museums of Scotland,
Queen Street, Edinburgh EH2 1JD

Address for Subscriptions:
John Donald Publishers Ltd, 138 St Stephen Street,
Edinburgh, EH3 5AA, Scotland

ROSC is published annually. It is a well-illustrated journal.
Price £5 per issue

Published with the aid of a generous grant
from an anonymous donor.

Phototypeset by Burns & Harris Ltd, Dundee.
Printed and bound in Great Britain by Bell & Bain Ltd, Glasgow.

Editorial Notes and Comments

The *Review of Scottish Culture* (*ROSC*) has been widely welcomed in its first year. Its combination of accurate, fresh information and readability has been favourably commented on, and, unlike many journals which live by subscriptions alone, it is selling in the shops. We shall continue to produce good material, and in addition, we intend to develop 'Editorial Notes and Comments', so that up-to-date events and projects can be made known. In this context we wish to draw attention to two bodies whose activities are having a beneficial effect on the quality of the landscape of Scotland.

The first is the *Farm Buildings Association*, a UK body organised into regional branches. We learn from the President of the South of Scotland Branch, Tony Winkle, FRICS, himself a practical farmer with a small farm in Peeblesshire, that a Farm Buildings Award Scheme is to be inaugurated in 1985. This relates to farm buildings or groups of farm buildings in the South of Scotland, erected or extensively altered since 1980. A similar scheme has been running in the North Area for many years. The Scheme is of considerable importance in encouraging farmers, architects and planners to think hard about the ways in which improvements can be matched with their surroundings, and deserves to be more publicly known.

The second is the *Saltire Society's Patrick Geddes Planning Award*. Patrick Geddes made Scotland one of the pioneering nations in modern environmental planning. In conjunction with the Royal Town Planning Institute, the Saltire Society is keeping the cultural traditions of Patrick Geddes alive through this award, the purpose of which is to promote public interest and to encourage professional excellence in the art of town and country planning. The multi-disciplinary nature of planning is fully reflected in the composition of the adjudication panel, which covers the

> Royal Incorporation of Architects in Scotland
> Royal Scottish Academy
> Institute of Directors
> Scottish Society of Directors of Planning
> Royal Institution of Chartered Surveyors
> Saltire Society
> Institute of Civil Engineers
> Royal Town Planning Institute
> Royal Scottish Geographical Society

The Panel is chaired by the Rt Hon Lord Fraser of Tullybelton.

The first awards were made at Saltire House on 25 January 1985. There were 27 entries from all over Scotland. The winning entry was that of the Lesmahagow Environmental Action Project, planned and executed by Clydesdale District Council in association with the Scottish Development Agency and the Scottish Civic Trust. When presenting the award, Lord Fraser quoted the panel's assessment as follows:

> Prior to the project, Lesmahagow was a community in severe decline with a run down environment, and the panel found the initiative quite outstanding as an example of what can be achieved by all parties concerned working together to tackle problems on a broad and integrated basis. Through a comprehensive programme of work (including landscaping, housing improvement, provision of rehabilitated industrial premises, establishment of a branch library, creation of recreational facilities and upgrading of the local school) Lesmahagow has been remarkably transformed into an attractive community in which to live and work. We regard the project as a significant contribution to the art of town and country planning in Scotland.

Three other projects received commendations: the Loch Lomond Local (Subject) Plan, the Lochore Meadows Land Reclamation Project and Country Park, and the Urban Conservation Strategy for Moray. Lesmahagow's reward was a bronze plaque cast from a portrait medallion of Patrick Geddes sculpted by the French artist Georges Durand. Authors of all successful entries received illuminated certificates specially designed for the Patrick Geddes Planning Award by Campbell Sandilands, a young artist from Scone, who is pursuing postgraduate studies at the Duncan of Jordanstone College of Art in Dundee.

We wish also to draw attention to *The Eric Cregeen Fellowship Fund*. Eric R. Cregeen died in 1983, in the prime of a busy life. As Assistant Director of the Manx National Museum he was responsible for a comprehensive survey of Manx life and tradition. As Resident Tutor in Argyll for the Extra-Mural Department of Glasgow University he organised classes and lectured throughout the Argyll mainland and islands. He helped to form many local history societies, undertook a number of important archaeological excavations and carried out invaluable work on the records of the Argyll Estate. In the School of Scottish Studies, as Lecturer, Senior Lecturer and Reader, he was responsible for research and teaching in the field of social organisation, contributing a wealth of data on tape, film and photograph to the oral and material culture archives. He pioneered the combination of written and oral sources for the study of Highland and Hebridean communities and was a founder and leading member of the Scottish Oral History Group.

His breadth of view and multidisciplinary approach and his capacity for kindling enthusiasm and a spirit of enquiry in those with whom he was associated, marked his life and work. It is appropriate that he should be honoured through the establishment of a fund to support fellowships on research topics allied to his own wide interests, allowing students and scholars to become better acquainted with Scottish material, and researchers based in Scotland to make use of resources in other countries.

Contributions to the fund should be sent to: The Eric Cregeen Fellowship Fund, School of Scottish Studies, University of Edinburgh, 27 George Square, Edinburgh EH8 9LD, made payable to 'The School of Scottish Studies, University of Edinburgh', endorsed on the reverse with the words 'The Eric Cregeen Fellowship'. Deed of covenant forms are available.

Readers may help the cause of Scottish history and culture in other ways too. Two important Dictionaries should be mentioned, one of which, the *Concise Scots Dictionary*, was published in 1985. This is the first one-volume dictionary ever to cover the Scots language from the earliest records to the present day.

It is in the main an updated distillation of two major works, the *Scottish National Dictionary* and the *Dictionary of the Older Scottish Tongue*. It is simpler to use than the parent dictionaries, though it will guide readers to their use. Its wealth of information has been arranged to be as clear as possible. A full Introduction includes a detailed guide to the use of the Dictionary and also a history of the Scots language.

The Dictionary itself contains not only meanings, but also spelling variants; pronunciation, where this is likely to cause difficulty; grammatical information; dating; geographical distribution; idioms and phrases; etymologies; specialist vocabulary, for example legal and mining terms; and details of Scottish life past and present.

The *Concise Scots Dictionary* defines the Scots language as the language of Lowland Scotland, from Shetland to the South-West and the Borders. It gives meanings, pronunciations, and origins of all classes of Scots words from the twelfth century to the present day including:

Dialect words, such as Aberdeenshire farming terms
Words used by famous authors such as Dunbar, Burns, Scott and MacDiarmid
Words in general use, such as:

— Scots words with no English equivalent	e.g. dreich
— Scots words with English equivalent	loch
— Words with different meaning in Scots from southern standard English	close
— Words for Scottish objects, customs, institutions etc.	kilt, first-foot, Court of Session

The Dictionary has been produced in Edinburgh by a team of lexicographers under the auspices of The Scottish National Dictionary Association Limited. The Editor-in-Chief is Mairi Robinson. It is published by Aberdeen University Press, who also publish the *Dictionary of the Older Scottish Tongue* and distribute the *Scottish National Dictionary*. The price is £17.50.

The second Dictionary is the *Dictionary of the Older Scottish Tongue* (*DOST*). This very basic source not only gives meanings and etymologies, but in addition, every sense of every word is illustrated by quotations. There are about two million of them, taken from hundreds of printed and manuscript sources of all kinds. If a reader looks up a word, and studies the quotations, he will often get an astonishing amount of accurate insight into the word's background. The

Dictionary is an absolute treasure-house of information, on every aspect of Scottish life and culture.

Publication began in 1931, and from then till about 1980 it was done through the University of Chicago Press. This link with the United States was due to its first editor, Sir (then Dr) William Craigie, who was for a time Professor of English in the University of Chicago. His scheme for a dictionary of Older Scots, covering the 600 years from the 1100s down to 1700, went back to 1915 when he first wrote about his intention in a private letter to a friend, William Grant. By 1921, he had a paid assistant working on it. It is a measure of the vision of this very enterprising Scot that he was also editor of the *Dictionary of American English*.

Dictionaries of quality take much time and much dedication to produce. Sir William Craigie kept on editing *DOST* until 1954, when he was 86 years old. Long life and lexicography, apparently, go together. The editorial mantle was taken on increasingly, from 1948, by A. J. (now Professor) Aitken, of Edinburgh University. Harry Watson is now the main editor. The work is carried on in Edinburgh, and publication is being undertaken by Aberdeen University Press.

DOST is still far from being completed. Since 1931, five volumes covering the letters A to P have been published. The speed of production of the small and hard-working staff was reduced by 1980 due to shortage of funds brought about by cuts in university grants. Tremendous efforts have to be made to ensure that this great work, important not only for the Scots language but for all users of English in all its shapes and forms, is completed from A to Z as quickly as possible.

A major means of getting funds to maintain staffing levels has been through the setting up of the *Friends of the Dictionary of the Older Scottish Tongue*. This body was launched in March 1984 by the Countess of Strathmore. Initial funding came from the Graham Hunter Foundation, Inc., and that Foundation is continuing to give an annual grant for five years. The Friends are now providing money for two additional posts, though only on the basis of limited-term contracts.

Much more help is needed for continuity and greater speed. Readers of *ROSC* who wish to be associated with this great enterprise should send their donations to Dr A. Fenton, Secretary of the Friends of the DOST, at the National Museums address.

Finally, we congratulate the National Museum of Antiquities of Scotland on acquiring for the nation *Bonnie Prince Charlie's Silver Canteen*. This remarkable 'picnic-set', as the papers described it, consists of a 7 in. high by 4⅜ in. wide silver case, into which are ingeniously fitted two plain drinking beakers, no doubt for wine; a quaich-like cup for stronger spirits; two knives, two forks, two spoons, a cruet, a nutmeg grater and corkscrew and a combined marrow scoop and teaspoon, all of silver gilt.

The case and the beakers are fully marked, showing that they were made in Edinburgh by Ebenezer Oliphant, in 1740-41. Oliphant was a Jacobite, the 8th son of James Oliphant, 5th Laird of Gask. He was born on 7 March 1713, and was apprenticed to James Mitchelson, goldsmith in Edinburgh, on 13 September 1727. He became a well-known goldsmith, producing outstanding work of which the National Museum has several examples, including a gold and enamel ring with the initials of 21 Jacobite martyrs. He died in 1798. Recent research suggests that the Canteen may have been found amongst the contents of the Prince's covered wagon at Culloden, and given by the Duke of Cumberland to his ADC, George Keppel, Lord Bury, son of the 2nd Earl of Albemarle. It remained with the Albemarle family until 1963, when it was sold to a Scottish collector.

It then passed through a number of dealers' hands, and in 1984 there was a real danger of its export to America. The National Museum lodged a successful objection with the Export of Works of Art Committee, and was allowed three months to raise the money. To do so, it set up a public appeal launched by the well-known actor, director, broadcaster and writer, Tom Fleming. Public support was extremely gratifying. The Queen Mother and Prince Charles both contributed, and a personal message was received from Her Majesty the Queen. Over 600 individuals, business firms, banks, trusts and societies sent contributions from home and abroad. The National Heritage Memorial Fund and the Fraser Foundation gave very substantial help. The Glenmorangie Distillery Company Ltd., by making a grant and guaranteeing to underwrite the deficit, made it absolutely sure that this outstanding work of art, with all its historical associations, should remain in Scotland.

All those who donated so generously can feel well pleased at having played a role in preserving such an important part of our cultural and historical heritage.

Figs. 1-2. Prince Charles Edward Stuart's Travelling Canteen, made by Ebenezer Oliphant, Edinburgh, 1740-41. The contents are ingeniously packed into a container only 7 in. high by 4⅜ in. wide.

As we go to press, we learn of a new initiative to commemorate Dr I. F. Grant. An appeal has been launched to establish 'The I. F. Grant Memorial Library', at the Highland Folk Museum. It will concentrate on books and journals dealing with the subject matter of the Museum; that is, Highland history and folk life, and comparative material. Contributions should be sent to The Curator, Highland Folk Museum, Duke Street, Kingussie, Inverness-shire PH21 1JG, marked 'I. F. Grant Memorial Appeal Fund'. Cheques should be made out to the 'Highland Folk Museum'.

The Editors

Contributors

David G Adams Librarian, Angus District Library and Museum Service, Arbroath

Andrew Barlow National Museums of Scotland

Dana Bentley-Cranch Art Historian, London

Iain G Brown National Library of Scotland

David H Caldwell National Museums of Scotland

Hugh Cheape National Museums of Scotland

P Anne Clarke National Museums of Scotland

Valerie E Dean National Museums of Scotland

Alexander Fenton National Museums of Scotland

A F Fraser Professor of Comparative Physiology, Memorial University of Newfoundland, Canada (formerly Senior Lecturer, Royal (Dick) School of Veterinary Studies, Edinburgh)

Rosalind K Marshall Reference Section, Scottish National Portrait Gallery

Peter Robinson Scottish Development Department

Chris S Seaton Department of the Environment/Property Services Agency, Project Architect (Museums and Galleries)

Gavin C Sprott National Museums of Scotland

Geoffrey Stell Royal Commission on the Ancient and Historical Monuments of Scotland

Caroline R Wickham-Jones National Museums of Scotland

Charles W J Withers Department of Geography, The College of St Paul and St Mary, Cheltenham

Contents

	page
Editorial Notes and Comments	v
Contributors	ix
Rosalind K Marshall The Wearing of Wedding Rings in Scotland	1
Chris S Seaton The Book Designs of Talwin Morris (1865-1911)	13
Iain Gordon Brown 'Plaister Gimcracks': the Handicraft of Allan Ramsay the Poet	19
A F Fraser The Plague in the Grass (grass sickness in horses)	23
Charles W J Withers William Marshall, Agricultural Writer, in Scotland	31
David G Adams Notes on Long-Line Fishing from Arbroath, Ferryden and Gourdon	37
Gavin C Sprott Who Were the Sailormen?	43
Alexander Fenton Food on Sunday	53
Geoffrey Stell Destruction, Damage and Decay: the Collapse of Scottish Medieval Buildings	59
Peter Robinson Tenements: the Industrial Legacy	71
Dana Bentley-Cranch An Early Sixteenth-Century French Architectural Source for the Palace of Falkland	85
Caroline R Wickham-Jones, P Ann Clarke and Andrew Barlow A Project in Experimental Archaeology: Avasjö 1982	97
David H Caldwell and Valerie E Dean Post-Medieval Pots and Potters at Throsk in Stirlingshire	105
Hugh Cheape Dr I F Grant (1887-1983): The Highland Folk Museum and a Bibliography of her Written Works	113
Reviews	127

The Wearing of Wedding Rings in Scotland

Rosalind K Marshall

1. Numbering of fingers.

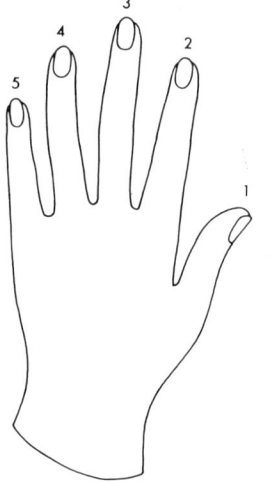

2. Ring terminology.

The wearing of a ring as a token of love and commitment is of ancient origin. In Western Europe it dates back at least to Roman times, and Isidore of Seville, writing in the early seventh century A.D., explained that the ring was 'given by the espouser to the espoused, either for a sign of mutual fidelity or still more to join the hearts by this pledge'. Originally, the ring was placed upon the bride's finger at her betrothal, not her wedding. However, such importance was attached to its giving that the ritual soon became part of the marriage service itself.[1]

From surviving examples, portraits and documents, we have evidence of four distinct types of betrothal and wedding ring used in Scotland before 1800. The earliest has the well-known design of two clasped hands forming the bezel. This device, popular from Rumania to England, is known as the fede, from the Italian phrase 'mani in fede'.[2] A number of interesting medieval fede rings are preserved in the National Museums of Scotland, and two fifteenth-century examples are fairly typical. One has the clasped hands motif rendered in silver by means of somewhat primitive craftsmanship, a series of straight

3a, b. Fifteenth-century fede ring, National Museums of Scotland, NJ 72.

1

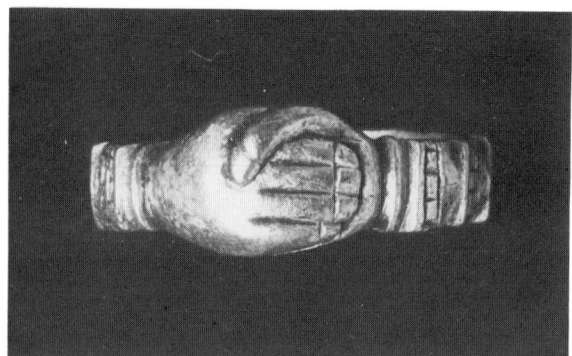

4a, b. Fifteenth-century fede ring, National Museums of Scotland, NJ 61.

lines indicating the middle fingers, which are encircled by hook-like thumbs and small fingers. The
hoop of this ring is very broad, with a narrow, raised
cable pattern decorating the upper and lower edges. It
was found in Earnscleugh Water, Lauder.

In the second ring, the hands are much more
delicately modelled, with short, incised strokes indicating the fingernails of the hand on the left. Round
the outside of the hoop are panels with the letters 'II
IESUS NA', an abbreviated form of the often-used
inscription, 'Iesus Nazarenus Rex Iudeorum'. These
and other rings in the National Museums' collection
are so large that they must have been worn by men,
although one or two are of a size to fit a woman's
finger. Not all were actual betrothal rings: some were
more casual love tokens, presented by a donor who
would later marry someone else.

The materials used, as well as the varying quality
of the workmanship, indicate that fede rings were
popular throughout society with all who could afford
them. Some are of the relatively inexpensive copper
and brass-gilt. More are of silver, and occasionally a
jewelled fede ring was made. For example, a list of
some of James VI's jewels, compiled in 1606, mentions 'ane great ring of gold, enameled, sett with fyve
diamondis with hand in hand in the middis, callit the
espousall ring of Denmark'. This was unusual,
though, for the typical fede ring is simply a plain hoop
with a decorative bezel but no gems.[3]

Jewelled betrothal and wedding rings of a rather
different design were, however, popular from the later
Middle Ages onwards. These did not incorporate any
particular device, but consisted of a gold hoop with
one or more precious stones forming the bezel. Thus
we find that when James V married Princess

Madeleine of France, he paid 1100 crowns for 'ane
grete diamant sett in table for the Quenis spousing
ring'. (The term 'in table' refers to the way in which
the stone was cut, with a flat top.) The princess died
not long after her wedding day, but James soon re-
married and spent a more modest 300 crowns 'for ane
ring witht ane diamand to be the Quenis Grace
spousing ring'.[4]

This ring may have been placed on Mary of Guise's
finger at her betrothal, her proxy wedding in France or
the subsequent ceremony in Scotland. Contemporary
descriptions do not provide any precise information as
to the occasion, and the term 'spousing ring' is
ambiguous. Certainly, the betrothal in Scotland was
known as 'the spousals', but the verb 'espouse' was
often used to mean 'marry'.[5] Pre-Reformation terminology must therefore be treated with caution, and it
is perhaps safest to follow the contemporary usage and
employ the term 'spousing ring' without attempting to
translate it into a modern equivalent.

As it happens, we do know that when Mary, Queen
of Scots married Lord Darnley in 1565, it was at her
wedding that she received her spousing ring. Thomas
Randolph, the English ambassador, attended the
ceremony and reported that 'the rings, which were
three, the middle one a riche diamonde, were put
upon her finger . . .' A few months later, fearing that
she might die in childbirth, Mary made a will and in it
bequeathed to her husband the 'bague de diamant,
esmaille de rouge' with which he had espoused her.[6] It
seems that he in turn had received from her a signet
ring bearing the royal arms of Scotland and the initials
'M' and 'H' entwined above a love knot. This ring was
found at Fotheringhay Castle and is now in the
Victoria and Albert Museum, but although it is

5a, b, c, d, e. Group of fede rings, National Museums of Scotland, NJ 16, 18, 41, 57, 51.

engraved with the date 1565, it would not have been given at the wedding ceremony. There was no provision in the service for the giving of a ring to the groom, and any such gift would be made by the bride before or after the marriage service.[7]

Unfortunately, Mary's own ring has not survived, nor is there any visual representation of it, for in none of the authentic portraits of the Queen does she wear any ring at all. Of course, even when jewelled rings of this period do exist it is frequently impossible to identify them as spousing rings. Unless they have an inscription inside the hoop or the fede device at the back, opposite the bezel, they are identical in appearance to rings worn for purely ornamental purposes.[8] The same problem affects rings worn in portraits, although occasionally one does seem to suggest itself as a possibility because of some unusual feature of its design.

A picture of Lady Agnes Keith, Countess of Moray, is worthy of particular scrutiny for this reason. Painted in 1561-2 to commemorate her wedding, it shows her clad in a fashionable velvet and satin gown with a splendid array of jewellery. The Earl of Moray had

originally been betrothed to an infant heiress, but after making evident to all his 'long love' for Lady Agnes, he finally followed his 'hartis inclination', as he himself put it, and married her instead. Since this was a love match, it would be reasonable to suppose that the new Countess would wish to display her ring, so it is interesting to observe upon her hand a tablecut diamond in a gold scroll-work setting of unusual intricacy. Above it is a guard ring, always a sign that the companion ring was of particular value.[9]

Any suggestion that this may be a spousing ring can only be tentative, but whatever its status we know from documentary evidence that the gem-set hoop retained its popularity well into the seventeenth century. When she made her will in 1644, Anna, Marchioness of Hamilton, bequeathed to her eldest son 'my greit diamont ring' which his father had given her and which she kept carefully in 'ane velvet keis'. Again, in 1687 when the Episcopalian Earl of Panmure married Lady Margaret Hamilton, he paid £432 for 'a fine seven stone diamond ring' which he purchased on the eve of the wedding.[10]

By the end of the sixteenth century another type of love ring had made its appearance, and it is immediately identifiable because it took the form of a jewelled heart. This design was fashionable in England and France in the sixteenth century, and the earliest Scottish example noted so far appears in a portrait of Janet Scott, widow of Sir Thomas Kerr of Ferniehirst.[11] Painted in 1593, Janet wears a long dark veil over her hair and stands beneath a motto which reads 'Ubi amor, ibi fides' (Where there is love there is

6a. *Agnes, Countess of Moray* by Hans Eworth; in a private Scottish collection.

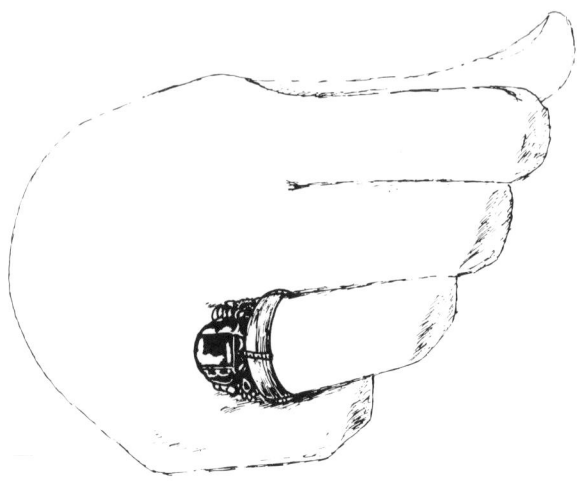

b. Detail, right hand.

7a. *Janet Scott, Lady Kerr of Ferniehirst* by an unknown artist; in the collection of the Duke of Buccleuch and Queensberry K.T.

b. Detail, right hand.

fidelity). On the small finger of her right hand she wears a ring with a heart-shaped stone resembling a peridot. It is set in gold, with delicate bows on the shoulders of the hoop. Janet also has a fine diamond ring protected from loss by a black mourning guard ring, so the exact function of the heart ring is uncertain. It was probably a betrothal ring or a love token rather than a wedding ring, but whatever the truth of the matter, the symbolism of the heart is obvious.

About twenty years after Janet was painted, Jean, Countess of Roxburghe, sat to an unknown artist. Not only is her portrait a sensitive rendering of the lady herself, but it records a wealth of fascinating costume and jewellery detail, including a ring with a very large bezel in the shape of a crowned heart. The design is elaborate, with small, oblong stones outlining the central heart. The crown is likewise set with small stones and the hoop is composed of rectangular gems set in gold.[12] Similar in design but without the crown is the splendid ring seen in the 1625 portrait of Anne, Countess of Winton,[13] while a picture dated 1626 completes the quartet. Painted by the Aberdeen artist

George Jamesone, it is a full-length representation of Anne, Countess of Rothes, and her small daughters. The only ring the Countess wears has a bezel with petal-shaped stones set in gold to form the crown above a large heart.[14] In these three portraits the gems are almost certainly diamonds. They are rather blacker in colour than might be expected, but that is largely attributable to the method of stone-cutting. It was not yet possible to cut gems brilliantly, and table-cut diamonds reflect less light than their modern counterparts, especially if seen against dark garments.

After the late 1620s, the heart-shaped ring disappears from Scottish portraits although references can still be found in documents. A list of Lady Anna Montgomerie's jewels, drawn up when she died in 1632 a few months after her wedding, included a diamond ring 'with foure diamonds in the forme of a crounit heart', and as late as 1645 the Earl of Eglinton was purchasing 'ane turquois ring in ane heart way'.[15] By the eighteenth century, the heart device had been transferred to the luckenbooth brooch, which became the favourite love token. Fancy rings with romantic connotations remained in fashion too, though, and the

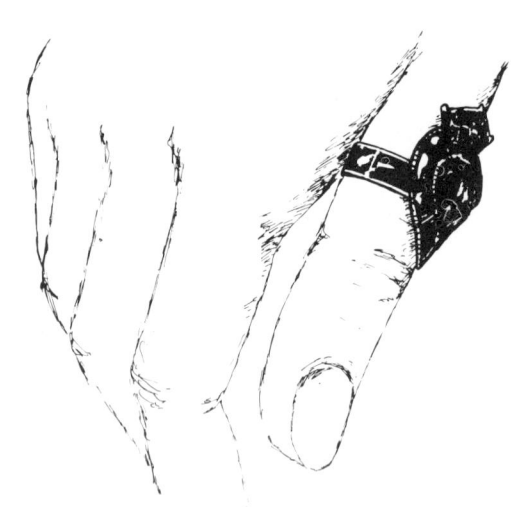

b. Detail, right hand.

8a. *Jean, Countess of Roxburghe* by an unknown artist; in the collection of the Grimsthorpe and Drummond Castle Trustees.

b. Detail, right hand.

9a. *Anne, Countess of Winton* attributed to Adam de Colone; in the collection of the Scottish National Portrait Gallery.

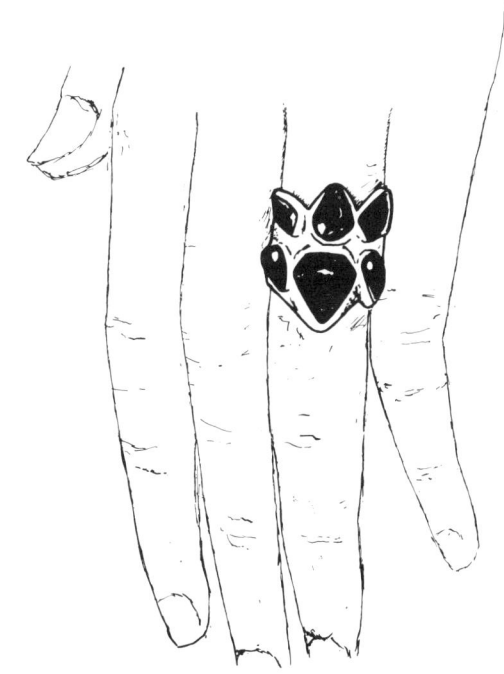

10a. *Anne, Countess of Rothes and her daughters* by George Jamesone; in the collection of the Scottish National Portrait Gallery.

b. Detail, left hand.

National Museums possess a charming example in which two elegant gold hands hold, not a heart as might have been expected, but a cluster of four pearls surrounding a small round emerald. As an additional decorative touch, a tiny ring with a green stone adorns the forefinger of the gold right hand.[16]

Despite the continued liking for fancy love rings, the usual wedding ring at that time was the fourth and final type, a plain gold hoop. English evidence suggests that it may have pre-dated the jewelled spousing ring, and certainly when Mary Tudor surprised contemporaries by choosing a plain gold band when she married Philip II of Spain, one explanation of why she had done so was 'because maydens were so maryed in olde tymes'.[17] Be that as it may, not until the seventeenth century did the plain wedding ring find favour again in Scotland, and it may be that Presbyterians preferred this austere version. Not all plain hoops were spousing rings, it must be noted. Ladies quite often possessed a number of plain rings, and Margaret, Countess of Findlater, was far from unique in owning '5 gold woups [rings], plain and enambled'.[18]

11. Eighteenth-century ring, National Museums of Scotland, NJ 81.

Those which were given as love tokens usually had an inscription engraved inside the hoop. This might take the form of a motto, and in 1696 when Jean Cook complained that William Johnstone had deserted her, she drew the commissary court's attention to the fact that he had given her 'a big gold ring with the inscription "constant love"'.[19] It was also customary to inscribe the initials of bride and groom inside the ring, and an example in the National Museums is typical. Made in Edinburgh, it has the letters 'J.S:A.R.', with the date 'September 4th 1747'.[20] Rings of this type with similar inscriptions have remained in fashion right up to the present day, although in recent years the hoop has often been broader and flatter, with an engraved design on the outside.

Having identified the various types of betrothal and wedding ring, we can now consider the tantalising problem of where exactly the ring was worn. The obvious place to seek information would seem to be in the portraits of the time, yet any study of the pictorial evidence is beset by unexpected difficulties. The Reference Section of the Scottish National Portrait Gallery at present records slightly over 1000 female portraits from before 1800,[21] yet of these a mere thirty-five show rings of any description, and from a total of fifty-eight rings altogether, only eighteen may with some confidence be identified as spousing rings. Now of course a number of pictures show head and shoulders only, while in others the lady's hands are concealed by flowers, draperies, accessories or even by other sitters. Nevertheless, the number is startingly small.

Time and again, ladies gaze serenely down from their canvases, hands elegantly disposed but completely bare of ornament. No satisfactory explanation of this phenomenon — which is not exclusively Scottish — has yet been put forward. We know from accounts that many of the ladies concerned possessed fine collections of finger rings, and the notion that Presbyterians disapproved of all jewellery is easily refuted. Not only are there bills recording the purchase of splendid jewelled rings by Covenanting countesses, but ladies famed for their strong religious convictions appear in their portraits bedecked with necklaces, earrings, hair ornaments and brooches.

It could be, of course, that the explanation lies with the working methods of the artist. The fashionable portrait painter had not time to paint every inch of a picture himself and would simply sketch in clothing, arms and hands for his assistants to complete. They did this in the studio, in the absence of the sitter, and so they could not observe any rings worn, but the same applied to bracelets and brooches, yet these appear frequently in pictures. Moreover, not every artist

could afford to employ drapery painters, and in any event the same artist would show rings in one or two of his paintings but not in others.

The mystery remains unsolved. The element of artistic licence does not negate portraiture as an historical source any more than the subjective element in documents nullifies the value of the written word. The experienced researcher is aware of these qualifying factors and makes allowances for them. The significance for our present study is twofold: we cannot assume that because few wedding rings appear they did not exist, but our chances of discovering which finger the ring adorned are gravely reduced. For instance, only two female Scottish portraits dating from before 1560 show any ring at all, and in neither is one worn on the right hand. This is a pity, for written sources make it clear that the fourth finger of that hand was where the spousing ring was placed before the Reformation.

This tradition went back at least as far as the seventh century A.D. when Isidore of Seville explained, 'The ring is placed on the fourth finger because a certain vein, it is said, flows from thence to the heart'.[22] He based this remark on the anatomical findings of Aulus Gellius in the second century A.D., but while his medical authority had been discussing the left hand, Isidore applied his conclusions to the right hand instead, and throughout the Middle Ages the fourth finger of that hand was the one selected.

The Roman Catholic Church gave precise instructions for the placing of the ring during the marriage service. First of all, it was blessed by the priest, who passed it to the bridegroom. The bridegroom held it in his right hand and took his bride's right hand in his left. With the words 'In the name of the Father' he put the ring firstly upon her right thumb. He then moved it to the forefinger of the same hand, saying 'In the name of the Son'. Transferring it to the middle finger, he added 'and of the Holy Ghost', then he put it on his bride's fourth finger, murmuring 'Amen'. There it remained for the rest of the ceremony.

This was to be the procedure until the Reformation. Possibly Archbishop Cranmer in England noticed Isidore of Seville's mistake when he was drawing up the Edward VI Prayer Book of 1549, for in it he was careful to specify that the ring should be placed on the fourth finger of the left hand, and he gave no instructions for its transference from one finger to the next during the ceremony. A more widespread

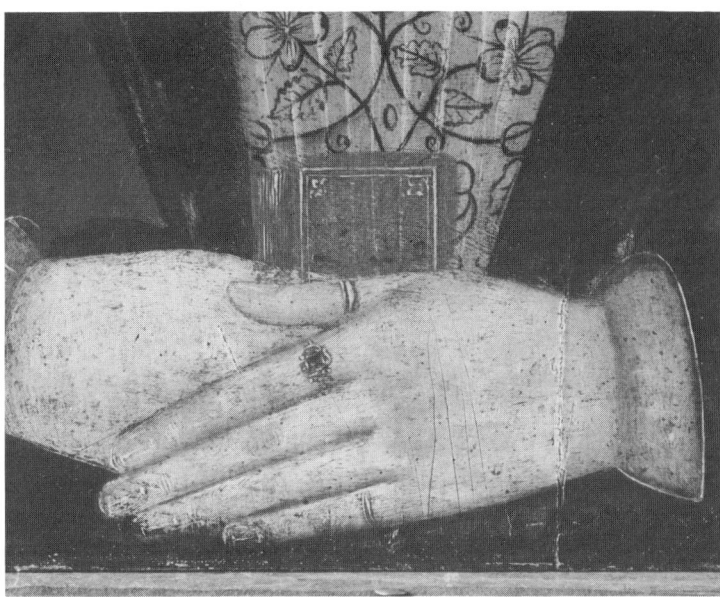

12a. *Mrs Esther Kello* by an unknown artist; in the collection of the National Museums of Scotland, on loan to the Scottish National Portrait Gallery.

b. Detail, left hand.

explanation of the change is that Protestants in their anxiety to do away with anything reminiscent of Roman Catholic ritual decided that the wedding ring must have a new position. In Scotland, the Reformers went a stage further and at first allowed no place at all in the marriage service for the giving of the ring. Similarly there is no mention of it in James VI's Prayer Book of 1617.[23]

It would be unrealistic to suppose that with the coming of the Reformation people abandoned the tradition of centuries and gave no spousing rings. Alterations in such personal customs do not come about overnight, and there must have been a lengthy period of transition. It is relevant to note that Lady Agnes Keith's elaborate diamond ring (Fig. 6) appears on the fourth finger of her right hand. Now, she married a leading Protestant and her wedding was performed by no less a personage than John Knox himself, but it did not take place in the very early days of the Reformation, so it remains probable that this is indeed a spousing ring, worn on the traditional finger.

Apart from the diversity arising from personal preference, a considerable state of confusion existed because of the differing forms of religious practice.

The 1637 Prayer Book of Charles I followed the English example and gave instructions for the ring to be put on the bride's left hand. Episcopalian Scots would comply with this ruling, but the Prayer Book was unacceptable to many, and convinced Presbyterians were now more likely to abandon the ring altogether because of their feelings about the rest of Charles I's ecclesiastical policies. Meanwhile, Roman Catholics continued to use the right hand and did not change the ring to the left until towards the end of the seventeenth century. Thus we can see the Roman Catholic Janet Scott with her jewelled rings on her right hand (Fig. 7), and the Roman Catholic Countess of Winton displaying her heart-shaped ring (Fig. 9) on the fourth finger of her right hand.

To compound the confusion, some ladies decided that the best place for the spousing ring was the thumb. Samuel Butler alluded to this curious custom, writing in his satire *Hudibras*, published in 1668,

> Others were for abolishing
> That tool of matrimony, a Ring
> With which th'unsanctify'd Bridegroom
> Is marry'd only to a thumb.[24]

Indeed, as late as 1693 a character in Thomas Southerne's play *The Maid's Last Prayer* proclaimed of a suitor, 'Marry him I must, and wear my wedding ring upon my thumb too, that I'm resolved on'.[25]

Pictorial evidence records this practice in Scotland also. One painting which may be relevant is the portrait of Mrs Esther Kello, the famous calligrapher. Dated 1595, which was about the time of her wedding, it shows three rings on her left hand. One has an amber-coloured stone set in a conventional quatrefoil bezel: such rings are seen in many Western European portraits of the time. On her small finger is a plain double hoop, and on her thumb is another double hoop. Unfortunately, her hand is held at such an angle that the ring is turned away from the viewer, but it appears to have a bezel. Only the edge is visible, and even in the original painting it is difficult to discern. This is a pity, for it might be the only example found so far in a portrait of a Scottish gimmel or double hoop spousing ring.[26]

This is speculation, of course. More convincing proof comes in the form of a slightly later picture by George Jamesone. Dating from about 1635, it shows his own family. His wife is prominently placed in the centre of the canvas, holding flowers in her hands, and

14. *Anne, Duchess of Hamilton* attributed to David Scougall; a plain ring which is probably not a spousing ring; in the collection of the National Trust for Scotland at Brodick Castle.

13. *Self-portrait with wife and child* by George Jamesone; in the Fyvie Castle Collection.

on her right thumb is a plain hoop which must surely be her wedding ring.[27]

During the seventeenth century, a number of jewelled and plain rings also appear on the small finger of either hand — no fewer than thirteen out of a total of twenty-seven, as compared with seven on the fourth finger of the left hand, two on that finger of the right hand, three on thumbs and two worn other than on the hands. Some of these rings on the small finger may have been spousing rings, probably most were not. It is impossible to tell, because in design they are no different from purely ornamental rings, and if the originals had an inscription inside the hoop, it is forever hidden from our gaze in the painted image. One fact is certain: no rings at all at that period are worn on the middle finger or forefinger of either hand in the pictures examined in this survey.

Despite the wide variations in the seventeenth century, made more complex by the changes from Episcopalian to Presbyterian practice in the Church of Scotland, it seems that by 1700 or so the fourth finger of the left hand had become the accepted place for the spousing ring, which was now almost invariably a plain hoop. During the eighteenth century, rings almost vanish from portraits altogether, but at the turn of the century there is a sudden change, and from 1800 onwards dozens of ladies are shown with plain wedding rings on the fourth finger of their left hands. Moreover, from about 1830 these rings are often accompanied by a jewelled engagement ring of the type familiar to us today.

The explanation of this abrupt alteration in fashion is elusive, but perhaps some conclusion may be drawn from their very absence of rings in earlier portraits and their unexpected reappearance. Before the late eighteenth century transport was poor, women tended to stay in their own locality, and in a small community everyone knew everyone else. The ring was a love token symbolising the promise made between two individuals, rather than being an outward sign of the woman's marital status. Since it was a precious possession, both financially and emotionally, it is quite probable that it was not worn regularly after the wedding but was put away carefully in a 'velvet keis', in the drawer of a cabinet, or worn on a chain around the owner's neck. In an imaginary portrait of a sixteenth-century lady, Jamesone shows a ring in

16. *Lady Majory Edmonstone* by George Jamesone; in a private collection.

precisely that position. Admittedly the picture is fanciful, but the artist made strenuous if not altogether successful efforts to represent the costume of the period, and there is no reason to suppose that the wearing of the ring was entirely his own invention.[28]

By the early nineteenth century, with increased mobility, a rising population and many people moving from country to town, there was much more social interchange between strangers. It was therefore useful to indicate publicly that a woman was engaged or married, and so the ring came to be worn for a new purpose. No longer was it merely a private symbol of affection between espouser and espoused. It did, of course, preserve that function, but it had also become an outward sign to society at large that the wearer was a married woman, committed exclusively to one particular partner and enjoying a specific status as his wife.

15. *Catherine, Countess of Melville* by Sir John Medina; in the collection of the Earl of Leven and Melville.

Acknowledgements
Illustrations appear by kind permission of the private owners listed in the captions; the Trustees of the National Museums of Scotland and the Trustees of the National Galleries of Scotland. The author is also grateful to the Duchess of Buccleuch and Queensberry, the Earl of Moray, Mrs A. Dundas-Bekker, Miss Lorna MacEchern, Mrs Dana Mayer; and the staff of the National Museums for their helpful cooperation.

References

1. Charles Oman, *British Rings, 800-1914* (London 1974), 36; C. C. Oman, *Catalogue of Rings* (Victoria and Albert Museum 1930), 16-17; Phillis Cunnington and Catherine Lucas, *Costume for Births, Marriages and Deaths* (London 1972), 118-9; Ernle Bradford, *Four Centuries of European Jewellery* (London 1953), 131.

2. Oman, *British Rings*, 38-9; Guido Gregorietti, *Jewelry throughout the Ages* (London 1969), 166, 198; O. M. Dalton, *Franks Bequest Catalogue of the Finger rings in the British Museum* (London 1912), 161ff.

3. National Museums of Scotland, rings NJ72 and NJ61; see *Proceedings of the Society of Antiquaries of Scotland* lv (1920-1), 20; *Angels, Nobles and Unicorns: Art and Patronage in Medieval Scotland* (Edinburgh 1982), 93; see also rings NJ16, 18, 41, 57, 71; Thomas Thomson, *A Catalogue of Royal Inventories* (Edinburgh 1815), 329.

4. *Accounts of the Lord High Treasurer of Scotland*, ed. T. Dickson and Sir J. Balfour Paul (Edinburgh 1877-1916), vii, 14, 56.

5. Rosalind K. Marshall, *Virgins and Viragos: a history of Women in Scotland, 1080-1980* (London 1983), 27-8.

6. Thomas Wright, *Queen Elizabeth and her Times* (London 1838), i, 202; *Inventaires de la Reyne d'Escosse* (Bannatyne Club 1863), 112.

7. Oman, *Catalogue*, 94, no. 559; S. Maxwell and R. Hutchison, *Scottish Costume, 1550-1850* (London 1958), 175.

8. *Princely Magnificence: Court Jewels of the Renaissance, 1500-1630*, ed. A. Somers Cocks (Victoria and Albert Museum 1980), 92, no. 125e.

9. Portrait by Hans Eworth in a private Scottish collection; Roy Strong, *The English Icon: Elizabethan and Jacobean Portraiture* (London 1969), 94; Roy Strong, *Hans Eworth: A Tudor Artist and his Circle* (National Portrait Gallery, London, exhibition catalogue 1965), 6; *Registrum Honoris de Morton* (Bannatyne Club 1853), i, 9; Maurice Lee, *James Stewart, Earl of Moray* (New York 1953), 97-8;

10. Hamilton Archives, M14/3/3; Scottish Record Office, Dalhousie Muniments, GD45/18/983.

11. In the collection of the Duke of Buccleuch and Queensberry K. T. at Bowhill, Selkirk.

12. In the collection of the Grimsthorpe and Drummond Castle Trustees.

13. In the collection of the Scottish National Portrait Gallery.

14. In the collection of the Scottish National Portrait Gallery.

15. Scottish Record Office, Eglinton Papers, GD3/E/8/746; W. Fraser, *Memorials of the Montgomeries* (Edinburgh 1859), i, 271.

16. National Museums of Scotland, NJ81.

17. Letter of John Elder in *Chronicle of Queen Jane and two years of Queen Mary* (Camden Society 1850), 141, quoted in Oman, *British Rings*, 38.

18. Scottish Record Office, Edinburgh Commissary Court Register of Testaments, CC8/10/16.

19. Scottish Record Office, Edinburgh Commissary Court, CC8/5/1 f.395ff.

20. National Museums of Scotland, NJ129.

21. This comprehensive archive of approximately 30,000 photographs of portraits receives additions of some 500 photographs each year, so further examples of spousing rings will be recorded in the future.

22. Oman, *British Rings*, 36.

23. *Ibid*; Cunnington and Lucas, 121.

24. Samuel Butler, *Hudibras* (London 1668), Part iii, Canto 2, vv 303-6.

25. Cunnington and Lucas, 121.

26. In the collection of the National Museums of Scotland, on loan to the Scottish National Portrait Gallery; Gregorietti, 198.

27. In the Fyvie Castle Collection.

28. In a private collection.

Calendar of State Papers relating to Scotland, ed. M. J. Thorpe (London 1858), i, 563.

The Book Designs of Talwin Morris (1865-1911)

Chris S Seaton

It may come as a surprise to admirers of the 'Glasgow Style' to know that fine examples are still to be found in return for a modest outlay in the form of book cover designs from the period. These covers are the work of Talwin Morris, art director to the firm of Blackie and friend of Charles Rennie Mackintosh and his circle.

In the 1890s the large Scottish publishing houses were still, for the most part, family concerns built up during the earlier part of the century and run on paternalistic lines. The energy and business acumen of the directors of these firms ensured a success which often outstripped that of their London counterparts, and takeovers by Scottish firms were not unusual. The 'Big Five' could be said to comprise Blackie, Collins, Nelson, Blackwood and Chambers, while Constable, Maclehose, Foulis, Oliver and Boyd, Bartholomew and Ballantyne were noteworthy amongst the numerous smaller firms.

The passing of the Education Act in 1872 had opened up vast new markets in school text books and what are referred to as 'reward books' or school prizes. The whole climate was one of change and innovation, and the scene was set for the revolution in design which was to accompany it. Walter Blackie and Son were doubly fortunate in that they possessed far-sighted directors whose sound business sense was equalled by an awareness of the artistic trends of the time.

By 1893 the first issues of *The Studio* were already influencing the course of graphic design through the medium of Beardsley's illustrations. These were to break the stranglehold of Victorian formalism and bring a new fluidity which William Morris and his disciples had been incapable of achieving.

At this time Talwin Morris was pursuing a career as an assistant art director to an upmarket weekly London journal called *Black and White*, having gravitated to publishing following a brief apprenticeship in an architect's office (Beardsley coincidentally followed this route also). He successfully applied for the advertised post of art director with Blackie's and began work in May 1893. Thus was forged the link of Morris, Blackie and later Mackintosh which would eventually result in the commission for Hill House. Morris's style was already noteworthy for its delight in a delicate sinuous line and well-designed lettering. Early contact with Mackintosh and his circle introduced him to the symbolic motifs of which *The Universe* (1896) (Fig. 1) is almost a complete résumé. There is an earlier design for this which owes more to William Blake than the Glasgow Style.

Such was the volume of work that many titles had to be commissioned from other sources. These were

1.

13

often provided by 'The Silver Studio', a London-based design studio, and often incorporated figures. These were something which Morris eschewed. If he did not incorporate his monogram, then another characteristic trademark of two dots slightly separated from a third is a useful means of identification.

In 1897 *The Studio* published an article on the Glasgow group in which Morris received equal if not greater critical appraisal than Mackintosh for all aspects of his work including metal and fabric design.

Morris carried out freelance commissions for other publishers such as Maclehose and Cassells. For the Cassells *Battles of the 19th Century* (2 vols. 1896) he designed no fewer than 150 chapter headings which are outstanding testimony to his inventive use of line and lettering to create an appropriate theme.

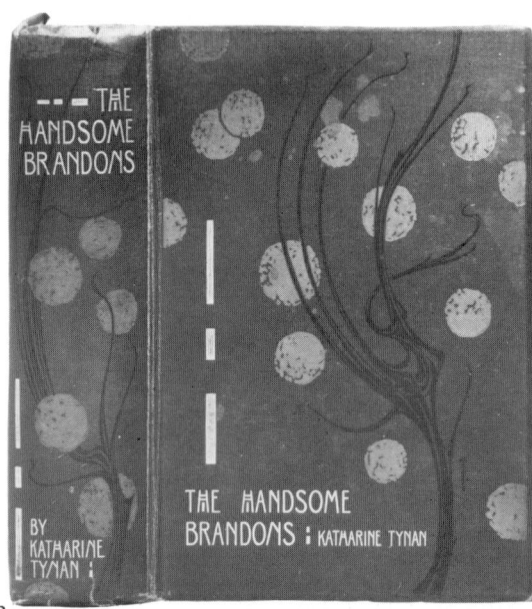

2.

The Handsome Brandons (1899) (Fig. 2) is a good example of a Morris cover for the 'reward' series covers showing some Japanese influence and proving that he was his own man in design terms.

In 1898 a new offshoot of Blackie's called the Gresham Publishing Co. was formed. This was to handle large-format subscription series and Morris was in charge. Although he had a quantity of widely acclaimed work behind him, the next phase in his career really marks his arrival as a mature designer.

It is difficult to choose between the numerous examples from this period, but mention must be made of such designs as *Gladstone* (4 vols. 1898), *The Book of*

3.-4.

the Home (4 vols. 1902) and *The Modern Carpenter and Joiner* (8 vols. 1902) (Fig. 3). The 'Red Letter' series (Fig. 4) of small-format poetry books under the

Blackie imprint testify to Morris's attention to detail and come in a variety of bindings: leather, vellum and cloth. Morris also designed the endpapers and title pages, the latter with varying degrees of success.

In the larger-format Gresham my own favourites are the *National History of Plants* (2 vols. 1902) (Fig. 5), a masterly design in which Morris exploits his facility with form and lettering to give an impression of space where width is restricted on the spine. The background is a dark blue with a rich green and gold lettered design. *Modern Power Generators* (2 vols. 1908) (Fig. 6) shows the economy which Morris could bring to a cover design and is quite undated and fresh seventy-five years on. The background here is olive green with a black and gold design. Other Scottish publishers were definitely influenced by Blackie products, and one can find the evidence on titles by Nelson and Collins around the early 1900s and continuing after Blackie had altered their style. No one approached the ease and authority of Morris, and these other examples were merely imitative.

Two similar designs, *The Cabinet of Irish Literature* (4 vols. 1902) (Fig. 7) and *Poetical Works of Robert Burns* (4 vols. 1909) cannot be classed a typical Glasgow Style but are nevertheless beautifully produced in green and red bindings with an overall gold repeat pattern of convoluted lines reminiscent of Celtic ornament.

So far I have been unable to trace any photographs

6.

of Morris, but Mary Newbery Sturrock is, happily, able to recall meeting him. Her memory is of a tall pale-complexioned man, who favoured the dress of the artist of the day, in cloak and wide-brimmed hat. He died aged only 46 and was succeeded by A. A. Campbell at Blackie's. The style of covers had changed to one of solid symmetry often with classical figures totally in keeping with the solid Edwardian spirit of the times. The Glasgow Style was out of favour, but Morris's designs were to persist on Blackie school text books well into the 'thirties and 'forties, and it is interesting to speculate on the countless embryonic designers moved to creative doodling by them on long afternoons in class (Fig. 8).

Morris was instrumental in helping to raise to an art form the design of cloth bindings, until that time disregarded by the practitioners in fine tooled leather bindings. His particular facility with integrating lettering in the overall design excels the work of other more celebrated artists of the time. Beardsley and Crane both executed covers for limited editions where the lettering is merely an adjunct to the design.

The exact extent of Mackintosh's collaboration with Morris is still unclear, but enough evidence exists to testify to the collaboration in graphic design. For the Glasgow International Exhibition of 1901 Mackintosh created a pavilion in the Moorish Style for Pettigrew

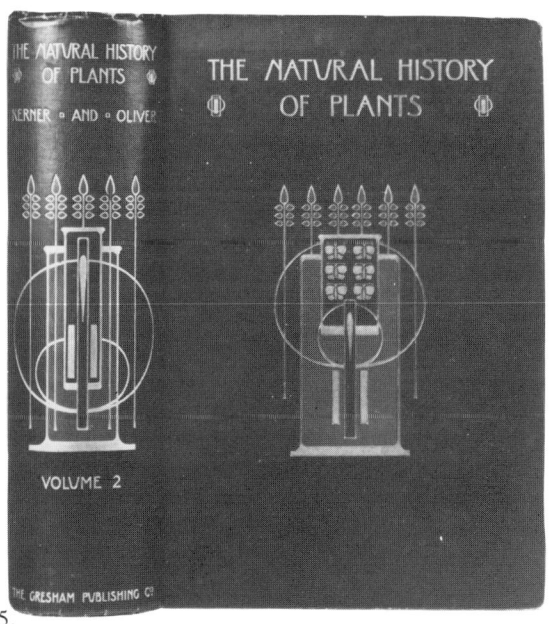

5.

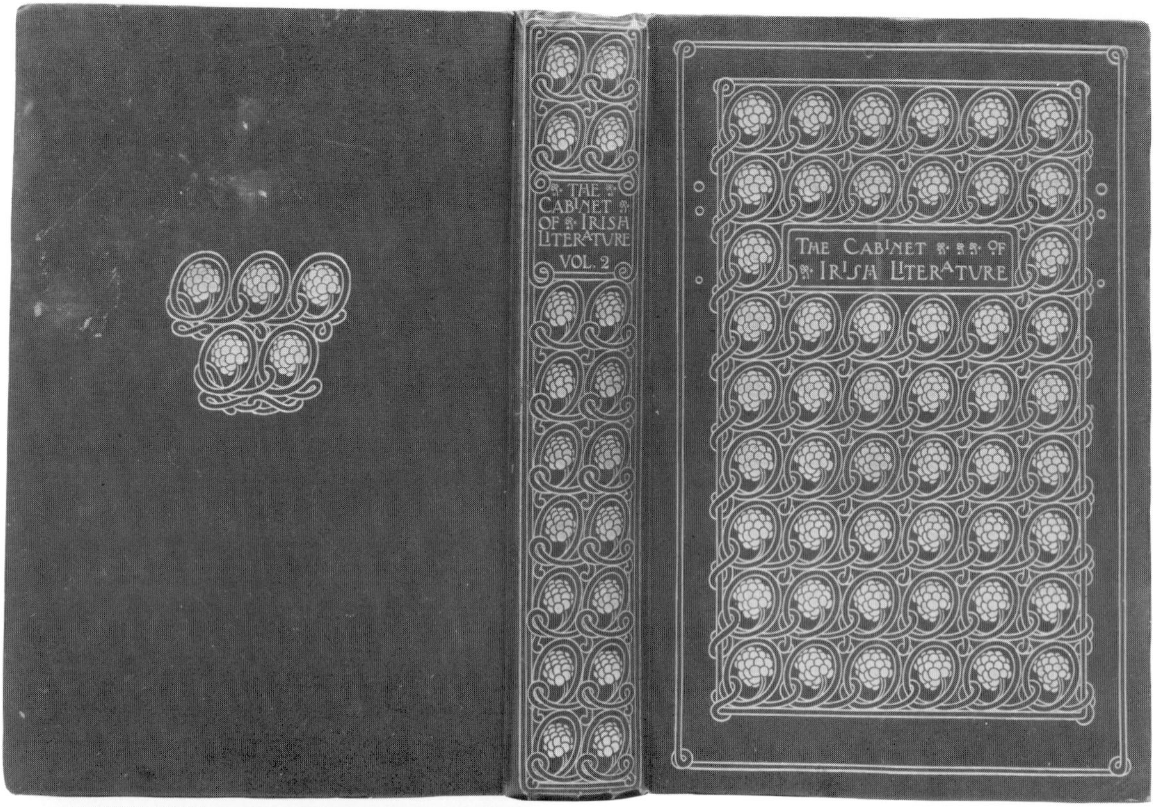

7.

8.

and Stevens, and the accompanying poster extolling the virtues of the new department store was designed by Morris.

The first exhibition of the work of Morris was held in London in October 1983. This was organised by Gerald Cinamon (Chief Designer, Penguin Books), author of an impressively researched series of articles on Morris in the quarterly journal of the Charles Rennie Mackintosh Society. The exhibition catalogue will, hopefully, form the basis for a comprehensive inventory of his work in book design and other fields.

Much remains to be discovered about this member of the Glasgow group before he can be placed accurately in context with his contemporaries who jointly helped create the style so closely identified with a great city at the height of its influence.

Sources

Cinamon, G., compiler, *Talwin Morris Exhibition (23 August-2 October 1983) Catalogue* (William Morris Gallery, London).

Howarth, T., *Charles Rennie Mackintosh and the Modern Movement* London 1977 (2nd ed), 23-24.

Larner. G. and C., *The Glasgow Style* (London, 1979), 11-12.

Newsletter of the Charles Rennie Mackintosh Society Glasgow 1981 (Winter No. 28; Spring/Summer No. 29; Autumn No. 30).

S., E. B., Some Designs for Cloth Bindings. In *The Studio* XV (1898), 41-44.

Taylor, J. R., *The Art Nouveau Book in Britain* (Edinburgh 1979), 127-30.

White, G., Some Glasgow Designers and their work. In *The Studio* XV (1897), 231-233.

'Plaister Gimcracks': the Handicraft of Allan Ramsay the Poet

Iain Gordon Brown

The exhibition 'Poet and Painter', held in the National Library of Scotland to commemorate the tercentenary of the birth in 1684 of Allan Ramsay the elder and the bicentenary of the death exactly a century later of his son Allan the painter, had as its theme each of the Ramsays' interests in that art which the other made his especial province. The poet was discussed as a man concerned with the visual arts, and the painter was examined as a littérateur. Some fresh insight into the interrelationship of the arts in eighteenth-century Scotland was provided by an exhibition which considered at an appropriate anniversary moment a remarkable instance of the involvement of an artistic poet father and his poetic painter son with what were known in Augustan aesthetic theory as the 'sister arts'.

During research for the Ramsay exhibition certain evidence for the elder man's interest in handicraft came to light. The poet's letters were closely examined for all references to the visual arts, and several which alluded to his own practical experience of making works of art, or more properly craft, were identified as being of special interest. One actual example of his handiwork has also been discovered, and this was displayed in the exhibition; and a further item also now falls to be considered in a brief account of the material remains of the art of Ramsay the poet. These objects have the additional curiosity of being, so far as is known, the only surviving memorabilia of either of the two Ramsays.

The middle and later years of the 1730s saw first the obstruction and ultimately the failure of the poet's plans for a theatre in Edinburgh. His letters of this period contain allusions not only to the frustration of his theatrical project but also to his gradual withdrawal from commercial life as a bookseller and to a general disenchantment with literature. These attitudes are well expressed in a letter to Duncan Forbes of Culloden:

> Will ye gie me something to do here. I pass a sort of a half idle scrimp life tending a trifling trade that scarce affords me the needful . . . Bookselling good for Nothing, poetry that's faild me . . .'[1]

From these disappointments he sought diversion. One major outlet was his active promotion of his son's career: as the present writer has shown, the poet followed the young painter's progress with keen interest and attempted to the best of his ability, and in a variety of ways, to advance him in his quest of 'rhino and renown'.[2] But the elder man also indulged his own artistic tastes by way of distraction from ambitions thwarted. His enterprising mind turned to the promotion of sales of pictures and *objets d'art*, and his ventures in this field are attested by advertisements in *The Caledonian Mercury*, for example in the issues of 25 November 1736 and 14 February 1740. (In February 1740 the poet can also be found advertising in *The Caledonian Mercury* mezzotints by Faber of his son's new whole-length portrait of the second Duke of Argyll. From about this date the poet occasionally signed letters 'Allan Ramsay primus', for he was aware that from then on, when the name was mentioned, another individual and another talent had to be considered every bit as much. And so, in this newspaper advertisement, the public is informed that prints of a picture by 'Allan Ramsay junior' are to be obtained from 'Allan Ramsay senior in Edinburgh': a perfect instance of the two Ramsays' names being used together, and of 'senior' attempting to assist 'junior' to the limit of his power.) Furthermore the poet found satisfaction and release from the pressures of the commercial and literary rat-race — the desire for retirement and for a life of virtuous ease is a recurring theme in his letters of this period — in the exercise of his manual talents. That he had ability in the area of practical arts and crafts should come as no surprise, for he had, after all, practised the skilled profession of wigmaking before turning to literature. Tradition in the family of one of his closest friends and patrons preserves the memory of the old poet making children's toys.[3] But it was in the production of a series of plaster of Paris plaques decorated with casts of coins or intaglio gems that he took the greatest pride and pleasure; and it is these, together with the associated literary evidence, which it is the purpose of this note to discuss.[4]

Ramsay first mentioned his 'gimcracks' in a letter of 15 October 1734 to his great friend and patron Sir John Clerk of Penicuik:[5]

> I send you likwise ane Esay being the first tryal of mine of two Bas-reliefs done in Clay & brunt into a Brick one from a Medale of your own and a Cleopatra. The fancy pleases me because it is one way of making such things durable at the same time that I can make them as sharp as thrown on sulphur or plaster.

Some months later the poet again referred to his 'art of casting', this time in the remarkable letter which he sent to the Lord Provost of Edinburgh soliciting government aid to enable his son to pursue his artistic training in Italy. Ramsay had been doing some name-dropping in suggesting how such favours might be obtained. The Lord Advocate was his friend, he told Patrick Lindsay; and so was the great Duke of Argyll's brother:

> My Lord Ilay does not disregard me (dinna Laugh). I had his Lordship in my closet the day before he left this place near two hours making Bas-reliefs, he was much pleasd with my art, lugd out some courious antique Gems which I took molds of, and promised to bring me a Box full the next time he came doun.[6]

On 27 May 1735 Ramsay informed Clerk: 'I am much improven in my arts of casting, bronzing &c this Spring. It has opened a fine field of amusement to me . . .' With this letter he enclosed an example of the craft of which he had clearly become very proud:

> I am subject to the common quality of Gimcrackers, that of fancying every one should like what pleases themselves, which engaged me to send you a specimen of my casting of Medales, having purposly chosen some Scots coins of low & wore impression for I can be sure to bring my coppys out as sharp as the originall. One of

the litle Tables shews one side the other the Reverse as they are numberd from 1 to 16. A complete Series of Grecian, Roman & British Coins done in this manner 30 or forty on a Table would ornament a Closet extreamly well with Basreliefs interspersd . . . I am ashamed to give you the trouble but if it were a diversion to you any morning to range on your Charter house table all your best old and modern medals and count them up and send me a loan of them for a day or two they shall be returnd safely with setts of them of my doing either plain or bronz'd . . .[7]

The specimen of Ramsay's 'casting of Medales' to which its articifer here refers still survives in the Clerk collection at Pencuik House, Midlothian, though its identity was until recently unknown and its author-ship had remained unrecognised. The plaster plaque in question bears on its back the incised signature 'A Ramsay' (the initial letters being written as a ligature) and the place and date of manufacture, 'Ed^r. 1735'. The casts are of coins of four sovereigns: Charles II, William III, Anne and George I. The plaque, which measures 13.5 by 11 cms, has a field painted dark red and a black-painted raised edge; the coins are coloured in simulation of the originals (Figs. 1, 2).

Ramsay mentioned, in the letter to Clerk just quoted, his belief that casts of this type of ancient coins

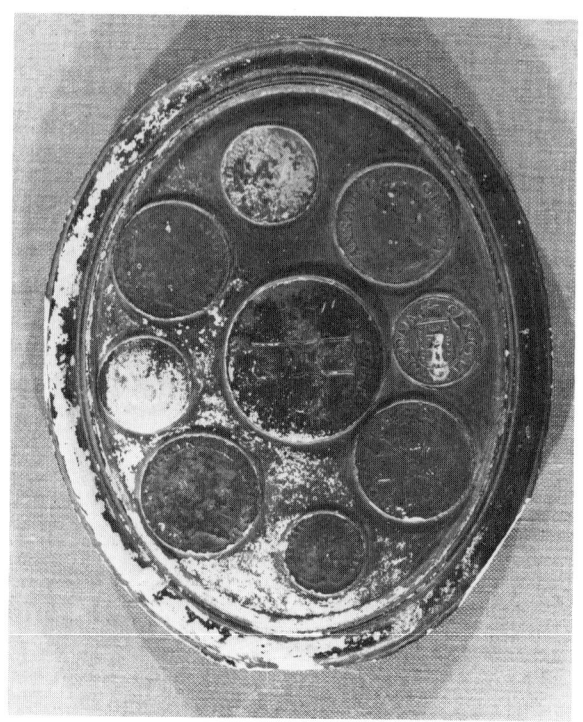

1.

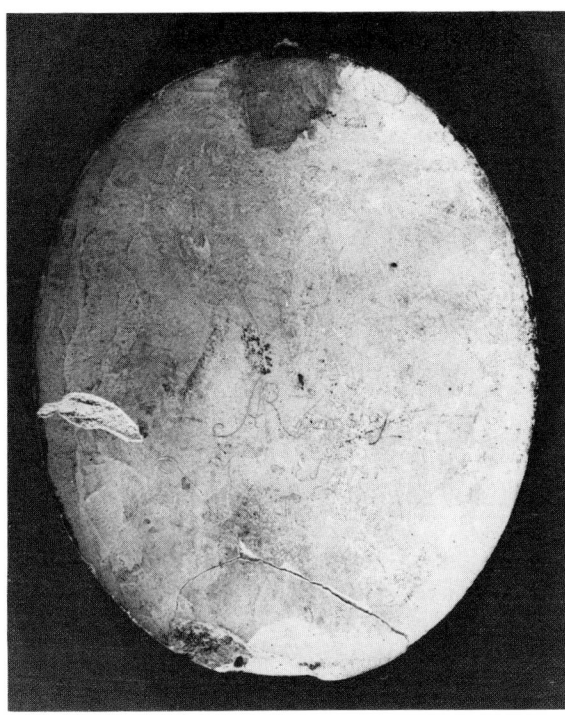

2.

'would ornament a Closet extreamly well with Basreliefs interspersd . . .' What exactly did he have in mind? The evidence suggests that the poet did indeed make plaques of a historical series of Roman coins. A draft of a poem in one of his composition books in the British Library[8] dates from 1735. This verse was addressed to 'the Countess of Eglingtoun with the bass-relief Bustos of the 12 Cesars'. Susanna, Countess of Eglinton was one of Ramsay's principal patrons, and the recipient ten years previously of the dedication of *The Gentle Shepherd*. Now he addressed her thus:

> These first Imperial twelve who blaze
> so bright in antient story
> Who did by noble conquest raise
> old Rome to all her Glory
> Attend your Ladyship in Bust
> were they in Being now
> Sure Julius or the great Agust
> would share the world with you.

Between such 'tables' of coin-impressions might hang 'Basreliefs'. An indication of what Ramsay meant by these is offered by a letter to Clerk of 31 October 1738:[9]

> I herewith send you a Dozen of the most curious Bass-reliefs that ever I had. I had them lately from abroad

they are well worth half crowns the pice but if you like them take the set for a Guinea or less if you think proper.

He added by way of postscript:

> The Bass reliefs being taken from the antique statues I need not tell you their names you'll know them at first sight only for form I shall name them as named to me — 1 Apolo — 2 Venus — 3 Hercules — 4 Dejanira — 5 The faun — 6 The flora — 7 The Vestall Virgin — 8 Jupiter & Io — 9 Jup. & Leda — 10 Nymph & Satyr — 11 Inigo Jones — 12 a Cupid from Corregio. The small ones to the Bargin.

Old Allan, so endearingly consequential, and enthusiastic in his interests in coin-plaques and classical plaster bas-reliefs, could not restrain himself (even when writing to a man of Clerk's known antiquarian learning), from giving gratuitous information. It must be admitted that the letter implies that these particular casts were not in fact of Ramsay's own manufacture but were simply imported and retailed by him at a time

3.

when it pleased him to think of himself as the sort of art dealer Clerk's own grandfather had been a century before. The possibility remains, however, that the poet did actually cast little classical plaques of a type similar to that of the Venus (from the series mentioned above) which has very recently been discovered at Penicuik House (Fig. 3). This pleasing piece of gimcrackery is the only known survivor of those objects which illustrate Ramsay's ideas of decoration in an idiom which reflects well the self-consciously classical mood of his pastoral verse and Horatian epistles.

References

1. National Library of Scotland, MS. 2968, f. 25 (15 April 1736); cf. A. M. Kinghorn and A. Law, eds., *The Works of Allan Ramsay* (Scottish Text Society) Vol. IV [hereafter *Works*, IV], p. 203, Letter 45.

2. See generally Iain Gordon Brown, *Poet and Painter: Allan Ramsay, father and son, 1684-1784* (Edinburgh 1984), and *id.*, 'Allan Ramsay's rise and reputation', *The Walpole Society*, L (1984).

3. Brown, *Poet and Painter*, p. 10. See also Rosalind K. Marshall, *Women in Scotland, 1660-1780* (Edinburgh 1979), p. 8 and plate 4.

4. I am grateful to Sir John Clerk of Penicuik, Bt. for permission to quote from the Clerk of Penicuik Muniments in the Scottish Record Office, and also to reproduce the photographs which illustrate this article.

5. SRO, GD18/4339; cf. *Works*, IV, p. 198, Letter 40.

6. NLS, Adv. MS. 23. 3. 26, f. 19; cf. *Works*, IV, p. 200, Letter 41.

7. SRO, GD18/4340; cf. *Works*, IV, p. 201, Letter 42.

8. Egerton MS. 2023, F. 14; cf. Kinghorn and Law, eds., *The Works of Allan Ramsay* (Scottish Text Society) Vol. III, p. 235.

9. SRO, GD18/4342; cf. *Works*, IV, p. 210, Letter 52.

The Plague in the Grass (grass sickness in horses)

A F Fraser

While Britannia ruled her global empire, it was a time of great peace in Scotland. Throughout the pleasant summer months of 1910, Scottish horses grazed their native fields as usual, when free from work. Year by year in their hundreds of thousands they had seasonally rusticated like this in well-earned temporary freedom. But this was to be the last summertime of good fortune in the untroubled life of the Clydesdale. The era of working horses living in complete harmony with the native environment was, in a sense, drawing to a close. The countryside of Scotland would never again so safely harbour countless idle horses grazing their lowland fields. In the late spring of the following year a fatal illness struck them from nowhere. Its first blow fell on the east coast.

The disease, quickly to be named grass sickness, was unknown in the world until, in May 1911, some military horses grazing in the parish of Barrie, near Dundee, contracted a strange malady and died. The illness was like no other, and local vets were puzzled.

1. The great pre-potent Dunure Footprint. Many of his progeny became grass sickness victims.

The new ailment gradually touched more and more spots on the eastern side of the country as the grazing seasons followed each other. It spread stealthily.

At first grass sickness did not progress far from Dundee, although it occurred in an increasing number of adjacent parishes, affecting Clydesdales and other work horses there. During the years of the First World War, the disease spread inland to Central Scotland and northward. Perthshire became affected, as were the counties of Aberdeen and Angus. Soon after the Great War's end the sickness became prevalent among horses in Fife. It encroached on the Highlands by appearing in arable pockets of Inverness-shire and Ross-shire. As new areas became involved, the disease took the form of localised epidemics, around Brechin and Forfar, for example. In 1920 fierce outbreaks also affected such northeastern strongholds of the Clydesdale horse as Turriff, Banff, Moray and Nairn.

In due course the spread took a southerly direction, affecting Galloway and the Border regions. It spilled over into northern England from there. Although they seemed relatively unaffected for a while, the central lowlands of Scotland experienced more and more cases until, in 1928, Ayrshire suffered severely. An epidemic along the Ayrshire coast, taking in the surrounding districts of Ayr and Girvan, showed that virtually all of mainland Scotland had now been covered by the inexorable progress of the disease over a span of seventeen years.

The advance of grass sickness was continuous, eventually reaching the Orkney Isles by 1938. Although neighbouring areas became affected, adjacent grasslands were not always involved one after another. Rivers such as the Tay and the Spey had checked the progress of the disease for several years. Ranges of hills, too, such as the Campsies, seemed to act as barriers to its spread. Nevertheless, an annually progressive advance took place, leaving increasing numbers of horses dead in its wake and uncounted tragic circumstances for horsemen and farmers. It was estimated that the annual toll of horses reached fifteen hundred, and immediate replacements on that scale were out of the question. Ploughmen lost jobs and homes. By 1929, grass sickness had taken all of agricultural Scotland into a grip which was not be released as long as horses were the main work force in the country. Thousands of once-fit horses fell as its victims.

Other farm livestock were unaffected by this disease, and it was clear that only the horse and horse-kind were susceptible to grass sickness. Even a few individuals of the donkey, the Przewalski horse and the zebra later became affected in Britain. Although it was the Clydesdale which suffered in greatest number, other breeds of horse were just as prone. Perhaps the Shetland Pony had some immunity; comparatively few of them succumbed in affected areas. In all breeds, foals and very young horses less than a year of age were only rarely affected. Evidently they had some form of juvenile immunity which certainly had not been acquired from their vulnerable mothers. Three to six year old horses showed the highest incidence.

Identifying the disease was not difficult. It had very characteristic forms and, especially after the event, there was no confusing it with other miscellaneous illnesses of horses. The main character of the illness was that the whole digestive canal, from throat to rectum, ceased to function, as though on physiological strike. With this event came some distress and a gripping mental depression. The primary signs of the disease were inability to swallow and some regurgitation of grassy stomach contents (being 'sick' in the Scots idiom). There was also sweating, quivering of muscles, arrest of urination and poor evacuation of the bowels. Sometimes in drawn-out cases the inactive intestines would later produce scant, hard droppings resembling grass golf balls with black coating.

The illness usually followed one of two courses — the acute type, which was severe and short, and the chronic type, which slowly worsened over weeks or months. Some other cases were sub-acute and were of an in-between type. The start of the illness, however, was similar in all types; the horse had difficulty in swallowing food or water and became sluggish. These first signs became dreaded by horsemen. When watering the horse a suspicion would start when the water was not being gulped well. (It is usual for a big working horse to take in about forty strong gulps at one drinking.) Water which had been drunk would start to run back out of the mouth and nose. At this the horse would retch, as though to be sick; sometimes it actually vomited, which is a virtually impossible act for a normal horse. The disease was well named by farmers. Another early sign was a pitiful attempt to chew and swallow food. This too would be brought back; or a horse could choke on its own food.

With the first signs soon went a depressed state which became a stupor which was unlike the sharp-witted working Clydesdale respected for its responsiveness. The knowledgeable horseman knew what he was dealing with by that time — another 'grass case'. To be sure, the horse could be roused with a sharp command, but other signs would develop. Muscular tremors were commonly shown, some got stomach pains, some produced a foamy mass of sweat under the tail, some became generally distressed. The acute cases rapidly got worse and could die as quickly as in twelve hours, or go on for several days. The chronic case would completely cease to drink and would have little or no appetite while it stood to the bitter end in its huddled posture as the muscles wasted away progressively. In the hindquarters the flesh shrank and became very hard. The contour of the chronic case was striking, for the abdomen became so severely contracted that the horse took on a shape like that of a greyhound — 'herring-gutted' was a graphic term sometimes used.

Some farmers had a sick horse destroyed humanely and quickly but others, for a while, did not in the forlorn hope that the animal might recover. A few —

about four percent — of the chronic cases appeared to do so. It was true that some did not die and that some regained the appearance of good health, but they could never work again. Those few which appeared to recover never had their former stamina or strength. In due course it became routine to destroy a grass sickness case as soon as a diagnosis could be confirmed. Sometimes a blood test would be carried out to make the diagnosis a positive one; it became shown in the detailed research that no fewer than ten different biochemical constituents of normal blood increased in quantity during the terminal phase of the illness.

Although there were cases in a few spots in England and Wales and on the western seaboard of the mainland of Europe, it was very largely Scotland's own problem. Certainly, no other country had it in epidemic form. An average of two and a half percent of the population of horses in Scotland died each year from it. The affliction clearly had some specific cause which was most likely to affect a horse at pasture. Equally clear was its spread by some special agent,

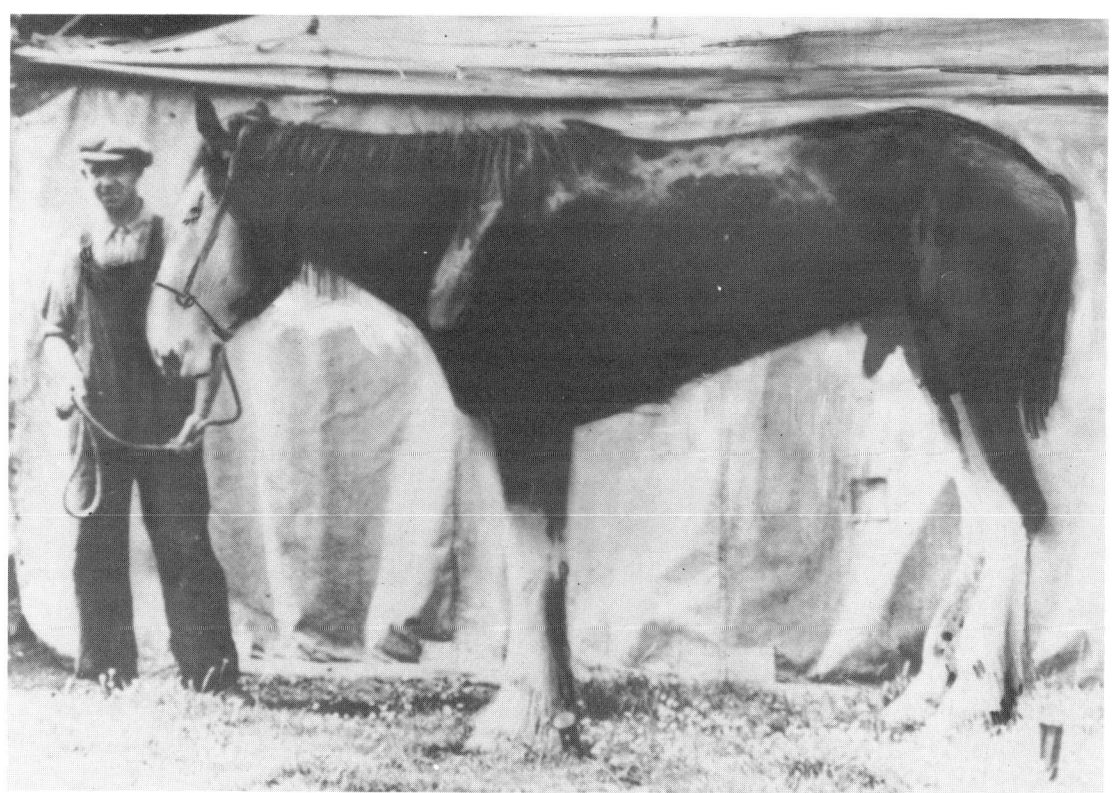

2. A typical case of chronic grass sickness. Photo: A. Brownlee.

such as wild life, or natural agency, such as wind. A pasture which showed a case one year might not show further cases in the succeeding years. Altogether, a great deal came to be known about it but the precise cause was not to be found. The illness remained incurable and continued to erode the Clydesdale breed as premium stallions and pregnant mares were counted among the victims.

The prevention · of grass sickness was evidently possible by permanent stabling; there was safety in hay, and the town horses therefore escaped the plague. It was an extremely uncommon event for a horse in a city or town stable to take the illness. While the grass sickness epidemics encircled the cities of Aberdeen and Dundee, virtually for two decades, the horses of these cities — which must have numbered over eight thousand in that space of time — escaped with only a rare case. Even when grass was cut and taken into the stable, horses which ate it did so with impunity. The street horses in the cities of Aberdeen, Glasgow and Edinburgh were never therefore in jeopardy, so the

problem remained on the farm and attracted surprisingly little concern in urban circles. Of course, the man in the street had the Great Depression on his mind while the horseman on the farm fretted over grass sickness.

For the investigators into its causal factors the mysterious condition of grass sickness left many pointers. Particularly tantalising were the seasonal clues. The great majority of cases occurred after the horse had been put out on grass pasture for two weeks or more. The state of the grass seemed significant, for the first cases each season were in areas or fields where the growth was most advanced. If a district had its springtime grass growth ten days ahead of another, that district would have its first 'grassers' ten days before the other. Again, it was commonly found that horses were attacked a few days after they had been transferred from one pasture to another. In each season, cases started to occur about the middle of May, but the peak incidence of the disease was in the month of June, when about seventy-five percent of cases

3. Clydesdale stable scene. Safe from danger in the grass.

occurred. After June the seasonal epidemic would decline sharply to autumn, by which time very few new cases would develop.

Farmers and horsemen became anxious about grass sickness when the weather was particularly fine. In periods when the weather was sunny, warm and dry, numerous cases would break out in the countryside. When there were spells of foul weather with cloud, rain and chill, the numbers of cases dropped. Again, more cases occurred in the open countryside than in fields near industrial areas.

The nature of the illness had a strange seasonal feature. At the height of the summertime epidemic, cases were mostly acute in nature, with the rapidly developing illness ending soon — and sometimes extremely quickly — in death of the afflicted horse. In other times and seasons of the year most cases took a chronic form, which was quite different by the manner in which the animal wasted away slowly, over weeks or even months, before the inevitable end.

But clues concerning the casual circumstances were confused in many obscure bizarre features. In some years the pattern would change. The disease would no longer seem linked to the weather, to the growth of the grass, or to any geographical distribution. Some few cases would occur in horses kept outdoors in winter. Symptoms too would change. Acute cases would not quiver or sweat, and more were reported to recover. Several cases could occur together on a farm which had never experienced it before and would not record it again in subsequent years. An area where many cases had developed in previous years would suddenly be free of any. One farm could be without any cases while others immediately around it suffered badly. In one farm several horses would become sick at one time while on another only a single case would develop out of a large number of horses similarly exposed. The veterinary authority of the day, however, did not believe that all these variables were a matter of chance. Professor Russell Greig in Edinburgh declared, 'There is little, if any, doubt that these are not chance occurrences, but there is some fundamental law, as yet imperfectly understood, which governs their manifestations'. In due course the great search was intensified to seek out the 'fundamental law' which apparently governed this plague. The quantity of negative findings continued, however, to grow.

The nature of grazing land seemed as though it must surely hold the secret. The possibility of some toxic environmental factor at work in the disease was also given serious consideration. The veterinary researchers exploring this line of thinking at that period were some decades ahead of their time. Today in medicine there is wide awareness of the real threat to health in toxic environmental substances, but this degree of public health awareness did not exist in the years between the world wars. The environment was not then perceived to be the vital theatrical stage to the animal and human play which we now see it to be. With the mature notion that a major disruption to health could result from discrete and subtle chemical interference, a mixed body of scientific investigators explored the guilty acres.

Several different lines of enquiry were pursued in painstaking studies which went on over many years. In some cases the lifetime's work of an able researcher was invested in some singular aspect of the problem. Poisonous plants in the grass, chemical imbalances in the soil, toxic chemical changes in the pasture, were considered in detail and subjected to experimental enquiry. But the affected pasturage of the country's length and breadth was so varied in every aspect that many well-founded suspicions had to be discarded through lack of their persistent implication. Evidence which is circumstantial in nature has the inherent defect that it must be absolutely consistent in all events to be reliable. This is true in science as in the judgement of human affairs. The cause of this disease defied logical investigation.

Minute traces of potentially toxic substances, either contained in the pasture or produced by its plant life, were more difficult to eliminate. But here the enquiry was discouraged by the fact that a horse weighing close to a ton would surely need a significant quantity of any toxic substance to be affected so severely so quickly. In some instances it was clear that the animal suffered the acute form of the illness after only two days on the grass. The many feeding experiments, in which suspicious substances were fed to horses, were all destined to failure by the fact that the natural disease was only contracted at pasture. It did not occur in the stable, even when freshly cut grass was fed. This simple feature of grass sickness nullified many investigations which were dependent on experimental reproduction of the typical illness in the stable by unavoidable ingestion of substances selected in the field.

The disease was essentially a pastoral phenomenon.

It totally resisted every attempt to transfer it to the laboratory. Frustrated researchers did not appear willing to accept philosophically the hard evidence that the causation was integrated in the grassland. At least they did not generally resign themselves to shifting their laboratory work to the fields and parks and make laboratories out of them. This might have been done in the attempts to reproduce or transmit the problem under controlled conditions. It was the only flaw in the campaign of enquiry which was otherwise complete, given the knowledge and technology of the time. The study of plant pathology — the disease of plant life itself — was to develop later. Similarly, virology, and its enormous parent subject of microbiology, was to undergo both evolution and revolution in the half-century following. The early efforts of total research into the cause of the grim harvest of Clydesdale casualties each year were nevertheless valiant.

What the research might have lacked in its scientific depth — by today's standard — was compensated by its breadth, which involved extensive enquiry and much documentation. On what types of farms did it occur? Was there a common characteristic of the geography or geology of farms affected by grass sickness? No, it was in time ultimately found to be associated· with every conceivable type of land and farm. It was encountered at all elevations from sea level to foothills. It was found with equal regularity on good land and bad land, well-drained fields and marshland, lush new grass and scant old grazings, weedy grass and fine turf, fertilised and unfertilised pastures. It was as common on flat lands as on hillsides which faced every point on the compass. It could occur on muddy fields and even, rarely, on fields frozen under snow.

The types of grasses implicated in the disease also seemed very likely to hold answers. But extensive regional botanical surveys in 1927 and in 1938 failed to shed any light on the problem. For a time, however, it seemed that wild white clover might be the culprit. It appeared to be present on many of the offending fields and it had only been widely introduced to Scottish pastures about the time when the first cases were discovered. But, while clover was common where the disease occurred, it was also common in many places where it had never occurred. Suspicion also fell on the buttercup for some time, before it eventually completely excluded itself from some cases. No single type of grass or weed was consistently found to be present in the pastures involved in the disease.

The nature of the soil itself was considered. Intensive soil analysis was performed on samples from scores of farms and their implicated fields. But again, this failed to show consistent findings. The variations in these soils were as wide as in soils from unaffected areas. Researchers turned away then from grassland and searched for likely micro-organisms instead. The true cause had to be a germ since they concluded that 'there exists no correlation between the type of pasture concerned and the occurrence of the disease'.

Innumerable attempts were made to isolate organisms from the blood of acutely affected horses, but all failed. Even when large quantities of blood from affected horses were transfused into the blood of healthy horses, transmission of the true disease did not occur. It was then thought that a substance produced by an organism, an extract and not the organism itself, might be the cause. Sure enough, it was found in 1933 that one particular bacterial toxin was found in the intestines of some affected animals. This led a large-scale attempt in 1937 to immunise working horses against that bacterium (a clostridium) and its poisonous product. The experiment, conducted on a national scale, involved 4,500 blood tests and included over 2,000 horses. Some were injected and others, which were companions to these horses, were not injected. The experiment began successfully: the injected horses were immune to the toxin; but soon grass sickness affected their group as much as the group of horses not immunised.

Every conceivable angle was studied. Healthy horses were fed sweepings and insects from affected fields. All manner of potential causes were injected and pumped into experimental horses. The search included every conceivable poison and parasite. The most exotic, outlandish and unlikely agents were tested as the cause, but without a successful reproduction of the disease unnaturally. By an exhausting process of elimination, the likely causal agent was deemed a virus. With this conclusion and with fewer cases as horses become scarce in time, the search lost its impetus under a cloud of disappointment.

The ghostly past of grass sickness still haunts old stable buildings and chills the memories of farmers and horsemen, mostly now grown very old. Some never lost the picture of great lusty horses, on whom so much depended, fading in distress to thin 'herring-gutted' creatures. The sight of an afflicted work companion refusing to eat or drink, standing with its hind quarters backed into a corner and becoming more shrunken in appearance day by day, could remain as a vivid scar on the memory. To the grief of a horse-lover, the general distress and rapid end in the acute case was matched by the progressive mental depression and the gradual physical termination of the chronic. Some horsemen who had seen all this were glad enough when the epidemics diminished and ended as the tractors arrived in force. The changes in their lives and values, from the traditional ways to mechanisation on the farm, were easier to bear. Grass sickness, it could be said, invited the tractors onto the scene, for the fear of it was real in the agricultural society reliant on the draught horse.

A little more is known today about the mystery. Sophisticated research has shown that degeneration of protein-producing particles within certain nerve cells supplying the bowel is evidently responsible for many of the clinical features of grass sickness, such as the loss of stimulation, function and movement in the digestive tract. This nerve damage is caused by a toxin in the blood of affected horses. The paralysed state of junctions along segments of the intestines and the dilatation of sections preceding such junctions are characteristic of the basic *post mortem* findings in grass sickness. These forms of bowel defect can now be recognised as a state of 'generalised achalasia'. Achalasia is a bowel disorder involving segmental constriction, and several achalasias are known in human diseases caused by viruses and blood parasites. The loss of certain nerve cells due to a toxic agent can cause the stomach's entrance and exit to be closed off, with severe swelling of the stomach and the gullet. As a result tears and stretch damages would (and did) affect these parts. Other junctions of the digestive canal could also be affected with achalasia, giving the symptoms of paralysis of the throat and of the large intestine. In any case which survived, these alimentary

defects would be permanent and there would be limited absorption from the damaged digestive system. This is probably why 'recovered' animals never could regain their fitness.

The primary cause is still as much a mystery as ever. The spread around the country would seem to have been the work of some other creature — a transporter, or vector. In the '14-'18 war years, when much was neglected in rural Scotland, a small, overlooked animal, such as a mole, a hedgehog or field mouse, might have been somehow responsible for some of the spread. A vector might or might not have suffered some form of the illness itself and may have been a continuing reservoir for it. It may at times have died out in places, to the relief of the horses there. Such a state of affairs is not impossible in the world of biology. Something like it is seen in a brain disease of horses in the American continent which is caused by a virus transmitted by mosquitoes feeding from egrets and other birds — which harbour the disease and suffer it themselves. So there might have been some similar explanation for the weird pattern painted by grass sickness which spoiled the Clydesdale's grand finale at home.

Novel grass sickness cases (which might be different achalasias) are being discovered far beyond Scotland, and it could become a world problem in time. In Scotland the ailment is still present, with ponies the main victims now. Only a full solution to the problem would satisfy science and allow the development of some protection for those horses which dwell in vulnerable places. Future research may find the cause, such as a neurotropic virus, but the ten thousand prime horses which suffered and died of this plague in Scotland will remain a black statistic in equine history, proof that neither nature nor fate is necessarily fair. The army of willing work horses in Scotland's fields deserved better, even in the hard times of those lean years.

William Marshall, Agricultural Writer, in Scotland

Charles W J Withers

William Marshall was one of the greatest of all commentators on the agricultural economy at a time when many people were documenting and directing changes in the rural scene. Kerridge considers Marshall 'certainly the best of all English agricultural writers',[1] and Horn, his biographer, regards Marshall as a critically important figure in Britain's agricultural history.[2]

He was born in Yorkshire in 1745 and died, in the same county, in 1818. Virtually his whole life was spent either managing, observing, or writing about the agricultural interest during a period of major changes in farming practice. Marshall's monument in Pickering records how 'he was indefatigable in the study of rural economy'.[3] His deep knowledge of the subject is reflected in numerous publications,[4] which to one observer at least, are to be preferred to those of Arthur Young, Marshall's great rival, for their 'arrangement and greater practical knowledge'.[5] Marshall was also a prime mover behind the establishment of a Board of Agriculture. Yet his influence was most keenly felt in English agricultural circles and with one exception, all Marshall's works deal with the rural economy of different parts of England. In a period when changes in Scotland's agriculture were no less dramatic than those affecting England, it is interesting that someone of Marshall's stature should have shown so little concern with 'the georgical element' in Scotland. No firm reason can be put forward to account for this relative neglect: Marshall pursued his surveys of England's rural economy in great depth, and it may be that after detailing agricultural affairs in England he intended to turn his attention to Scotland, and perhaps also to Wales, but never did so through lack of time. He hints at this in his *The Rural Economy of the West of England* (1796). In noting that he has 'at length obtained a GENERAL VIEW of the ESTABLISHED PRACTICES OF ENGLAND', he goes on to remark: 'And, altho' I have had a partial View of those of SCOTLAND, it is not my intention to extend my Remarks to that part of the Island, or to Wales, until I have, in some measure, *rounded my plan*, with respect to ENGLAND'.[6] It may be also that works such as Home's *The Gentleman Farmer* (1776), Wight's six-volume *The Present State of Husbandry in Scotland* (1778) and several texts on the agriculture of regions such as Berwick,[7] Angus,[8] and Galloway[9] made a Scottish survey by Marshall along the lines of his work for England unnecessary. It may simply be that Marshall's overriding concern with England and the physical impossibility of surveying agriculture in every district and region meant he had little time (though no lack of interest) to devote to Scotland.

Marshall's only work on Scotland is his *General View of the Agriculture of the Central Highlands of Scotland*, a relatively short survey of sixty-eight pages, published in London in 1794. In effect, the 'Central Highlands' were synonymous with the Perthshire estates of the Earl of Breadalbane with whom Marshall stayed for four months during the summer of 1792 and for a shorter period in 1793. The connection between the two men and between Marshall and the management of affairs on the Breadalbane estates is crucial. In 1792, there arose a serious disagreement between the Earl and John Campbell, his factor, over renting policy, the rendering of services and the management of the estate. Marshall was caught up in the affair and, eventually, was called upon to advise the Earl. In 1793, Marshall again visited the area and involved himself with matters of sheep breeding. It was at this time also that moves made by Marshall to establish a Board of Agriculture were to be successful (though not for Marshall himself). His work on Scotland appeared as a 'tribute to the Board'.[10] For a number of reasons, then, Marshall's *General View . . .* merits study. This note examines the work in relation to Marshall's other publications and his importance as a whole, but more particularly, focuses upon the way in which, in places, his survey of the agriculture of the Central Highlands was influenced by his being a close witness to problems associated with the improvement of the rural economy in the area. Such a note is interesting for the light it casts upon the man and his work. Marshall would perhaps have been the first to agree: he himself wrote how 'a reviewer ought to decide on the internal evidence of the work before him, yet some knowledge of a writer's experience, especially while writing on a practical and difficult art, may serve to lighten the labour of criticism'.[11]

Marshall's interest for us today and his influence amongst his contemporaries stems from two sources: his publications, and his involvement with the Board of Agriculture. His first published work — *Minutes of Agriculture Made on a Farm of 300 Acres of Various Soils near Croydon* — appeared in 1778 and was based on his first real experience of farm management. It was followed by works on *Agriculture and the Weather* (1779), the *Black Canker Caterpillar*, and *Planting and Ornamental Gardening* (1785), but he is best known for his surveys of the rural economy of England, the first of which, *The Rural Economy of Norfolk*, appeared in 1787. Others followed at regular intervals, each focusing on different parts of the country, and each characterised by a thoroughness and detail born of careful observation and deep knowledge: on York-shire (1788), Gloucestershire (1789), the Midland Counties (1790), the West of England (1796), and the Southern Counties (1798). Despite the county bases on which they were published, Marshall based his works on what he called 'districts'. As he wrote in his *The Rural Economy of the West of England*, '. . . in examining a Country, like England, with a view to the existing state of its AGRICULTURE, and the other branches of its RURAL ECONOMY, the arbitrary lines of Counties are to be wholly disregarded . . . *Natural*, not *fortuitous* lines, are requisite to be traced; *Agricultural*, not *political* distinctions, are to be regarded'.[12] Marshall adopts the same plan in his work on the Highlands, and while, in places, he talks of the Highland hills as one district, he also recognises local differences in soil, vegetation, and agriculture. Strath Tay, for example, he refers to as the 'Garden of the Highlands'.[13]

Almost every aspect of agriculture, and the factors bearing upon it, was examined: from the geology, the geographical situation and area, through the laying-out of estates, the extent of leasing, the propagation and management of woodlands, enclosures, farm sizes, the amount of competition between farmers in different districts, the management of grasslands, orchards, harvested crops and vegetables, to new breeds, the nature of the tenantry and the degree to which the rural economy was suffused with a 'spirit of improvement'.

Marshall was one of the first to realise that farmers needed guidance in the adoption of innovations and in the improvement of techniques, and that, for the most part, no such assistance was forthcoming: 'It has long been justly complained of, that whilst every attention has been paid, & every possible encouragement given, to *trade*, yet that Agriculture, has been totally neglected'.[14] In his *Rural Economy of the Midland Counties* (1790) he wrote: 'I think it right to intimate the probable advantages which might arise from a BOARD OF AGRICULTURE; — or, more generally, of RURAL AFFAIRS; to take cognizance, not of the state and promotion of AGRICULTURE, merely; but also of the CULTIVATION OF WASTES and the PROPAGATION OF TIMBER: bases on which, not Commerce only, but the political existence of the Nation is founded'.[15] After a period of delay, Marshall's scheme was adopted (though he was not the only motivator), and in 1793 the Board of Agriculture was established with Sir John Sinclair as President and Arthur Young as Secretary.[16] It was against this background that Marshall arrived in Scotland, at Taymouth in Perthshire, in 1792.

The problem on the Breadalbane estates centred upon the rents set for two farms in particular, Finlarig and Boreland, in Killin parish.[17] The persons most involved in the dispute over the new renting policy were the Earl himself, and John Campbell, his factor. Campbell, though himself based in Glenfalloch in the south-west of the county, seems in his position as factor (and what Marshall was later to call 'ground officer') to have acted on behalf of the tenants of the farms in question. In January 1792 Campbell wrote to the Earl of Breadalbane protesting that 'the rents spoke of as intended to be put on these Two Farmers were in his opinion higher in proportion to their value than those of the rest of your Lordship's farms in the neighbourhood'.[18] Not only was the rent itself increased, the new lease imposed the ending of tenurial services and payment in kind.

The tenantry of the farms, and of the estates as a whole, were divided into several groups: small tenants, crofters, and cottars. Under the previous leasing arrangement, those holders of land lower in the hierarchy had performed labour services for the others, chiefly at harvest, and, more regularly, at the cutting and carrying of peats. The Earl of Breadalbane was proposing the abolition of such services as part of general improvements on his farms. In his reply to Campbell, dated 23 January 1792, he wrote: 'Whatever rents I shall put on my farms I shall take care no good Tenant will have any cause to complain of them'. In the same letter Breadalbane remarks: 'I should consider myself as incurring the suspicion of extreme folly was I to diminish or underrate the value of my Estate'.[19] He expected an annual rent of £150 per annum for Boreland. We are not told about Finlarig, but Boreland farm was mixed in nature, containing arable and pasture: 'a considerable Grazing is annexed to it which contains upwards of Eight Hundred Sheep'.[20] Part of the intended improvements involved enclosing some of the grazing land. This enclosure, together with the extinction of rights and the displacement of population it entailed and the associated cessation of labour services, signalled new ways in the management of Highland agriculture. It was this, rather than the increase in money that Campbell, acting either in the interests of the tenants, or for some undisclosed personal reason, felt unable to sanction.

Breadalbane clearly had a high regard for his factor and tried to win him over to the proposed new policy. In the final lines of his letter of January 23, the Earl points out that 'Considerable offers over the rent fixed has [sic] been offered for Boreland, but I have given you the preference on more moderate terms and what I consider rather under the value of the farm than above it'.[21] In the February of 1792, Campbell again protested to the Earl, asking why the renting policy had been altered in such a way. Breadalbane's reply suggests his patience was wearing thin: 'These are the rents I proposed if they are not agreeable to the Tenants or if they think them too high tell them from me they may remonstrate'. He goes on, however, to deny them even that: 'I can read a petition but a remonstrance I shall through [sic] in the fire'.[22]

There is no evidence to suggest that such a petition or remonstrance was actually drawn up, or, if it was, whether Breadalbane ever received it. In any case, Campbell could not agree to the new policy, and on 12 March 1792 he resigned. The Earl appealed to him over this 'unexpected resolution': 'I am sorry for it was by no means my intention having never impeached or even suspected your abilities, integrity or honour . . . I trust your good sense will induce you again to resume the charge'.[23] Campbell continued to correspond on such matters as the Crinan Canal and the leasing of mines on the estate, but he never resumed his position as factor. In April 1792 he wrote to the Earl through an intermediary: 'he requests me to mention to your Lordship that having resolved to confine his attention chiefly to his private affairs and to that of his immediate Relatives He resigns your Lordship's business at Inverary and desires me to make his best acknowledgements and wishes to know who is to be his successor'.[24] There the affair ended.

Later that year Breadalbane issued a circular to his estate factors, the wording of which suggests that the proposed policy had been accepted:

> Now my Estate is settled upon improving Leases, I expect that for my Interest and the Welfare of the Tenants you will by precept and example encourage them to go on cheerfully, so that by strictly attending to the regulations of the Lease they may in two or three years be enabled to live more comfortably. And that they may not want further inducement I propose giving a few premiums to those who improve best — second best and third best in the Several Districts; for this purpose you will keep Memorandums of what you observe going on in your officiary and be ready to Report to me when I call for it after my return to the Country.[25]

Horn (1982) has hinted at the influence of Marshall in this circular.[26] Perhaps more evident is the influence *upon* Marshall, as it is reflected in places in his *General View of the Agriculture of the Central Highlands of Scotland*, of the dispute between Breadalbane and his factor. Of course, much of what Marshall includes in his survey of the Central Highlands follows a pattern that was laid out in earlier publications and continued in later ones. It is no surprise, therefore, to find paragraphs devoted to enclosures (or, in the case of Perthshire, to the lack of them), to rents, and to subdivisions amongst the tenantry. But, in places, Marshall seems to be mindful of the affairs on the Breadalbane estates, and the way they were changing in the early 1790s, in his survey.

The Highlands were, in Marshall eyes, still largely unenclosed: 'we rarely meet with regularly inclosed fields, as in southern provinces; nor are the separations which occur (those of plantations and other kept grounds excepted) considered, or intended, as fences against sheep, which still overrun the country during the six months of winter, when the entire district may be said to lie in the most perfect state of common'.[27] Of the level of rents charged in the area, Marshall observed that many of the smaller estates 'may have been raised to something near their rental value: but the larger, I believe, remain at rents much below the real value of their respective soils; even when the disadvantages of situation and climature are taken into the estimate'.[28] It is difficult to know for certain if Marshall was thinking of Breadalbane's comments to Campbell concerning Boreland when he wrote this, or if he was making a general observation on Perthshire. The same must be said also of Marshall's comments on the tenantry. After briefly documenting the small holding size of the average tenant and the crofters in the area, Marshall turns his attention to the cottars: 'And still below these rank the Cotters, answering nearly to the cottagers of the southern provinces, except that, in the Highlands, they are attached, like the crofters, to the tenant, or joint-tenants, on whose farm they reside; receiving assistance and returning for it services'.[29] Given Marshall's association and acquaintance with the Earl at exactly the period the latter was introducing changes to his estates that sought the removal of labour services and the promotion of competition amongst the tenantry, it is likely that Marshall was influenced in what he wrote by what he had observed at first hand. And, of course, he would be likely to view the old practices as more representative of Highland agriculture than the new ones since he was not in a position to judge the success of the proposed new measures.

In general, Marshall's brief account of Highland agriculture was 'sensible and perceptive'.[30] In the several 'Principles of Improvement' he proposes towards the end of the work, Marshall is sufficiently in tune with the changes in the rural economy of the area to appreciate the consequences of new policies of management. In appreciating that enclosure will precipitate migration, Marshall urges that improvement be in everyone's interest, not merely the landowner's: 'Permit the present inhabitants to live in the county; and endeavour to make it the interest of everyone to assist in its improvement'.[31] The growing of potatoes and the establishment of woollen manufactures were recognised as important agencies in this overall change. Marshall also wrote on the wasteful practice whereby each tenant cut, carted and dried his own peats or did so as part of labour services. He proposed 'manufactures of peats as of bricks and tiles', and urged that centrally positioned sheds be erected to hold half a year's consumption of peat. And lastly, in directing these and other changes, Marshall considered a good foreman an invaluable asset: 'Make choice of a GROUND OFFICER who is capable and willing to set the requisite examples'.[32] Marshall may only have been advocating the need for reliable information and supervision in directing change in Perthshire just as he did in the case of his surveys of other areas, but it is difficult to avoid the conclusion that the case of Campbell had coloured his opinions regarding the diffusion and implementation of 'the spirit of improvement'.

The picture that Marshall affords us of Highland agriculture is admittedly limited in comparison with other sources of the period, not least perhaps Sinclair's *Statistical Account of Scotland*, published in twenty-one volumes between 1791 and 1799. But what is interesting is that through Marshall's work on the Central Highlands and his involvement in the affairs of the Breadalbane estates, we may glimpse, however fleetingly, the type of changes and activities that underlay a crucial period in Scotland's rural past. And after all, it is through such small-scale, unspectacular changes that Scottish country life has evolved and changed.[33]

References
1. E. Kerridge, 'Arthur Young and William Marshall', *History Studies* (1968), 2, 44.

2. P. Horn, *William Marshall (1745-1818) and the Georgian Countryside* (Oxford 1982), 2-3.

3. *Dictionary of National Biography*, XXXVI (1893), 252.

4. Some twenty-three separate works in all. A list is appended in Horn (1982), 87. She does not, however, mention Marshall's *Arbustum Americanum, the American Grove, or an Alphabetical Catalogue of Forest Trees and Shrubs, natives of the American United States*, which the *Dictionary of National Biography* states was published in 1785.

5. J. Donaldson, *Agricultural Biography* (London 1854), 64.

6. W. Marshall, *The Rural Economy of the West of England including Devonshire and parts of Somersetshire Dorsetshire and Cornwall* (London 1796), I, xxvi.

7. A. Lowe, *General View of the Agriculture of Berwick* (London 1794).

8. Mr Roger, *General View of the Agriculture of Angus* (London 1794).

9. J. Webster, *General View of the Agriculture of Galloway* (London 1794).

10. W. Marshall, *General View of the Agriculture of the Central Highlands of Scotland* (London 1794), ii.

11. W. Marshall, *A Review (and Complete Abstract) of the Reports to the Board of Agriculture from the Midland Department of England* (London 1815), 398.

12. W. Marshall, *The Rural Economy of the West of England . . .* , 1-2.

13. W. Marshall, *General view . . .* , 11.

14. National Library of Scotland, MS 641, f. 148 (Probably from J. Sinclair; undated).

15. W. Marshall, *Rural Economy of the London Counties* (London 1790), I, 222.

16. P. Horn (1982), *op. cit.*, 29.

17. Scottish Record Office (SRO), Breadalbane Papers, GD 112/40/10/6/9. Horn has these references incorrectly catalogued in her biography.

18. Ibid.

19. SRO, GD 112/40/10/6/10.

20. Ibid.

21. Ibid.

22. SRO, GD 112/40/6/12/2.

23. SRO, GD 112/40/6/11.

24. SRO, GD 112/40/6/17.

25. SRO, GD 112/40/10/6/23, ff. 1-7. All these folios are the same, as quoted in full in the text.

26. P. Horn (1982), *op. cit.*, 27.

27. W. Marshall, *General View . . .* , 16.

28. *Ibid.*, 26.

29. *Ibid.*, 32.

30. P. Horn (1982), *op. cit.*, 30.

31. W. Marshall, *General View . . .* , 51.

32. *Ibid.*, 60.

33. A. Fenton, *Scottish Country Life* (Edinburgh 1976), v.

Notes on Long-Line Fishing from Arbroath, Ferryden and Gourdon

David G Adams

These notes put on record information gathered from fisherfolk in Arbroath, Ferryden and Gourdon. Work with three types of long-lines is discussed (Fig. 1).

Place	Strings per Back	Hooks per String	Total Hooks
Arbroath	7	200	1400
Gourdon	12	100	1200
Eyemouth (Berwickshire)	10	100	1000

The number of hooks used in Arbroath and Gourdon appears to have been higher than for most parts of the east coast, though even there variations were possible. It is said that at Gourdon and Ferryden seventy to eighty hooks formerly made up a string, of which there were fourteen to a back, giving a total of 980 to 1120 hooks per line.

The hooks hung from lengths of hemp cord called *snoods* (Arbroath (A): *sned*; Ferryden (F): *snod*; Gourdon (G): *snud*). At one time they were spun by the fishers but latterly were factory-made. These were tied by a clove hitch to the *back* with two inches or so plaited to stiffen them. To the loop was tied the horsehair *tippet* (A), *tuppence* (F), or *tippin'* (G), made of two strands of horsehair each of about 15 to 18 hairs. These were usually spun by retired men using a *tippin' stane*, a spinner with an iron hook fixed in a lead disc. The hook was then bound or *beat on* with strong linen *beatin' thread*. The combined length of the snood and tipping was about 36" to 40", the tipping being about 22" (Fig. 2). The hair used had to be from a horse's and not from a mare's tail, as in the latter case the urine was believed to weaken the hair. Black or brown horsehair was the commonest obtainable but a preference for black was expressed at Ferryden and Gourdon, apparently because they usually fished on a dark rocky hard bottom. At Gourdon it is said that at Stonehaven and elsewhere to the north there was a preference for white horsehair since they fished on a sandy bottom. The reason for the use of horsehair is not at all clear. It was believed that it floated slightly

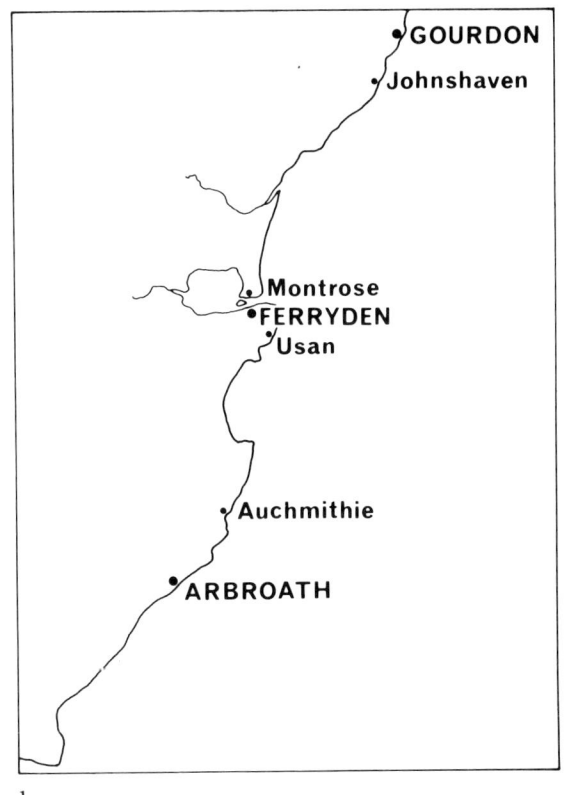

1.

Sma' (small) *lines* are the ordinary haddock lines as distinct from the great lines used to catch bigger fish. The line consists of the *back*, made from lengths of hemp cord spliced together by the fishermen. Each of these portional lengths was known as a *hank* or *string*, and each carried a certain number of hooks:

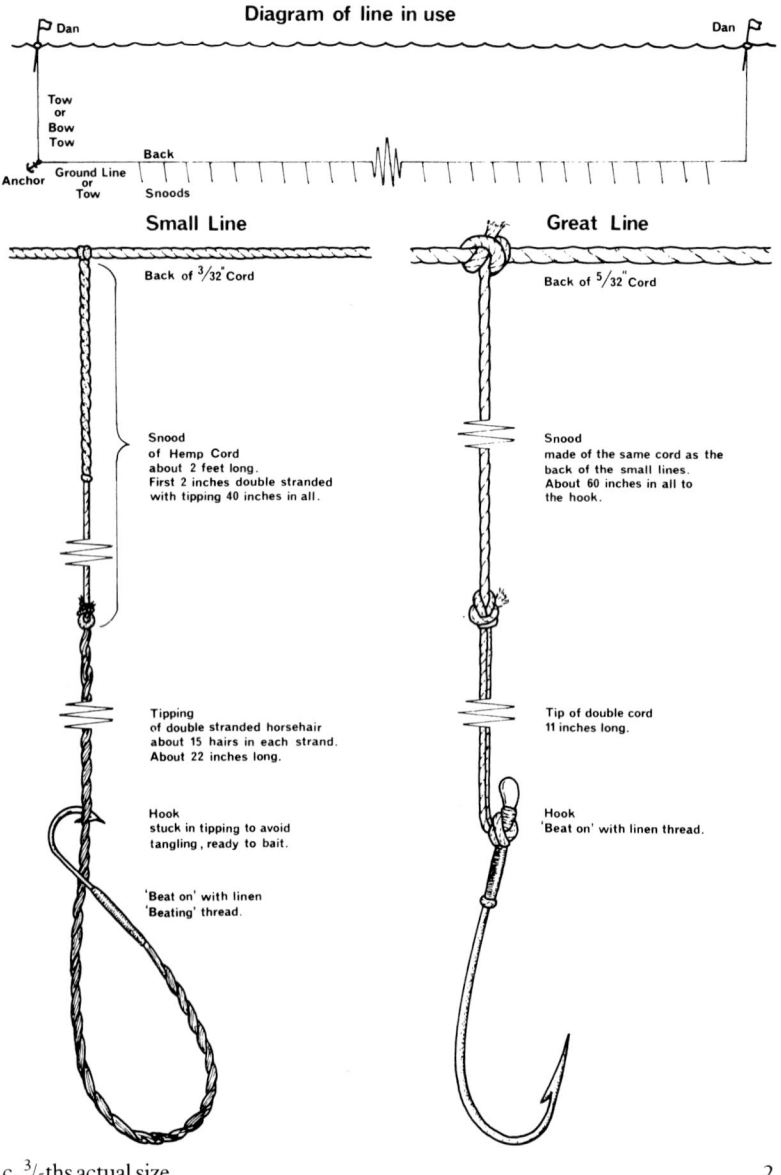

Diagram of line in use

Dan

Dan

Tow
or
Bow
Tow

Back

Anchor

Ground Line
or
Tow

Snoods

Small Line

Back of ³/₃₂" Cord

Snood
of Hemp Cord
about 2 feet long.
First 2 inches double stranded
with tipping 40 inches in all.

Tipping
of double stranded horsehair
about 15 hairs in each strand.
About 22 inches long.

Hook
stuck in tipping to avoid
tangling, ready to bait.

'Beat on' with linen
'Beating' thread.

Great Line

Back of ⁵/₃₂" Cord

Snood
made of the same cord as the
back of the small lines.
About 60 inches in all to
the hook.

Tip of double cord
11 inches long.

Hook
'Beat on' with linen thread.

c. ³/₅ths actual size

2.

and thus attracted the fish, but at the depth and time of day the fish feed it is unlikely that they would see the tipping at all and would locate bait by olfactory means. When synthetic orange coraline replaced horsehair it was at first tarred black until it was discovered that the bright orange made no difference to the fish. The horsehair, like the hemp cord and snoods, was supplied by Montrose Rope and Sail Works.

Each fisherman owned two lines, one being baited while the other was in use. A new line was bought every year. Lines were only shot twice, then *barked*,

i.e. soaked in water in which *cutch*, the bark of the East-Indian betel nut palm, *Areca catechu*, had been boiled up. This was done in large cauldrons usually by the shore. The process was repeated in a fortnight and afterwards every three weeks to remove the slime which built up, in order to give a good grip when hauling in the line. About twenty years ago nylon replaced hemp for the back, and coraline came into use for the combined snood and tipping, so that the whole is now referred to as the *snud* at Gourdon. The nylon lines are tarred only once a year and will last about fifteen years. The new materials were not sought by the fishermen, though the enforced giving up of the traditional materials has resulted in considerable labour saving. The contraction of line fishing also led to difficulty in the supply of traditional materials.

Each of the hooks had to be baited, usually with two mussels as the local Montrose basin mussels, the traditional source for the whole area, are small, and sometimes even three or four had to be used. Mussels were also bought in from the Tay or Leuchars in the last twenty years at Arbroath and Gourdon. About thirty years ago when there were enough line boats to warrant it, the Gourdon Fishermen's Association, set up about that time, sent a lorry to collect mussels from the Ythan at Newburgh. These were 'bonny big mussels' remembered with fondness as only one was needed per hook and so there was much less work in shelling and baiting. In one season twenty years ago spoiled edible mussels were brought into Arbroath from the beds at Morecambe Bay. Early this century shiploads were even brought in from Holland.

The 2400 or 2800 mussels required had first to be sheeled (cut from the shells), a job usually done by women at home, taking anything from three to four hours. The family assisted, children as young as three helping to gather limpets and sheel mussels. Sheeling and baiting used to be done in the house in winter and at the door in summer, but between the wars moved to sheds and outhouses. Young children were often placed in a barrel or large basket to keep them from wandering off and so interrupting the work. The mussels were sheeled with wooden-handled knives at one time made in Ferryden, or now with a cut-down table knife, into 2lb jam jars, the number of which gave a measure of how many were still needed, and then put in a wooden *mussel trough*. Baiting took another four or five hours, so the whole process, if done by one, could take up to nine hours.

When being baited, the line lies in a large round basket or *hamper* on the left of the baiter. On the right, tilted up slightly, lies the *scull*, originally a large oval wicker basket about 4 ft long, 3 inches deep at one end and tapering to nothing at the other. The last maker of wicker sculls at Gourdon died over ten years ago, and so oblong wooden trays, *backets*, are now used. There seems to be some evidence that backets were used in the Auchmithie-Arbroath area about 100 years ago. In baiting, the hook is first stuck through the *eye* of the mussel, the name given to the position of the large

addictor muscle which opened and closed the shell. The hook has then to be stuck through the dark brown *tongue*, the mussel's palp, to ensure it does not slip out. The *back* of the line is coiled in the deep end of the scull. The wooden sculls have a wooden crosspiece, and the first row of baited hooks is laid against this, the upper two-thirds of the scull being covered in a layer of newspaper upon which the mussels are laid, probably to prevent slipping on the shiny paint. The wicker sculls had to be covered in a layer of grass to prevent the hooks catching as the lines were shot. This was *bent* or *sea grass* (*Parpholis stigosa*) which has thin round stems and was pulled rather than cut. At Arbroath retired fishers gathered it on the West Links. At Ferryden it is said to have grown in a plantation above the village. At Gourdon it could be got at the shore just at the north end of the village, but twenty to thirty years ago the women used to make occasional expeditions to Sheilhill near Catterline to collect it. When wicker sculls were used, a crosspiece used to be made by twisting some of the grass and placing a piece of wood over it. At Gourdon this was called a *corsin' ging*, but at Arbroath where a piece of old hosepipe was laid on top, it was known as a *brig*. When completely baited the *back* of the line lies coiled in the bottom third of the scull while the other two-thirds is filled with neat row upon row of baited hooks, each attached by the tipping and snood to the *back*. In the past the baiting was done by one woman but in recent times at Gourdon another member of the family will sometimes turn up and bait alternate hooks, sitting at the opposite side of the line.

When the scull thus baited is handed over to the fisherman ready to take on board the boat, he lifts the coiled *back* up and over, and then checks over it, so that the snoods do not bunch together when the line is shot. This action was referred to as *settin' ower the line* (A, F), or *reddin' the back* (G), not to be confused with another process, *reddin' the line*. Each man of a boat's crew, usually five or six in the past, took a line on board. In the days when young laddies went to sea they started with a half line kept in a smaller half scull. The catch was usually shared equally between the boat's crew, with a share for the boat.

The lines are shot before dawn except in midsummer, so that the fish are attracted to the bait when they begin to feed at first light. Haddock, whiting and codling were and are the main catch. To commence fishing, a *dan* (a pole about nine feet long) is first put overboard, buoyed and weighted, with a brightly coloured flag at the top. It also carries a *tide licht* which is now battery-powered and switches off at sunrise. Until about fifteen or twenty years ago a candle within a small tin lantern was used. To the dan were attached three small *bows* (buoys) made of pig's bladders sealed with Archangel tar, and to these was attached about fifty fathoms of a tow with an anchor at the end. Plastic floats are used now. The bows were to prevent the tow pulling the dan over. At Arbroath a piece of old line useless for anything else, called a *bow tow* (also applied as a term of abuse for a useless person), was used. From the anchor runs about twenty fathoms of a *tow* (A) or *grund line* (G). To this is attached the first fishing line. The line was and is in some cases shot from the stern of the boat over a funnel of tinplate about four feet long, held on the left arm, and gripped by an internal wooden crosspiece. The boat then moves away from the anchored dan and the line pays out. At Gourdon now some of the boats have an H-shaped frame at the stern, over which the line is shot. At Arbroath the funnel was known as an *iron man*. The hand-held funnel gave good control over the shooting of the line, especially in sailboat days.

As one line is shot, the next is tied to it until all are shot. A second dan is then put overboard and the boat returns to the first dan to commence hauling in the lines. At Ferryden this was known as *hailing in*, and the end attached to the first dan was the *tissert end*, at Arbroath the *inmaist end* and at Gourdon the *in* or *tide end*. The other end, if anything, was the *oot end*. The lines are laid in a zig-zag pattern on the sea bed, always across the tide and preferably on hard bottom, since on a sandy or *saft boddom* the lines can travel and twist together, taking the crew hours to unravel ashore.

The zig-zag procedure was known at Arbroath as *feddin'* (folding) the line, and the turning point was the *bicht heid*. At Gourdon each part of the fold is a *bicht* or *wint*, each of which consists usually of a whole line. There are several ways of sailing in this process, usually *up sea*, *wast in*, due east and then inshore in a south-westerly direction. An alternative is *up sea*, *north in*, due east then inshore in a north-westerly direction. This was usual when men were fishing on the *shaald* (shallow) *water* and found boats working towards them instead of in the same direction (Fig. 3).

Hauling in one line takes forty minutes to an hour. At five or six lines to a boat as formerly, the whole process could take four or five hours. The fish are

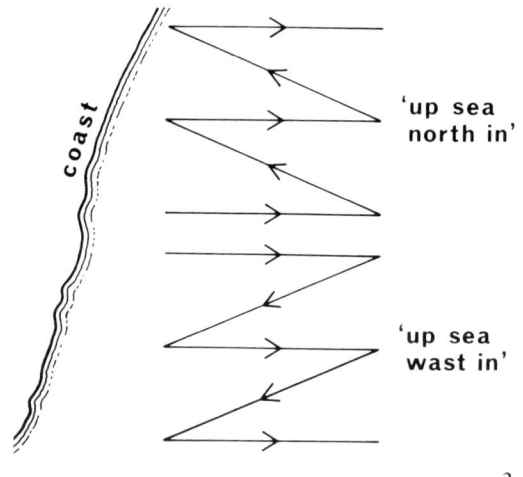

3.

taken off the hooks as they come aboard and the line is loosely coiled back in the scull. Each man takes turns to haul in half a line at a time, a marker every 200 hooks showing how many have been hauled in. Strips of red rubber are used as markers but coloured glass beads seem to have been used in the past. The same markers also give the baiter an idea of how many hooks have been baited or require baiting.

The next job ashore is *reddin' the lines* — removing old bait and the mess of starfish and clams attracted to the bait. Any missing hooks are replaced, a process which is referred to as *beating on wants* or *beating the wants*. The points of the hooks are stuck into the tipping to avoid tangling, and the line is coiled carefully in a large round basket or *hamper* ready to be baited again.

In the summer the lines were sometimes shot and left overnight about six or seven miles out off the Red Head from Arbroath in thirty fathoms of water on soft bottom. Lines and lobster and *partan* (crab) creels, called *sunks* at Arbroath, were formerly worked on the same day in summer. Nowadays at Gourdon line fishing is carried out in winter, and creel fishing in summer with strings of up to 240 creels worked from the largest boat. Gourdon, where nine men work five boats, and nearby Catterline where there is one boat worked by two men (in 1985), appear to be the last places on the east coast where the traditional long-lines are still used. There are a few young men at Peterhead who use a line with 500 hooks which they bait themselves with the large Ythan mussels. Otherwise Gourdon seems to be the last bastion of this age-old method of fishing.

The Sma' Gretlins

A seasonal variety of fishing about February and March, making use of the small lines with larger hooks and a variety of bait, seems to have been practised at Gourdon until about fifteen years ago. At Ferryden, where the fishing declined greatly between the wars (Gourdon expanded its line fleet at this period), this seems to have died out much earlier. At Arbroath no one had any clear recollection of it. Perhaps the interest in herring fishing there meant it was abandoned long ago. It may be the 'near great fishing' as practised at Johnshaven, between Gourdon and Montrose, described in the *Old Statistical Account* of the parish of Benholm. As haddock is in roe at that season, large codling was the main catch. The fish go off mussels at that time of year, and so the more easily available common mussel (*Mytilus edulis*), *lug* (lugworm, *Arenicola marina*), limpets (*Patella vulgata*) and *rampers* (ragworm, *Neries sp.*) were also used at both Ferryden and Gourdon, the lug and rampers being dug from the shore at Gourdon and from Montrose Basin. At one time boxes of lug were sent up to Gourdon by train by men who dug them from the Basin. The lug and rampers were baited live and sometimes the bait even crawled off the hooks, the lines being baited by the women in a scull as with the ordinary sma' lines. At Gourdon *slavery buckies* (dogwhelk, *Nucella lapillus*) were smashed with a hammer and cut in half, while at Ferryden a local variation was *clipes* (beadlet anemone, *Actima equina*), got from the rock pools at Scurdyness.

The Great Lines

Fishing with *gretlins* (Arbroath, Ferryden) or *gritelins* (Gourdon) is referred to locally in the mid-eighteenth century at Johnshaven where, as at most places, larger boats were used in midsummer, going out thirty to fifty miles in calm weather and staying out several nights. The *back* of the gretlins was made with heavier calibre hemp cord, about 5/32″ as compared with 3/32″ for the sma' lines. The snoods were of the same cord as for the *back* of the sma' lines and were set farther apart, at different distances according to the species fished for. The snoods were fixed to the *back* in a different way, the line being pierced and the snood pulled through and tied round it. The tipping was of two strands of lighter-calibre cord, and the hooks, which were three or four inches or larger, were also *beat on* with linen thread. The lines were not baited in a scull but coiled in a quarter-cran basket which had cork around half the edge, into which the hooks were stuck. The hooks were baited as the lines were shot, usually with pieces of herring or other fish. *Inkies* (cuttlefish, *Sepia officinalis*), often found in creels, were excellent bait for cod. At Ferryden twenty-five score (500) hooks were used, but at Gourdon 1,000 hooks per line were used. The gretlins were used in spring and early summer, after which sma' line fishing resumed. The catch was the great fish, cod and ling mainly, but also large halibut and skate.

The gretlin fishing seems to have died out at Ferryden by the inter-war period. Between the wars, the Gourdon men used larger boats out of Stonehaven harbour, which could be left and entered at any time with ease. They first fished offshore locally and then went to the Clyde via the Caledonian Canal and fished out of Campbeltown. Some Arbroath boats did the same and their herring boats would turn to the gretlin fishing if the herring was poor. The Montrose Bank, about twenty-eight miles out, was successfully fished for a couple of seasons after the war by men of Arbroath and Gourdon, and was then abandoned for good. Large trawlers out of Aberdeen used great lines off Rockall until about a dozen years ago, and one Anstruther boat practised this form of line fishing until July 1984.

Acknowledgements
I am grateful to the following informants:
Arbroath: Brian Bruce, Willie Smith, Willie Teviotdale.
Ferryden: Joe West.
Gourdon: Mr and Mrs Alex Welsh Senior, Alex and Rena Welsh, Mrs Mellish, Jackie Soutar and Jim Scott.

Alex Welsh senior was a ploughman and foreman on a small farm before joining the crew of a line boat in the late 1920s when the industry was expanding. His wife was the skipper's daughter. Both in their mid-70s, Alex Welsh junior and his wife Rena were both born into fisher families and are aged about 55. Mrs Mellish, aged about 60, was my main informant on the bait used in the sma' gretlins. Jackie Soutar, who is 85, was the informant on the great line fishing. Jim Scott, also in his mid-50s, gave information on the sma' gretlins. Joe West of Ferryden, aged 83, has never been to sea for a living but was a joiner. He comes from an old fisher family and has made it a lifetime hobby to collect the terminology, fishing lore and history of Ferryden. Brian Bruce of Arbroath is only 38 but was one of the last of the line fishers there, having gone to sea with his father before leaving school. He is now a lecturer in sea-survival at Robert Gordon's Institute of Technology, Aberdeen. Willie Smith and Willie Teviotdale are both retired fishers.

Sources

Coull, J. R.,   Fisheries in the north-east of Scotland before 1800. In *Scottish Studies* 13 (1969).

Gove, R.,   *Gourdon in the 19th century* (pamphlet) (1983).

Mather, J. Y.,   Aspects of the linguistic geography of Scotland: III Fishing communities of the east coast Part I. In *Scottish Studies* 13 (1969).

Who Were the Sailormen?

Gavin C Sprott

In 1934 H. M. Tomlinson wrote: 'when a man ventures round Cape Horn in a sailing ship for the experience, we expect a book from him as long as his voyage. These days we usually get it. Forty years ago a man would have been thought weak in the head who went round Cape Horn under sail for the fun of it. . . . Seamanship and the elements it had to meet . . . had acquired hardly more romantic merit than navvying'.[1] Well, that was a kind of backhanded prophecy, because with books such as *The Railway Navvies* and the *Navvy in Scotland*, the navvy, along with the cohorts of *Peasant Studies*, now has his place in the sun. Moreover, the wheel has perhaps come full circle. Basil Lubbock (of *The Last of the Windjammers* fame) has been criticised for his *chatter*. The life was not romantic, we are frequently reminded, but hard, terrible, dangerous and often boring. But as the years lengthen between ourselves and the last days of commercial deep-sea sail, how do we know?

There are striking parallels to be found between the attitudes of sailormen and the farming folk of the east coast of Scotland, and no doubt others elsewhere: perhaps a broad cultural inheritance that should not surprise us. The point in this instance is the curious parallel between the enthusiasms of the old horsemen, and what the author has known of his own family's attitude to their sea-going experiences. Under much fashionable interpretation, the records of the old-time farming point to a life of hard toil, exploitation, virtually no holidays, poor housing and low wages. But whether or not this was in fact so, people seemed to survive it with the most remarkable cheerfulness. Without denying the hardships, the memory tends to be a positive one — great ploughing matches, interesting horses, eccentric farmers, talented blacksmiths, a vigorous communal and social life, and innumerable pranks and hoaxes. Hearing the criticism of Lubbock's *chatter*, his talk of famous ships and legendary passages, anecdotal tit-bits about masters

and mates, it occurred to the author that that is not unfamiliar. There is this childhood memory aboard a ship in Glasgow Docks, the author's grandfather and two of his former shipmates yarning about old times. In fact, tales told to a child of the old windjammers, supplemented by later reading of what he wrote, only confirmed this impression of a life that was undoubtedly hard, but not without its own compelling interest, which was not a romantic after-thought, but a positive experience to the participants.

In this instance, a triangle of sources is considered that might shed light on shipboard life to see how they corroborated or conflicted — official documents

1. Capt. John Sprott, with Henrietta Twentyman, his first wife, and a friend, at the harbour at Harrington, Cumberland, post 1850. Shipowner and master mariner, he was lost in the Irish Channel in 1886.
Photo: Author's possession.   SEA/C.12370

2. The Barque *Geltwood*, 1056 tons, off Holyhead 1876, from a painting by J. Witham. She was the second of three sisters built by R. Williamson & Son, Workington, 1875-7. The *Inglewood*, 1043 tons, was first, and the *Mallsgate*, 1043 tons, was third. No expense was spared in the building of the *Mallsgate*, said to be one of the finest barques of her day both for appearance and speed. The loss of the *Geltwood* off South Australia was a *cause célèbre*, as it was at a remote place, and the locals plundered the wreck without reporting it, and the question was asked, did they refuse help to, or do away with, any survivors that got ashore? As the vessel foundered 1,000 yards out in a raging sea, this was unlikely. The wreck was discovered in 1983 with much of the general cargo remaining.
Photo: Author's possession.   SEA/C. 6447

relating to crews at the time, the memory of family involvement in deep-sea sail, and the recorded memories, partly of the author's family, partly of those they knew or who were associated with their ships.

In the broad spectrum of deep-sea sail, it is possible to make certain general distinctions of kind. The journal of Willie Hall recalls a voyage to the Brazil coast in 1863 in the barque *Wings of the Morning*, 344 tons. She was sailed by her owner, with his nephew and heir for mate, who, as he said, was 'fond of fun' — quite in contrast to a bigger ship, where a brother-in-law addressed the master as 'sir'.[2] It was a cosy atmosphere. When the crew lampooned his uncle in doggerel verse, the mate 'had literally to get into a quiet corner and kick and punch himself hard to prevent him from bursting with laughter'.[3] At the other end David Bone remembered the *Loch* liners on which he served on the colonial, i.e. Australian trade,

where at least from the Glasgow end, the crews, far from being scraped from the barrel, were composed of experienced hands who would come about the ship at the quayside 'luikin for a sicht'. But in between the fairly small ships and the regular passenger-carrying liners were the cargo-carrying merchantmen, making up the bulk of the deep-sea sail mercantile marine, and among these, in the last quarter of the last century, were the ships of the author's father's family.

The *Geltwood* was launched at Harrington on the Cumberland coast in 1876. A sister ship to the *Inglewood*, she was 1056 tons net register, a graceful three-masted barque sporting a skysail on the main. On her maiden voyage she was commanded by Frederick Harrington. It was to be Harrington's last voyage before he retired,[4] and on the 14th of March 1876 the *Geltwood* sailed from the Mersey for Melbourne. On board was Harrington's wife, Mr

Nelson, a well-known Carlisle architect, first and second mate, carpenter, bosun, steward, cook, fourteen able seamen, and the large number of seven apprentices. As we shall see, these thirty souls never reached Melbourne.

The likelihood is, apart from Harrington and his wife, the first mate (significantly a Robert Brocklebank from Harrington), and perhaps Mr Nelson the passenger, these thirty people could hardly have known each other. The second mate and the bosun might have bumped into each other in the same lodging house at 12 Pitt Street in Liverpool. Before sailing, Brocklebank and the steward had also lodged in the same street, but in different houses. Only two of the crew had recently shipped in the same vessel, the *State of Alabama*, from the Clyde. The bosun would have known the master and first mate by repute, coming from Harrington himself, as also might have John Stockton, a seaman from neighbouring Workington. Four of the able seamen came from Liverpool, but not one of their foc'sle shipmates had a birthplace in common, coming from as far apart as Inverness, Swansea, Dublin, Deptford and Halifax, Nova Scotia. You could not even say they had a preference for any particular kind of vessel. Of these fourteen able seamen, seven were off steam or auxiliary steam vessels of widely ranging tonnages. Only four of the able seamen had recently shipped on vessels broadly similar to the *Geltwood*. Even if in some cases the mention of previous vessels was a fiction, as will be considered later, the point of virtually no previous association holds.[5]

A pretty disparate lot, you might say. As the *Geltwood* was a newly launched vessel, this offered no test of whether men stayed on ships from previous voyages. The answer generally is an emphatic no. The *Inglewood*, launched the previous year, had a long and prosperous life, scattered over nineteen years, but hardly one of the foc'sle crowd shipped on her for two consecutive voyages.

The American Felix Riesenburg described the start of a voyage: 'an odd lot of humanity dumped their few belongings on the foc'sle deck, strangers all, excepting a few who just deserted from the British bark *Falls of Ettrick*, men jumbled together by strange fate, and destined to long months of close companionship — of hard knocks and endless days and nights of unremitting labour'.[6] Why were they strangers? In a nutshell, because they were paid off at the end of each voyage, if

they had not already deserted at the intermediary ports. It might be at least six to eight weeks or more before the same vessel would sail again. This applied to the mates as well as the men, although the former sometimes did remain with the same ship. The pattern of continuity that obtained in many small family-run coastal traders was impossible with deep-sea sail. Even when the ownership was in small towns or in the country, the ships sailed from the larger ports where the labour market was large, anonymous and impersonal. In 1905 Capt. James Barker (who was apprenticed on the *Ravenswood*, originally a Sprott ship) had to recruit a crew for the ship *British Isles* at Cardiff for a voyage to Pisagua in Chile: 'I obtained my crew without much difficulty or delay from among five hundred men grouped together in the enclosed ground surrounding the Marine Board building. Standing at the head of a flight of stone steps I looked down upon a vast sea of faces'. He looked them over, made his choice, the men followed him into a room in the offices where they were signed on before the Shipping Master, and joined the ship the next day.[7] This element of the initiative of choice often lying with the master is hinted at in a curious way in the crew of the *Geltwood*. Captain Harrington was an RNR man. Almost half his seamen were also naval reservists — possibly ex-naval men who kept the connection for the bounty. In other crew lists naval reservists are a comparative rarity — either because there were no reservists, or the men did not declare that, because the master had not made a point of asking. This was obviously a point of importance to Captain Harrington, and it appears as an element in his choice of crew.[8]

The other major means of recruitment — through the waterfront boarding-houses — offered the seamen even less element of choice than simply being asked by the master. There at least the man could say *no*. The boarding-house system was notorious. The crew members were seduced by the boarding-house *runners* on the promise of a few days' riotous living on the understanding that either the money due to them or the advance they would get on signing on another ship would go to the boarding-house. Alternatively if they were ashore without any of these conditions, they were still liable to be drugged and come to in the foc'sle of an outward-bound windjammer for which service the master would have reluctantly paid the appropriate *blood money* to the boarding-house master. It was a system that flourished more in the colonies, the US

3. Crew of the Barque *Archibald Russell* 2048 tons. Built by Scott's of Greenock for Hardie & Co., Glasgow in 1905, she was the third last sailing ship to be launched on the Clyde. She was bought by Capt. Erikson of Mariehamn in 1924 and was broken up on the Tyne after Hitler's war. This shows the crew in port in 1918. Back row, left to right: ordinary seaman: cook, an American: ordinary seaman: the steward, a half-caste from the mid-west of the US: four apprentices, Scots: three able seamen, Scots: Front row — able seaman, Norwegian: Mr Cameron, the mate and former master with the Loch Line: Capt. Buchan, Scots: John Bruce, acting 2nd mate, Scots: carpenter, Norwegian: able seaman, Scots.
Photo: Capt. John Bruce   SEA/C. 10722

and on the west coast of South America, where labour was short, and the conscience of Victorian philanthropy had not yet provided sailors' homes. The boarding-houses were one of those institutions which were universally condemned but survived with the acquiescence of the victims, which perhaps tells something about them. Ally Bone recalled that some sailormen 'gave you the idea that it was a great honour to be shanghai'd by such men as Jim Brady in Antofogasta. Tommy Moore of Buenos Aires, . . . or Tom Jenkins of the renowned "Shakespere" in Valparaiso'. There was no lack of women in the same business — Bremen Mary of Iquique ('Give de boys blindy to drink, de more they drink, the lest they eat'), 'Mother' Smyrden of Liverpool, 'Mother' Hall of the Black Diamond pub in Newcastle, New South Wales, or 'Mother' Rowley of Cullao.[9] As arbitrary you might

say, as picking a bunch of men from a jail, which actually happened, even on the swish *Loch Ness* under the command of Bully Martin, when David Bone shipped on her as second mate from Sydney in 1894 — perhaps the only example of Australian convicts being transported to the motherland.[10]

But how did things turn out when they got aboard? The dramatic descriptions do not paint an encouraging start: 'Sprawling on the filthy forcastle floor amidst the litter of the last debauch, the men lie as they have fallen, drunk to the misery of it all, putting out to sea in the way of sailormen since ever ships went out. The dark foc'sle, broken bottles, scraps of stale food, muddied clothes, and sodden bedding, lockers with putrifying meat left from the last voyage'.[11] Maybe so, or maybe not, for we cannot be sure it was always like that. The experience was powerful enough to be

4. The Ship *City of France*, 1200 tons, from a pen and wash drawing by David Bone. One of Smith's City Line, built in 1867, she was characteristic of the Clyde-built iron and later steel-hulled vessels that dominated the sailing ship routes of the oceans from the mid-1860s to the 1890s, and aboard which a whole generation of Scotsmen served as deep-sea sailormen. They combined the grace of the earlier clippers with the functional virtues and carrying capacity of a good workhorse. David Bone recorded his voyage on this vessel in 1890 in *The Brassbounder*, published in 1910.
Photo: From original in author's possession.   SEA/C. 12387

observe this time honoured ceremony of the sea. For better or for worse we were to be parcelled off to our respective task masters for the long months of the voyage ahead. The fate of friendships was to be decided, for watchmates are far closer than mere ship-mates'.[12] The process continued further: 'Frenchy was my first chum on the *Fuller*, and though for periods we drifted apart . . . yet we always came together again . . . the night that we paired off, on our first watch at sea, it seemed natural that Frenchy and I should . . . stump the deck in company'.[13] You cannot help but be struck by the extraordinary contrast between the random impersonality of the labour market and the sudden close companionship between perhaps six to eight men for several months on end. There is hardly a description of a voyage among the foc'sle crowd that does not bring out a theme of friendships and enmities — the ritual fights conducted in the lee of the forward deckhouses away from the eye of the afterguard, but probably with their knowledge. An exception is Claude Muncaster in *Rolling Round the Horn*, a description of a voyage from Australia to Europe on the *Olivebank* during her time as an Erikson ship between the wars.[14] Although Muncaster admired the Åland seamen, in his funny English way he never took the trouble to get to know them. By missing that vital element of characteristic companionship it is a picture without force. As Ally Bone remarked, 'a sailor's kist is his home' — a subtle box of tricks by which he revealed his identity to those he chose for his particular companions, by invitation to a private inspection of its contents, the half-made models of ships in progress, a particularly fine rope shackle, photographs, or a prized talisman of feminine interest on which confessions or yarns would be founded.[15] Muncaster was an artist to trade, yet he was never invited to decorate the underside of a kist lid of a shipmate as David Bone was, a useful social skill on a sailing ship.

Here let us return to the official documents. What did those sailormen have in common? Two things stand out quite clearly — age, and freedom from domestic ties. On the *Geltwood* already mentioned, the average age of the able seaman was 26.[16] On the *Inglewood*, her sister ship, in the same year, 1876, it was 24.[17] Another ship that is quite unconnected with these other two, the *Falls of Clyde* (one of the very fine Russell-built four-masters built for the Glasgow *Falls* line of Wright and Breakenridge, now preserved in

erected into a general image. But once the men had tramped at the capstan, the first sail had been set, the tug was astern, the drink had been sweated out and all the ropes and running gear had been neatly coiled down, a process of social organisation emerged, aided by the following ritual. All hands mustered aft: 'There was a feeling of uncertainty among the crew as we filed aft to the waist, standing in an awkward group about the main fife rail . . . The watches were about to be chosen. The two mates came down into the waist, and Captain Nichols stood at the break of the poop to

Honolulu), offers interesting corroboration. Of eighteen signings of crew over the years 1879-98, the average age for the able seaman was 29. It made little difference where they signed on — Glasgow, Dundee, Liverpool, London, Calcutta, San Francisco, Melbourne, Auckland, Cardiff, Port Elizabeth, Hull. There was little variation over these eighteen years. Of thirteen signings, the average youngest age was 20.5 and the average oldest was 46. Significantly, the oldest man was often quite a lot older than the next oldest, so the latter figure could give a false impression.

So quite clearly it was a young man's job. This is further borne out in two ways. One signing not included in these averages was a freak occasion in Liverpool in 1885, when for some reason (as yet unexplained) there were simply no young men available, and the average age of the seamen shot up from 29 to 56. This even applied to the officers, with the first and second mates 61 and 64 years old respectively. This was for a voyage rounding the Cape to Calcutta — not as hard as the Horn, but no cakewalk. But significantly, instead of the average sixteen to eighteen able seamen, they signed twenty-two, thus recognising the strength of the young men needed to work the ship.[18] Another point is the food. During this period, the provisions tended to be fairly standard on each vessel. The rations allotted to each man per week on the *Geltwood* were as follows: bread, 7lbs; beef, 6lbs; pork, 3¾lbs; and flour, 1½lbs:[19] a mighty lot of food, until you consider the work they had to do.

As to the lack of domestic ties, this is at least suggested by one simple fact, that although the officers, the sailmakers, cooks, carpenters and stewards quite often made an *allotment* of their wages — that is, a proportion to be deducted at source and paid to their dependants at home — in no one instance from several hundred cases did the records show that this was done by an able seaman. Even if faced with the inevitable desertions at Melbourne or San Francisco, the minimum length of these voyages was predictable, and in any case the owners usually profited, because the deserters forfeited any money due to them, so there was no reason why an allotment should have been refused to an able seaman. If the able seamen did have domestic obligations, then it appears they chose to ignore them. For the most part, like the bothy man on the east-coast farms, the average sailorman was footloose and fancy free.

But there is a puzzle. How did these men first get

involved? In the records, they are nearly all recorded as having served in a previous ship, including the occasional ordinary seamen, even the occasional *boys*. A first ship in the articles is extremely rare among the foc'sle crowd. There is the parallel of under-age recruits trying to lie their way into the Great War. Maybe the average youngest age of 20.5 for able seamen is just an average of not a few exaggerations. What's in a previous ship? — in the circumstances of signing, just a name.

If life was so hard, indeed why did they bother? 'The man that goes to sea for pleasure would go to Hell for a pastime' (Ally Bone). And yet there are those cults (for want of a better word) that fly in the face of good sense, the men who 'with nothing to inspire them, no ambition to lead them to more responsible or better paying positions', yet are possessed of 'manhood and superb courage [which] nevertheless enabled them to carry on through days of bitter suffering'.[20]

We can identify the imperatives of these cults in simple physical details: 'I have seen, standing out in the open at the unsheltered wheels of sailing ships, men clad in raiment too scanty to keep the warmth of life in the body of a galley cockroach . . . shrinking from the cold penetrating blasts of a Cape Horn gale blowing from the ice fields, these creatures have often been the objects of my commiseration'. The offer of warm clothing was almost always turned down 'often with the courageous declaration that that sort of cold was no inconvenience at all'.[21] The author recalls working on the railways and in a timberyard where protective clothing could have been had for the asking, but people laboured in the bitterest cold and with dangerous loads in ragged jackets and not a glove between them. It would have been *saft* to do otherwise.

It is difficult to account for the initial appearance of the seamen, but what of their disappearance, on average, by the age of 46, and for the generality, much younger? We can only conclude that they settled ashore, some of them perhaps to marry, and some as emigrants, using their engagement as a cheap form of emigration. Those technically 'deserting' in the colonies in particular were by no means all foremast hands, but often included apprentices, aged 15 and upwards. By so doing they forfeited the £25 odds premium their fathers had paid to the owners, but of course that would not be their concern. Edward Sprott

5. Making fast the foresail on the Barque *Garthsnaid* off the Cape of Good Hope, September 1923. The photograph was taken by Mr Turner, the mate, from the jib-boom. Out at the yardarm was Archie Leckie, one of the apprentices, assigned to that position because he was the shortest. With the upper tops'ls and main course furled, the barque is already running under shortened sail.
Photo: Captain Archibald Leckie   SEA/C. 10584

deserted in Melbourne, off a family ship, forfeiting the sure prospect of command within six or seven years, so presumably a new life in Australia must have seemed attractive.

But as John Sprott remarked, when discussing this aspect of youthful crews, 'but you always had your *old* sailors'. The *old salt* of popular imagination? That was the image of the tradesman — the sailmakers, carpenters, cooks — that sticks in the mind. As Ally Bone recalled of one character on the *Killoran*: 'Sails was the only one the Old Man [i.e. Captain] ever argued with. An order was sufficient for others. [He] was much too good a sailmaker and seaman to give either of the mates an opportunity to corner him, but he dearly loved a row with the skipper'.[22] Again, on the *Ben Rosail*, the captain and Sails 'were always quarrelling . . . their quarrels never came to anything, just two old seamen enjoying themselves'.[23] It is the vignette of a worthy — the development and perhaps even fossilisation of character and eccentricity that their specialist skills and continuity of service allowed them. This is borne out by the records. The numbers are so much fewer that averages would not mean much, but the ages range from young tradesmen who

have just served their time to old men. They often had families and dependants at home, as the allotments of wages show.

But what of the afterguard, the captain and mates? Here we will concentrate on only one, but very important, aspect. Much has been said of discipline, the poop deck tyrants, the hard nut mates. Here there is a danger of looking at the past through the eyes of the present, as we are all much more gentlemanly now, eschewing many of the former rigours of subordination. David Bone was a normal, indeed gentle man. Yet as the author remembers, he was never to be touched in his sleep — or he might take a swipe — an ineradicable reaction bred of his windjammer days when in certain circumstances you slept on your valuables, crippled potential thieves first and asked questions afterwards. Harry Sprott, first mate on one of his family's ships in the 1870s, was set upon by an unruly crew in Shanghai. He felled one after another with his fists until they desisted.[24] This physical roughness was just part of the age. The cohesion that underlay the discipline was provided by something else peculiar to a sailing ship at sea.

The sailorman had two things to contend with for

6. *Running the Easting down* in the Southern Ocean aboard the *Archibald Russell*, 1919. A heavy sea breaks over the port rail as the barque races with yards squared before the *roaring forties* on the way to Australia. This photograph was taken from the poop by John Bruce, then 2nd mate.
Photo: Captain John Bruce   SEA/48/38/22

That was skill. A seaman would settle for a hard mate rather than an incompetent one: 'One man may be easier, but give me the best sailor. A good sailor aft saves work for his watch forward'.[26] A master could drive his men to the limit if they and he had confidence in his skill. Bully Martin, under whom David Bone served on the *Loch Ness*, was one of the hardest drivers of his day, but as Lubbock says, 'he was such a consummate seaman, that in 45 years service as master [he] lost only a couple of men'.[27]

For there was this ultimate fact: if total disaster struck, the afterguard went as well. On land, if there was a famine, the servants would die before the masters, the peasants before the lairds. But on the night of 6th June, 1876, the barque *Geltwood*, driven before the worst hurricane that people could remember, foundered on a rock 1,000 yards from the shore of Rivoli Bay in South Australia. Not one of the thirty souls aboard survived. Ten years later, on another of his ships, John Sprott was swept from the poop to his death in the Irish Sea. The sea is no respecter of persons, and between master and crew that was the ultimate bond.

survival. One was what he would call *bad luck*, that is injury or worse from circumstances beyond his control, because of the weather, frostbite, losing a grip, falling spars and so on. The other was incompetent seamanship on the part of the master and mates. He could do nothing about the first except take care of himself, 'one hand for himself and one hand for the ship', resort to innumerable charms, and observe certain taboos. If the second — the seamanship of the afterguard — failed, then he became dangerous. Ally Bone remarked in admiration of a certain Mrs Davis who sailed with her husband, master of the *Killoran*, 'she could handle a ship as well as her husband'.[25]

Note
Some of those whose evidence is quoted had the following relationship to the author, and in large part knew or were known to each other.

Ally Bone	Lieut. Alexander, great uncle.
David Bone	Commodore Sir David, grandfather.
Felix Riesenburg	Author and friend of David Bone.
James Barker	Captain, one-time apprentice on *Ravenswood* built for Captain John Sprott.
Edward Sprott	Great uncle.
John Sprott senr.	Captain, great-grandfather.
John Sprott junr.	Bishop J. C. — father.
Harry Sprott	Great uncle.
'Bully' Martin	Captain J., under whom David Bone served as apprentice and second mate.
H. M. Thomlinson	Author and friend of David and Alexander Bone, and James Bone, great uncle.
William Hall	Great-great uncle.
Frederick Harrington	Captain, friend of John Sprott senr.

References

1. A. Bone, *Bowsprit Ashore* (London 1932), 7.

2. J. Barker, *The Log of a Limejuicer* (London 1934), 135.

3. William Hall, Journal No. 2, MS in author's possession.

4. Information: Heather Stewart-Booth, Hallett Cove, South Australia, 1982.

5. Archives Department of Cumbria County Council, TRS 1/593.

6. F. Riesenburg, *Under Sail* (New York 1918), 13. Although the tone of shipboard life on a Yankee windjammer was different — better food and tougher mates — the organisation was international. See Muncaster 1933 below, for life on an Åland vessel.

7. Barker, *op. cit.*, 132.

8. Archives Department of Cumbria County Council, TRS 1/593.

9. Bone, *op. cit.*, 147-8.

10. D. Bone, *Landfall at Sunset* (London 1955), 70.

11. D. Bone, *The Queerfella* (London 1952), 22-3. This seafaring novel contains a daft story but with interesting vignettes of shipboard life. However, by now they have become institutionalised into fictional clichés.

12. Riesenburg, *op. cit.*, 17.

13. Riesenburg, *op. cit.*, 25.

14. C. Muncaster, *Rolling Round the Horn* (London 1933).

15. Bone, A., *op. cit.*, 101.

16. Archives Department of Cumbria County Council, TRS 1/593.

17. Archives Department of Cumbria County Council, TRS 1/591.

18. Strathclyde Regional Archives, TD/37/96.

19. Archives Department of Cumbria County Council, TRS 1/593. .

20. Barker, *op. cit.*, 200.

21. Barker, *op. cit.*, 176.

22. Bone, A., *op. cit.*, 29.

23. Bone, A., *op. cit.*, 55-6.

24. Information: John Sprott junr.

25. Bone, A., *op. cit.*, 42.

26. Riesenburg, *op. cit.*, 17.

27. B. Lubbock, *The Colonial Clippers* (Glasgow 1948 ed.), 176.

Food on Sunday

Alexander Fenton

In 1975, a questionnaire on eating habits from 1900 to the present day was circulated through the Scottish Women's Rural Institutes. It included questions on Sunday meals, which are discussed here. The 161 replies covered most parts of Scotland.

Throughout the country, the emphasis being on rural districts, three basic meals were eaten: breakfast in the morning, dinner in the middle of the day, and tea or supper at about five or six o'clock in the evening. The actual times depended on various factors such as cattle milking needs and churchgoing.

Breakfast

At the present day, breakfast is heavily influenced by the wide use of packaged products, and possibly also by the nature of hotel meals, with which people are becoming increasingly familiar. This means the eating of fresh grapefruit, cereals such as All Bran, Cornflakes, etc, taken with milk, toast and marmalade, and tea or coffee, sometimes combined with grilled bacon. Bacon and eggs are widespread, less so sausage and eggs. Grilled bacon on toast, without butter, was a kind of prelude in the 1920s to the bacon and egg era.

For an older generation, porridge was eaten for breakfast if brose was the regular weekday breakfast, perhaps with a boiled, fried or poached egg as well. On the other hand, where porridge was regular on weekdays, it was replaced by bacon and eggs on Sunday. There were even farms where porridge was followed by bacon and eggs. The breakfast bacon was often of home-cured pork, from a pig cured in brine (with brown sugar, saltpetre and salt), the eggs were fresh or cured in waterglass, the butter was fresh in summer, or salted in winter, the milk came from the farmer's own cows, and the oatcakes were baked at home. Home-made potato scones were frequently fried to go with the 'ham and eggs'.

Sequences of change were noted by two professional households in the town of Oban, Argyll:

	1900	1940	1970s
a.	Bacon and egg, girdle scones, pancakes.	Bacon and egg, toast, marmalade, tea.	Cereals, grapefruit, bacon and egg, toast, tea.
b.	—	Bacon — or sausage and egg.	Bacon — or sausage and egg.

An estate worker's family in the Island of Mull, however, had:

	1900	1940	1970s
c.	Porridge and milk.	Porridge and milk.	Porridge, cereal, toast and tea.

A Lanarkshire family, one that enjoyed its food, had a late breakfast before going to church, and changes can be seen clearly:

	1900	1940	1970s
d.	Stew with sausage, scones, oatcakes, bread.	Porridge, bacon and egg, scones, bread and butter, tea.	Grapefruit, bacon and egg, scrambled egg, or kippers.

In coastal areas, fish formed an element, for example 'Finnan' haddock and poached eggs or, at an earlier period (around 1918), fried salt herring with oatcakes, bread and tea.

Differences may be observable between members of a family. A wife might stick to grapefruit and cereals, whilst her husband ate fried bacon sandwiches. If the father was at home, there would be a substantial meal of sausage, bacon, egg, toast and tea, but in his absence the girls preferred bacon sandwiches or cereals. Even with the whole family present, the parents might have bacon and eggs, or fried or boiled eggs with oatcakes and 'loaf bread', whilst the children — at least the younger ones — had bread soaked in milk and sprinkled with sugar, then boiled eggs, bread spread with jam or syrup, and tea. Such milksops were called *flannen* (flannel) *broth* in north-east Scotland. Such individual variations, however, cannot be easily generalised.

53

In towns, in the neighbourhood of bakeries, the availability of morning rolls led to the use of hot buttered rolls — or of bran scones as an earlier variant — and tea or coffee as a simple breakfast. An alternative was simply tea and toast.

From 1900 onwards, the broad emphases have moved from porridge to bacon and eggs (with additions like slices of black pudding and fried tomato), and latterly to processed, pre-packed breakfast foods, often accompanied by grapefruit which, though fresh, is nevertheless imported. Of bacon, a Banffshire informant said of the early 1900s, 'you didn't hear much about ham for breakfast at that time'.[1]

Coffee has increasingly taken the place of tea, though tea itself was not absolutely general, for as late as the 1870s it was noted that on some Aberdeenshire farms the men got one cup of tea on a Sunday morning,[2] and this custom lasted in north-east Scotland, and possibly elsewhere, till within the last fifty years.

Dinner

Dinner was basically of three courses: soup, a main course, and pudding. If there was soup, however, there might be no pudding, and if there was no soup, the pudding was more substantial.

Broths and soups played a large part in the diet. They were especially common as part of the main Sunday meal, above all in winter. The main types of soup were potato, with the meat cut up in it, lentil, hen or chicken, and mutton. Chicken soup was made with rice and leeks, whilst rice soup itself was made with meat stock and vegetables. Kail broth made with vegetables, including borecole as the main one, with or without the addition of meat, was so common that the name *kail* came to mean not only the broth itself, but also the whole main meal. It has been replaced by Scotch broth, which is started off with beef (often brisket) and marrow bone, or a hen, and large chunks of turnip and carrot. Barley and dried vegetables are also added.

Since meat was not always plentiful — and was for long confined to Sundays or special occasions — a mealy pudding might be boiled in the broth as a substitute or to let the meat go further.

In modern days tinned soup saves Sunday work. In the words of a Kintyre farmer's wife, 'we have also tinned soup on a Sunday, either tomato or kidney or vegetable. If it is tomato I make it with milk as it is more nourishing, if any other kind I make stock with a bone'. In this way, even canned goods could be eked out with less commercial products.

With all soups and broths it was customary to eat oatcakes, although this has been largely replaced by bread at the present day.

The main course could relate closely to the first, if boiling beef, mutton or a hen had been the base for the soup. Potatoes, turnips and carrots (boiled with the broth) and cabbage or cauliflower were the associated vegetables. Equally, if not more common in the twentieth century, however, has been roast meat or fowl. Roasting was evidently considered a mark of distinction, but with current increases in the price of meat, roasts have become less usual for Sunday dinner, although they may still be prepared if visitors are coming. Cheaper alternatives are, for example, pork chops, or braised steak, or steak and kidney pie.

Because many families went to church regularly in the rural communities, there was a tendency to prepare Sunday meals the day before, or else the roast, or a casserole dish, would be left in the oven during the service. If, for example, the meat course was to be rolled brisket, this was larded and put into an uncovered basting dish in a hot oven, to brown for half an hour. The fat was removed, and a little boiling water and seasoning added to the sediment, plus whole onions and chunks of turnip and carrot. The oven heat was reduced, and the lid put on the dish for slow cooking. In this context, refrigerators and deep-freezes also have a part to play. According to a lady from Kintyre, Argyll, 'I take out of the deep freeze on Saturday steak or pork. If it is steak, I brown it well with a little fat for about 2½ hours and add carrots, and make a brown gravy. If it is pork I either roast it or put it in a pot on the oven. If it is pork I make apple sauce made with apples well cooked, adding butter and sugar and lemon juice. You have pork either hot or cold. What is left can do for another meal. In Winter I mash the potatoes, in Summer they are boiled in their skins. I also have a vegetable, either cabbage or cauliflower or brussels-sprouts or peas'. Some, at least, of the vegetables, could also come out of the freezer.

Churchgoing could also lead to adaptations in mealtimes. One family in Aberfeldy, Perthshire, had their main meal after four p.m. In Aberdeenshire some folk simply had a 'little dinner' after church, about one p.m., consisting of little more than a plate of pudding. A Roxburgh family had broth and rice pudding with tinned fruit, biscuits and cheese in the middle of the day, with a main meal at night, but a light midday meal does not always presuppose a main meal later. In Stirlingshire a family had trifle and custard with fresh tinned fruit, scones, cakes and tea as lunch, with their main meal around five p.m., a 'high tea' consisting of cold roast with chips, bread, scones, cakes and tea. This inversion of the old meal order is not necessarily an imitation of upper-class arrangements, but rather is conditioned by churchgoing.

In some cases potatoes were boiled on return from church, to go with cold meat, but in others no potatoes were prepared at all on that day. Dinner might then consist of a plateful of stewing steak and vegetables, with bread as a substitute for potatoes, and tea to wash it down.

As a rule, beef was preferred to pork or mutton for the Sunday roast. In the days before electric, gas, or paraffin ovens, pot-roasting was frequent, using a stout cast-iron pot. Where peat was burned as a fuel, glowing embers laid on the lid gave a good, all-over heat.

Another aspect of the main dish is the use of dumplings. The kind of batter known as Yorkshire pudding is becoming more common as an accompaniment to the Sunday joint. It is more of an incoming element than an indication of a need to make the meat go further, although this was the intention with mealy dumplings, and with the flour dumplings or doughballs (Aberdeenshire: 'dough boys') that were boiled with stew or mince. Though doughballs, consisting of flour, fat and a little milk as a binding agent, are still not uncommon, the older mealy dumplings have largely disappeared.

Other kinds of main dishes were also made on Sunday. On an upland sheep farm in Kirkcudbright, for example, the available resources could lead to much variety: home-cured ham boiled, rabbit pie with mutton chops in it, a pot-roasted hen stuffed with oatmeal and onions, steamed fish (usually dried cod, or herrings) or sometimes burn trout. In the more Highland areas, venison was occasionally to be had. In general, however, roast meat or fowl has been the standard for the period around 1940-1970s, whilst the earlier emphasis was on meat or fowl boiled as part of the soup or broth-making process.

The third course varied according to circumstances.

In summer the sweet could be a light one such as stewed rhubarb or apples, jelly or junket ('yirned milk'), with fresh or tinned fruit and cream. Rather more substantial and very widespread were milk puddings such as semolina, sago, cornflour and rice, again with fruit and milk or cream. For more special occasions trifle was made, based on a home-made sponge or Swiss roll or bought trifle sponges, soaked in sherry, jelly or tinned fruit, custard, and whipped cream. Rhubarb and apple tarts or pies, and steamed-fruit puddings and dumplings made the most substantial elements of all. The last, though sometimes eaten on Sundays, were more usual for birthdays and for Christmas and New Year dinners.

For midday meals, some general points of change can be noted for the twentieth century in two professional households in Oban:

1900	1940	1970s
a. Soup; roast meat and vegetables; steamed pudding.	Soup; meat and vegetables; cold sweet, tea.	Soup; meat and vegetables; cold sweet, coffee.
b. Soup; roast gigot of mutton or pork, or haggis, or liver; steamed puddings, dumpling or stewed fruit (apples, prunes).	Soup; chicken or rabbit or steak pie; baked custard or stewed fruit.	Soup; roast or stewing beef, chicken, roast lamb or pork.

For an estate worker's family in the Island of Mull, changes were:

1900	1940	1970s
c. Fish (salt herring) and potatoes.	Mutton soup; meat and potatoes; barley pudding.	Roast beef; vegetables and potatoes; cold sweet.

A Lanarkshire family, much influenced by the church at the beginning of the century, has strongly marked changes in eating habits:

1900	1940	1970s
d. Glass of milk and a biscuit.	Soup or broth made of potato, lentil, chicken, or oxtail; mutton, rabbit, chicken or stew, potatoes and vegetables; milk pudding of rice, semolina or sago, or stewed rhubarb or gooseberries.	Light lunch of cold meat and salad; evening dinner of soup, roast beef and Yorkshire pudding, green vegetables.

The third meal of the day, called 'tea' or 'supper' (though the latter name can nowadays be given to a snack taken before going to bed), at five to six p.m., was generally fairly light. It was often more a question of baking than cooking, with *crowdie, crudes* (curds) and oatcakes, *bannocks* (pancakes) and scones, and tea, or salmon and salad, or a boiled egg and cheese and oatcakes.

Cooked meals were also quite usual, however. In the words of a Kintyre housewife, 'evening meal on a Sunday is about 6 o'clock. It consists in summer of a salad when lettuce and tomatoes are plentiful, mostly made with gammon or ham decorated with egg, or sausages and egg, or fried fish done with fish dressing and tea and scones and pancakes, and brown bread and butter and jam, home-made biscuits and home-made cakes'. Other possibilities were a cheese soufflé with toast, poached eggs, or macaroni and cheese. Here too, baking as well as cooking is in evidence, and it was an old custom to make further use of oatmeal in the shape of a *barm loaf*, as a change from the baking of scones and pancakes. This consisted of a pound of oatmeal, a good teaspoonful of bicarbonate of soda, a shake of black pepper and salt, a heaped teaspoonful of flour, a tablespoonful of syrup and another of black treacle, all mixed with buttermilk to a pouring consistency, and put into a well-greased cake-tin. This was baked for an hour in a slow oven, or put in a strong pot over a peat fire. It was then browned on top by having red peat embers placed on the lid.

In some families in Kincardine, and no doubt elsewhere, peasemeal brose followed by cheese and oatcakes made the Sunday tea.

Substantial meals could also be eaten, for example in Kirkcudbright, where one family regularly had rabbit and steak pie, bread and scones, and home-baked currant loaf.

Change in the course of the century can also be pinpointed. The two Oban families had:

	1900	1940	1970s
a.	Cheese, oatcakes, tea.	Cold meat, pies, eggs, bread, scones, cake (5.30 p.m.)	Cheese, meat, or boiled or scrambled eggs, salads, bread, scones, tea (5.30 p.m.)
b.	Cheese or boiled egg.	Tea and cakes, cheese, sardines.	Salads, cheese pudding, or fish.

In the Island of Mull, the estate family ate:

	1900	1940	1970s
c.	Oatcakes.	Tea and scones.	Tea and pancakes, cold meat, potatoes, biscuits and cheese.

The Lanarkshire family had:

	1900	1940	1970s
d.	Oatcakes, cheese, scones, tea, an apple.	Boiled egg or cheese, scones, bread, jam.	No data.

The Questionnaire evidence shows that tea has been gradually becoming more sophisticated and complicated in the course of the century.

The evidence brings out several factors which could be better appreciated against knowledge of the eating system in the previous century, for in the earlier part of the twentieth century (and still amongst conservative families) older traditions survived. In farming families in the nineteenth century, breakfast was often of porridge eaten with milk or ale, and tea was rare. Brose was sometimes eaten but farmers did not go to the extreme of having brose three times a day, as was the case with farm-workers living on their own in bothies. Brose continued to be much eaten, although this does not come out clearly from the Questionnaire answers, for these have been filled in mainly by farmers' wives. Nevertheless the emphasis on oatmeal in various forms — porridge, brose, oatcakes, stuffing for roast hens, in barm loaf, etc. — remains clear as a special characteristic of the Scottish diet.

Something of the conservative character of the country appears from the fact that tea, until the 1940s, could still be a Sunday treat for the men. Coffee as a regularly available alternative has come to the country districts only within the last fifteen to twenty years, as part of a flood of commercially produced tins and packets of processed and powdered foods and drinks that is levelling out differences in eating habits in different countries as well as in different parts of the same country.

The timings of meals also show a conservative character. Though breakfast has become later than the five or six a.m. of earlier days, nevertheless the eating of the main meal in the middle of the day is still substantially surviving, except where churchgoing circumstances demand something different. Only in the towns and amongst professional people is the habit of evening dinner a regular thing.

References
1. National Museums of Scotland, M.S. 1974, 22.
2. *Deeside Field* 1927, 33 ff.

Destruction, Damage and Decay: the Collapse of Scottish Medieval Buildings

Geoffrey Stell

'. . . Breaking and building
In the progression of this world go hand in hand.'[1]

During a century which has seen an awesome capacity for material destruction outstrip great technical advances in construction, architectural historians and archaeologists have become increasingly concerned about the fate of our historic environment. This concern has expressed itself in the practical issues of preservation, conservation and rescue archaeology, to which the history of destruction and neglect is appended, usually as a supporting moral argument.

Unpleasant as it may seem, however, destruction is a historical phenomenon in its own right, and the subject deserves disinterested attention on its own terms. Prompted by thoughts and experiences arising from a career devoted to the investigation of threatened buildings, my purpose in this article is thus to examine, from a historical as distinct from a technical viewpoint, the evidence for some of the calamities that are known to have befallen Scottish medieval buildings. Critical assessments of material damage in medieval Scotland are remarkably few,[2] and, although the history of the appreciation and protection of medieval ruins is reasonably well served,[3] there is no overall survey of post-Reformation destruction and neglect.[4]

Whilst obviously not immune from the universal effects of age and decay, medieval buildings nowadays command general acceptance as objects worthy of protection; compared to structures of more youthful age that stand in the middle of the preservation battleground they have suffered fewer premeditated casualties in recent decades, and then usually only in exceptional circumstances.[5] Distant in time and custom, they are generally viewed with objective curiosity, tinged perhaps with an element of romanticism or cruel realism. But the combined effects of dilapidation and man's destructive folly can still excite anger or despair among visitors to some of our major medieval churches.

Since Victorian times the preservation of ruins and the conservation of historic buildings for continued use have posed their own technical difficulties, which have been compounded by the modern problems of air pollution and traffic vibrations.[6] In many respects, however, the potential agencies of destruction faced by buildings today are similar to those encountered in the Middle Ages. Natural phenomena, especially extremes of weather, remain probably the strongest and most capricious forces to be reckoned with, either in terms of gradual erosion or immediate damage. Destruction wrought by man has taken a wide variety of forms: every age has suffered to a greater or lesser degree the effects of military activity, arson and vandalism, as well as the negative aspects of administrative 'planning' decisions. Whether caused by ignorance, carelessness or poverty of resources, building faults have also been a human responsibility, the results perhaps of poor siting, inadequate foundations and construction, or the lack of appropriate maintenance. Unforeseen accidents have always been an unfortunate random factor in human existence, often adding to the list of catastrophes of immediate and visible effect. The materially damaging results of longer-term social, economic, religious and environmental trends are not always clearly discernible to contemporaries, but, overall, have had a deeper and more widespread impact than any single event, however large. For these reasons the problem of redundancy usually affects whole categories of building at about the same time, hence the numerous deserted villages,[7] derelict castles and ruined religious houses[8] bequeathed by medieval Britain to the succeeding centuries, or the redundant farmsteads, industries, churches and country mansions that we have inherited from our more modern imperial past. Before the present century there have been few attempts to staunch these trends, and, like the dilemma of human unemployment, it still remains to be seen how far the problems of architectural redundancy are 'soluble' in the long term.

Within historic times the natural agencies of destruction in Britain thankfully have not included significant measures of seismic or volcanic activity which have created such widespread havoc in other parts of the world.[9] The effects of local earth or soil movements have not been uncommon, however, although the actual causes of subsidence and lateral movement are not always self-evident. Building deformities at Carlisle Cathedral, for example, may have been the result of the drying out and compaction of the site in the warmer climate before 1300, for no further movement has been registered since the middle of the fourteenth century.[10] No comparable case has yet been identified in Scotland where subsidence and related problems can most often be attributed to undermining or other similar causes of instability, natural or man-induced.

Some of the areas of greatest land surface movement are to be found in sandy coastal districts where wind, sand and sea have conspired powerfully to produce other dramatic and devastating effects. The medieval estate of Culbin was one of the most fertile and prosperous in the Laigh of Moray, often referred to as the 'granary of Moray'. The sand first encroached on the arable land there in 1676, and after the great storms of 1694-5 it was piled so high that 'there was not a vestige to be seen of his [George Kinnaird's] manner place of Culbin, yairds, orchyairds and mains thereof'.[11] Even more immediate in its effect was the severe southerly storm which in August 1413 overwhelmed the medieval township of Forvie on the Buchan coast, still buried beneath the famous dunes of the Sands of Forvie.[12] Among the Hebridean islands great blankets of sand, dunes and machair have covered settlements of all periods from prehistoric to early modern times. Blown sand led to the abandonment in the later eighteenth century of many of the numerous and large townships on the west coast of Tiree, then one of the most densely populated parts of this fertile island, leaving behind a medieval chapel

and burial-ground at Kilkenneth virtually alone in a sea of dunes.[13] A similar fate had overtaken the old parish church of Gullane in East Lothian which by 1612 was being 'continewallie overblawin with sand'.[14] Blown sand also blocked the coastal outlets of the Lochs of Strathbeg and Spynie in the North-east, thereby contributing to the demise of the communities at Rattray and Spynie.[15]

As the modern world knows to its cost, winds of gale force 9 and above on the Beaufort scale are quite capable of causing structural damage on their own account. There can scarcely have been a year without such occurrences somewhere in Scotland. One of the most famous victims was the openwork stone crown of the tower of King's College Chapel, Aberdeen, which in 1634 was 'thrown down by the force of a great storm', described in another account as 'ane gryt storme of snaw with horribill heiche wyndis'.[16] 'Ane horrible high wind', still a characteristic of the otherwise well favoured Laigh of Moray, was also reported to have blown down some of the remaining timber roof trusses over the choir of Elgin Cathedral in December 1637.[17] Most recorded cases of storm damage relate to communal and corporately funded public buildings. Hence, whilst numerous incidents affecting private houses may have passed unremarked, it is known, for example, that part of the tolbooth stair at Ayr was 'blawin down be storme of weddir' in 1615-16, and that the tolbooth at Tain had to be demolished and rebuilt after serious storm damage had caused the partial collapse of the old tower in 1703.[18] The actual circumstances surrounding such events are rarely described in detail, however, except in newspapers, for which the following report in the *Ayr Observer* of 25 February 1845 can serve as a nineteenth-century example: 'On Saturday night or early on Sabbath morning the tower of Brodick Castle fell with a terrible crash. The old castle had been injured by the late storms, and several of the lintels had been rent. Workmen were employed in repairing the damage — no fewer than sixteen persons being working on it on Saturday last. Providentially the fall occurred during the time when no one was about it. The tower was, in the judgement of scientific men, too heavy for the old building on which it was erected'.[19]

The number of unreported cases of damage caused by electric storms also remains incalculable, especially among tall ruined buildings. Its known effects have certainly not been negligible. Lightning striking church steeples or spires was the cause of some disastrous fires throughout medieval Christendom, and one of the worst affected buildings in Scotland was Glasgow Cathedral. At some date before 1406 the central timber spire was struck by lightning, and in the ensuing conflagration the bell-tower and the choir were ruined, possibly the vestry and chapter house as well.[20] Secular buildings too were damaged in this manner; as Sir Robert Sibbald picturesquely put it, 'the thunder broke upon the house of West-binny [West Lothian] some time agoe, and demolished some part of it'.[21] Our knowledge of the extent of the disaster is much more precise in a case such as Melville House in Fife, for which a letter dated 27 October 1733 contains a long list of items damaged by lightning.[22]

Torrential rains and floods are the concomitants of many storms.[23] Although some earth-and-timber castles in Britain and on the continent may have been sited and designed with a view to keeping them above flood levels,[24] other mottes proved particularly vulnerable to spates of floodwater. The early thirteenth century witnessed the erosion and effective destruction by this means of various buildings in Perth, probably including the royal castle,[25] and of the principal Scottish residence of the Bruce family at Annan, an event that was believed to have been a manifestation of a curse laid upon the lords of Annandale by St Malachy in about 1140.[26] Stone buildings on riverside sites faced similar hazards, even when protected by ditches and water-courses. Greenlaw lay so close to the east bank of the Kirkcudbrightshire Dee that, according to one account, 'sometimes the inundation of the river comes into his [the owner's] cellars and lower roomes'.[27] Few would have dared to build so close to the River Tweed and its tributaries in the Borders, or to the Spey and the Findhorn in the North, rivers which have gained a fearsome reputation for sudden and devastating floods.[28]

The structures at greatest risk were the river bridges. The major — and costly — structures crossed powerful and frequently turbulent waters, but few proved more troublesome than those which crossed the Tay and the Earn in the vicinity of Perth. The long, eleven-arched medieval bridge over the Tay at Perth had a particularly calamitous history in the sixteenth century, and after the destruction of all but one arch in 1621 the struggle to maintain this crossing

was eventually given up, not to be renewed until about 150 years later.[29] Problems with the Earn crossing were compounded by the fact that the bridge had been built across the curve of a meander where the river was gradually shifting its course and eroding the northernmost abutment. The first serious consequences were felt in January 1614 when 'the northernmost pend and bow of the Bridge of Erne fell down, being evil bigged from the beginning, filled only with clay and earth, and without any blind pend'.[30]

The effects of unfortunate choices of site and poor construction have been felt throughout the ages, and in urban or suburban contexts such defects have become popularly associated with the worst kinds of speculative building. A report of March 1657 on burnt property in the Cowgate, Edinburgh, for example, censured Thomas Robertson, a famous building speculator of his day, for badly constructing the walls of a tenement-building with 'stone and clay and small rubbishe'.[31] The hazards of urban sites were exemplified by the collapse in 1691 of a house gable on the north side of the Old Vennel in Glasgow 'occasioned through the springs of the tounes well ther'.[32]

Ruinous and decaying buildings in the burghs were also a hazard that could not be ignored (Fig. 1). In 1573 the bailies, council and deacons of Edinburgh served what was in effect a Dangerous Building Notice on John Lawson to take down within forty-eight hours the 'ruinous and decayed gallery . . . at the nether end of his great bigging' which overlooked the common passage of the Overbow.[33] Acts of Parliament were issued in 1594, 1644 and 1663 anent the repair or demolition of ruinous houses in royal burghs, and there were numerous local ordinances and reports arising from particular cases in many of the larger burghs.[34] Ruinous houses in Glasgow's Briggait caused much official concern in the 1670s; one group was described in January 1677 as being 'lyklie to fall . . . quhilk may be dangerous and hazardsuome to old people and bairnes', but it was not until September of the following year that masons and wrights were called in to take them down.[35] In some cases it was recognised that neighbouring properties were also endangered. In 1611, for example, the owner of a collapsed house in Lanark was charged with the repair of an adjacent building that had been pulled down in its fall.[36] According to a general report on the royal burghs in 1692, housing in many of them was described as being in a decayed, waste or ruinous

1. Airds Close, Grassmarket, Edinburgh, 1850
(from Drummond 1879, plate 88).

condition.[37] The coastal burghs in particular seem to have been afflicted with poverty and decay, but decaying and ruinous buildings may well have been a feature of most urban landscapes from the earliest times, worse at certain periods, in certain regions, and even within certain parts of a burgh, hence perhaps the appellation 'Rotten Row'.

Outside the burghs there have been many well-known cases of structural collapse but the reasons for their occurrence can merely be guessed at. The fall of a portion of the central tower of Elgin Cathedral in 1506 and the complete collapse of its restored successor in 1711[38] might be attributed to a variety of causes: this part of the church might have been seriously weakened by the fire of 1390 (see below) and the weakness left unremedied; alternatively, and perhaps more plausibly, the designs of the successive central towers might have been quite simply too ambitious in terms of their construction, foundations and siting, a fault shared by the towers of not a few English medieval cathedrals.[39]

The structural difficulties at Linlithgow Palace, a large building erected partly on forced soil, may have had similar roots. In 1583 it was noted that the west quarter of the palace was 'altogidder lyk to fall downe',[40] and in 1605 attention was drawn to the insecure and dangerous condition of the north quarter. Nothing was done, and so on 6 September 1607 the Keeper of the Palace had to inform James VI that 'betwixt thre and four in the morning, the north quarter of your Majestie's Palice of Linlythgw is fallin, rufe and all, within the wallis, to the ground; but the wallis are standing yit, bot lukis everie moment when the inner wall sall fall, and brek your Majestie's fontan'.[41]

Lack of regular maintenance obviously contributed in no small measure to decay and disaster, even among those buildings that enjoyed continued use after the Reformation. At the former abbey, later parish church, of Fearn in Easter Ross concern about the condition of the heavy slated roof was expressed in 1695, but, left alone for almost another half-century, the roof eventually fell on the congregation during divine service in October 1742. According to a contemporary report,[42] '60 people were killed, besides the wounded. The gentry whose seats were in the niches, and the preacher falling under the sounding board, were preserved'. Another account[43] relates that seventeen were killed on the spot, but others (number unspecified) later died from their injuries. The fact that there was no similar tragedy at Jedburgh is perhaps a cause of wonder, and a tribute to the vigilance of the principal heritors. For, despite progressive despoliation of the rest of the monastic buildings and despite actual and threatened collapses of adjacent parts of the church, it was not until 1875 that parish worship was transferred from the nave of the abbey church to a new purpose-built structure in the town.[44] Part of the great abbey church of Melrose had fulfilled a similar function until 1810, and it seems reasonable to suppose that it was no easy matter maintaining a safe and secure place for reformed worship among the ruins of these great monasteries.

The phases through which most secular buildings passed on their way to collapse and ruin simply remain uncharted. One of the more suggestive case-studies, however, is Duffus Castle in Moray where a substantial hall-building of fourteenth-century date was erected on a twelfth-century motte whose forced soil appears to have provided insufficient foundation

2. Duffus Castle, Moray, 1981.

(Fig. 2).[45] A considerable mass of walling has broken from the northern end of the hall and has slid down the slope almost in one piece. In the words of the official guide, 'large portions of the curtain wall round the bailey have similarly tilted forward or slid down'.[46] The dramatic collapse of the hall probably took place in the seventeenth century, but we do not know precisely when and under what circumstances. Its walls allegedly show traces of burning which have been ascribed to an incident in 1452, and not to the later phases of occupation.

Even when merely contributing to the processes of ruin and collapse, fire has always been one of the most potent agencies of destruction, especially in congested urban areas. Fires were endemic in all the major burghs, but Glasgow suffered particularly badly in 1652 and 1677,[47] and Edinburgh in 1700.[48] One spectacular casualty of this Edinburgh fire was a fifteen-storeyed building called Babylon which, according to one account[49] 'was ane immense heap of combustible matter upon a small foundation, and made a prodigious blaze'.

In Edinburgh the lighting of domestic fires in rooms 'wanting ane chymney for venting thairof' was prohibited in 1585,[50] and during the course of the seventeenth century a series of regulations proscribed the use of combustible materials for roof coverings, frontages and forestairs.[51] In Glasgow smithies, kilns, candle houses and sugar refineries with their attendant fire risks were encouraged to move out to the edge of the burgh,[52] and consciousness of such risks came to be shared by private builders in the countryside. It was explicitly for reasons of fireproofing that Patrick, 1st Earl of Strathmore, replaced in the later seventeenth century the canopied kitchen chimney that his father had installed in Castle Huntly; it had 'a timber brace carried up with patched straw and clay and was full of hazard for taking of fire, as indeed upon many occasions it did'.[53]

But, then as now, even the strictest fire precautions were no proof against accidents, carelessness or malicious arson. According to the Kalendar of Fearn, Milton Castle in Ross-shire was burnt out when a crow's nest in a chimney accidentally caught fire there in 1642,[54] and the source of some fires in Glasgow was traced back to alleged negligence or arson on the part of urban blacksmiths or their apprentices.[55] Some churches on the fringes of the Highlands suffered from arson in the course of local family or political disputes, and it is believed that fires involving the loss of human life took place under such circumstances at, for example, the chapel in Tain in 1427 and at Kilchrist in 1603.[56]

Perhaps the most infamous act of deliberate incendiarism in the whole of Scottish history was the burning of Elgin Cathedral in 1390 by the then king's brother, Alexander Stewart, 'Wolf of Badenoch', one episode in a phase of violent disorder in the North at the end of the fourteenth century.[57] This outrage provoked loud complaints from the bishop of Moray, and from the anonymous but possibly Elgin-based author of the short chronicle inserted in the register of the bishopric, an account that betrays an obsessive concern with lawlessness and disorder.[58] Whilst the seriousness of the crime, in principle, and the turbulence of the times probably cannot be denied, a clear unbiased assessment of the background to this event and its precise architectural effect are long overdue.

That parts of the cathedral church were seriously damaged is not in doubt. Payments for its repair were aided by royal annuities, by reparations from Alexander Stewart himself and by revenues from the vacant see in the early fifteenth century.[59] On the basis of the surviving evidence, the upper part of the west front was one of the parts worst affected, or as the official guide book so vividly describes it, 'The original gable with its group of lancets was destroyed by the intense heat of the conflagration which had raged furiously at this end of the Kirk'.[60] The partial collapse of the central tower in the early sixteenth century may also have been a longer-term effect of this episode, but the rest is conjecture. Much thirteenth-century architecture still survives, and there is no convincing proof to show that the later fifteenth-century reconstruction of the chapter house in exalted style, or the patronage reflected in the architecture and monuments of the south choir-aisle can be attributed directly or indirectly to the fire of 1390. In the sober judgement of MacGibbon and Ross,[61] 'It is evident from the style of much of the work that still remains that this catastrophe, terrible as it was, caused only a partial destruction of the cathedral'. It is also evident that the artist who has visually recreated the scene in a nineteenth-century engraving (Fig. 3) has carefully placed the blaze in that part of the church which, on account of the collapse of the central tower, no longer survives.

A recently published guide to Pluscarden Priory[62] assumes that marks of fire damage in those monastic buildings may also belong to the same campaign, so the 'Wolf's' reputation for fire-raising would now seem to have established itself beyond authenticated fact. On the other hand, the 'Wolf' has had at least one, somewhat unexpected, apologist. John Shanks, shoemaker turned custodian of Elgin Cathedral, declared[63] a grudging admiration for 'the boldness of spirit and determination of purpose which that noble malefactor continued to display under the trying and singular circumstances in which he was placed', precisely the same fierce qualities which the redoubtable Shanks himself displayed in guarding the sacred ruins against the youth of Elgin in the nineteenth century.[64]

It would of course be a mistake to underestimate the extent of fire damage in cases which had no political overtones. Following a serious fire in the nave of the cathedral priory of St Andrews in 1378, it took about seven years to complete the most pressing repairs and about sixty years altogether to refurbish the complete structure and its fittings.[65] The conflagration caused by lightning at Glasgow Cathedral occurred at some date before 1406, and it has been suggested[66] that restoration of the badly affected north choir-aisle may not have been completed until the episcopate of Archbishop James (I) Beaton (1508-23) over a century after the event. But restitution of a fire-damaged fabric might go far beyond the original; Melrose Abbey was rebuilt in a much enlarged and grander form after 1385,[67] and so too, it seems, were Linlithgow Palace and Church after 1424.[68]

In the sphere of military history, however, just as in the case of Elgin Cathedral, some caution should be exercised in the acceptance of claims or reports that buildings were burnt and destroyed. Most evidence of this kind relates to the war zones of southern Scotland that lay in the path of successive English armies. The incursions of 1523, 1544 and 1545 were undoubtedly the most damaging, and there are impressive lists and numbers of places 'brent' by the English armies under the Earl of Hertford in 1544 and 1545, including some 'brent by the flete upon the see'.[69] The precise results of most such burnings remain uncorroborated, how-

3. 'Destruction of Elgin Cathedral' (engraving by T. Allom and R. Sands from Beattie 1838, *2*, opp. p. 153).

ever, and may not have amounted to complete destruction, a term which continues to be loosely and misleadingly applied. Moreover, there is reason to believe that prior to the sixteenth century most campaigns, apart possibly from that of 1385, were of limited destructive effect. Even in 1385 with 'the whole country [i.e. the Scottish Lowlands] ruined . . . the people of the country made light of it, saying, that with six or eight stakes they would soon have new houses . . .'[70]

Then, as later, the large and wealthy Border abbeys were usually among the principal victims,[71] but monastic bias and military reports have continued to sustain the old, exaggerated traditions. Statements to the effect that Jedburgh Abbey, the most vulnerable of the frontier monasteries, was in 1297 wrecked, plundered and rendered uninhabitable by the English under Sir Richard Hastings have recently been described as a travesty of the facts.[72] It was probably just as much at risk from one of its own canons who in 1297 twice tried to set fire to the monastery and stole ornaments, books and vestments.[73] 'Thrice ravaged' in the fifteenth century, 'given to the flames' in 1523,

'burnt . . . for the second time' in 1544, and its destruction 'completed . . . a year later',[74] Jedburgh Abbey must have been in a sorry plight throughout the later Middle Ages. But the links between alleged war damage and repair work in the fifteenth century remain unproven, and, despite later calamities, the church was sufficiently complete to be used for an episcopal consecration service in 1552. It is thus conceded, somewhat inconsistently, that 'the damage done must have been confined mainly to the parts E. of the crossing'.[75]

Kelso Abbey, situated uncomfortably close to the strategic and contested castle of Roxburgh, suffered a similar chapter of disasters: in 1305 its charters and muniments were said to have been burnt; in about 1316 the monastery was considerably despoiled and the monks reduced to begging; a papal petition of 1420 referred to it being severely damaged by hostile incursions; in 1523 the gatehouse tower was destroyed, and again in 1542, 1544 and 1545 it was savagely attacked by the English, it being Hertford's professed intention 'to rase and deface this house of Kelso so as the enemye shal have lytell commoditie of the same'.[76] These last attacks were undoubtedly devastating, but as late as 1517 Kelso was afflicted only by the effects of decay and by what appear to have been occasional acts of malicious vandalism: according to a detailed description prepared in that year, the tower 'in the inner part at the choir' was then 'empty on account of decay and age'; the only architectural damage attributable to the English was in the cloister 'partly covered with lead and partly unroofed through the fury and impiety of enemies'.[77] Such vandalism gathered momentum after the Reformation, and the abbeys provided a rich, illicit source of building-materials, of which lead was one of the most prized. At Melrose Abbey Sir Walter Scott of Branxholme was accused in 1573 of thefts of this kind, and in his defence he claimed that he had removed the materials merely to save them from the English invaders![78]

There are of course numerous accounts of damage to castles brought about by besieging armies. In a well-known episode in 1230 Rothesay Castle on Bute was captured by Norsemen who 'bound over themselves shields of wood . . . hewed into the wall with axes, because the stone was soft; and the wall fell down after that'.[79] After a siege in 1304 the gate of Stirling Castle was found to be 'a great deal' broken,[80] but the physical effects of sieges are generally difficult to assess. And just how far should Robert Bruce's renowned policy of demolishing fortresses — and the successive phases of castle 'destruction' effected during the course of Anglo-Scottish warfare in the fourteenth century — be interpreted literally? The most authoritative account of the history of Caer-laverock Castle suggests, for example, that although there are still some remains of the stone castle which stood at the time of the celebrated siege in 1300, Bruce's demolition order of 1312 and the Scots' levelling of the structure (*ad solum prostravit*) in 1357 can be assumed to have been largely effective.[81] But the arguments do not amount to conclusive proof; here, as elsewhere, the interpretation of phases of destruction is perhaps rather too readily adjusted to suit suggested phases of construction.

What is abundantly clear, however, is that the use of gunpowder ordnance, ushered into Scotland by James II (1437-60),[82] considerably increased the destructive potential of field artillery and besieging armies. A contemporary account of his siege of Abercorn Castle in 1455 related how 'the king remanit at the sege and gart strek mony of the towris down

with the gret gun, the quhilk a Francheman schot right wele, and failyeit na shot within a faldome quhar it was chargit him to hit'.[83] In his own account of the one-month siege James confirmed that the towers of the curtain-wall had collapsed as a result of the continual blows of the 'machines'.[84] Abercorn did not survive this onslaught, but in some buildings structural damage caused by siege armies or marauding bands can still be seen. In 1574 Alexander Ross of Balnagown was ordered to make good 'the doune casting of the battelit towr of Catboll' by building up the vaults again, and the irregular construction of the vaulted interior of Cadboll Tower in Easter Ross almost certainly reflects this episode.[85] And among the numerous ruined buildings which provide mute testimony to the effectiveness of gunpowder artillery there is, for example, the stump of Inveravon Castle in West Lothian 'kest doune' by James II in 1455,[86] or the shattered remains of Dunivaig Castle on Islay which was pounded by besieging forces in 1615 and 1647.[87] The civil wars of the middle decades of the seventeenth century certainly caused much damage to many castles throughout the country, but the evidence merits more detailed scrutiny. To what extent, for example, was Brodie Castle in Moray 'destroyed' by Montrose's men under Lord Gordon after their victory at nearby Auldearn in 1645? The suggestion that 'some of the ancient parts have been preserved in the restoration which took place thereafter'[88] may, on further detailed enquiry, prove to be an under-statement.

During the Cromwellian period medieval ruins continued to provide a source of readily available building materials. Tradition asserts, for example, that buildings in the vicinity of Inverness, including Fortrose Cathedral, were plundered for the military citadel built there in the 1650s.[89] At Fortrose, as elsewhere, the programme of destructive quarrying had commenced shortly after the Reformation. In 1572 Lord Ruthven received a royal grant to remove lead from the church 'throw being . . . no parroch kirk bot ane monasterie [sic] to sustene ydill belleis'.[90] It had been the already unpopular houses of friars in the towns which had borne the main brunt of Reformation violence from as early as 1543,[91] but, in the words of the late Monsignor McRoberts,[92] 'the fact remains that, when the crisis of the reformation had passed, in Scotland, practically every single one of the larger churches was a complete or partial ruin and the lesser churches were shorn of their glory and very often damaged'.

The Reformation has indeed left an indelible scar on the architectural legacy of Scotland, but other less abrupt and violent changes have had even more profound effects. One measure of the thoroughness of social and agricultural reorganisation which took place throughout the Scottish countryside in the eighteenth and nineteenth centuries is that, unlike England, there is now virtually no upstanding farmstead, township or village which preserves part of its medieval character physically intact. The reasons for this lack of building continuity among the middle and lower ranks of rural society are deeply rooted in the economic, environmental and tenurial history of the Scottish landscape. On the other hand, the architecture of landownership in town and country has included numerous robust and sturdy medieval buildings which have withstood the ravages of time and man better than many elsewhere in the British Isles. The quality of stone building in Scotland was remarked upon by tourists and travellers from the later Middle Ages onwards, and the point was very well expressed by Daniel Defoe in the early eighteenth century. He considered that in Edinburgh 'the buildings are surprising both for strength, for beauty and for height; all, or the greatest part of freestone, and so firm is everything made, that tho' in so high a situation, and in a country where storms and violent winds are so frequent, 'tis very rare that any damage is done here. No blowing of tiles about the streets, to knock people on the head as they pass; no stacks of chimneys and gable-ends of houses falling in to bury their inhabitants in their ruins, as we often find it in London, and other of our paper built cities in England . . .'[93]

Notes and References

1. Christopher Fry, *The Boy with a Cart, Cuthman, Saint of Sussex* (2nd edn. 1945 (1st edn. 1939)), 22.

2. D. McRoberts, Material destruction caused by the Scottish Reformation, *The Innes Review*, 10 (1959), 126-72; J. Durkan, The Great Fire at Glasgow Cathedral, *ibid.*, 26 (1975), 89-92.

3. D. Murray, *An Archaeological Survey of the United Kingdom. The Preservation and Protection of our Ancient Monuments* (1896); G. B. Brown, *The Care of Ancient Monuments* (1905); Rose Macaulay, *Pleasure of Ruins* (1953),

355-6; S. Piggott, *Ruins in a Landscape* (1976), 133-59; I. MacIvor and R. Fawcett, One hundred years on! Ancient Monuments 1882-1982: a view from Scotland, *Popular Archaeology* (November 1982), 17-25; and *idem* in M. Magnusson, ed., *Echoes in Stone* (1983), 9-27. For England and Wales see also H. Honour, *Romanticism* (1979), 156-93; D. Watkin, *The Rise of Architectural History* (1980); M. W. Thompson, *Ruins, their preservation and display* (1981); and A. D. Saunders, A century of Ancient Monuments legislation 1882-1982, *Antiquaries Journal*, 63 (1983), 11-33.

4. M. S. Briggs, *Goths and Vandals, a Study of the Destruction, Neglect and Preservation of Historical Buildings in England* (1952); and see also J. M. Richards, ed., *The Bombed Buildings of Britain* (2nd edn. 1947).

5. E.g. the demolition of the castles of Elphinstone (East Lothian), Helmsdale (Sutherland), Cathcart (Glasgow), Flemington (Angus), the old bridge at Bridge of Earn (Perthshire), and numerous proposed demolitions.

6. See e.g. A. R. Powys, *Repair of Ancient Buildings* (1929); B. M. Feilden, *Conservation of Historic Buildings* (1982).

7. M. W. Beresford and J. G. Hurst, eds., *Deserted Medieval Villages* (1971).

8. C. Platt, *The Abbeys and Priories of Medieval England* (1984), 220-41.

9. R. P. Wilcox, *Timber and Iron Reinforcement in Early Buildings* (1981).

10. H. H. Lamb, *Climate, history and the modern world* (1982), 172, 188.

11. T. Thomson and C. Innes, eds., *The Acts of the Parliaments of Scotland* (1814-75), 9 (1687-1695), 479a; J. A. Steers, The Culbin Sands and Burghead Bay, *Geographical Journal*, 90 (1937), 498-528 at 500-1; and *idem*, *The Coastline of Scotland* (1973), 216-20.

12. J. B. Pratt, *Buchan* (1901), 22; Steers, *op. cit.* (1973), 235-41; Lamb, *op. cit.*, 185.

13. E. R. Cregeen, *Argyll Estate Instructions, Mull, Morvern, Tiree, 1771-1805* (Scottish History Society 4th series, 1 1964), xxvii, 2, 18, 89; R(oyal) C(ommission on the) A(ncient and) H(istorical) M(onuments of) S(cotland), *Inventory of Argyll*, 3 (1980), No. 298.

14. RCAHMS, *Inventory of East Lothian* (1924), No. 24.

15. K. Walton, Rattray, a study in coastal evolution, *Scottish Geographical Magazine*, 72 (1956), 85-96 at 90-4; A. G. Ogilvie, The Physiography of the Moray Firth Coast, *Trans Royal Soc. Edin.*, 53 (1923), 377-404 at 395-404; and H. B. Mackintosh, *The Lossie and the Loch of Spynie* (1928).

16. A. Mitchell, ed., *Geographical Collections relating to Scotland made by Walter Macfarlane* (Scottish History Society 1st series, 51-3, 1906-8) 2, 507; W. D. Simpson, ed., *William Kelly* (Aberdeen University Studies, No. 125, 1949), 71.

17. H. B. Mackintosh, *Elgin Past and Present* (1914), 66.

18. G. S. Pryde, ed., *Ayr Burgh Accounts, 1534-1624*

(Scottish History Society 3rd series, 28 1937), 261; G. Stell, The earliest tolbooths: a preliminary account, *P(roceedings of the) S(ociety of) A(ntiquaries of) S(cotland)*, 111 (1981), 445-53 at 453 and refs cited.

19. C. E. Whitelaw, The Castles, in J. A. Balfour, ed., *The Book of Arran*, 1 (1910), 241-51 at 243n.

20. Durkan, *op. cit.*

21. R. Sibbald, *History, ancient and modern, of the Sheriff-doms of Linlithgow and Stirling . . .* (1710), 28.

22. Scottish Record Office, Leven and Melville Muniments GD 26/13/276.

23. For the effects of increased rainfall in early four-teenth-century England see C. Platt, *Medieval England* (1978), 95 and refs cited; see especially the chronology of the water-table in J. R. Ravensdale, *Liable to Floods* (1974), 6-12. For the effects of climatic changes in general see also M. L. Parry, *Climatic change, agriculture and settlement* (1978), C. D. Smith and M. L. Parry, eds., *Consequences of Climatic Change* (1981), and Lamb, *op. cit.* According to tradition (Hugh Miller, *Scenes and Legends of the North of Scotland* (1835), 69-71), the medieval burgh of Cromarty suffered and eventually succumbed to the effects of marine erosion at some date before the eighteenth century, but it is not clear whether this was coastal inundation brought about by changes in sea-level (cf. Ogilvie, *op. cit.*).

24. E. J. Talbot, The Defences of Earth and Timber Castles, in D. H. Caldwell, ed., *Scottish Weapons and Fortifications, 1100-1800* (1981), 1-9 at 4-5.

25. W. Goodall, ed., *Joannis de Fordun Scotichronicon cum Supplementis et Continuatione Walteri Boweri* (1759), 1, 528; A. A. M. Duncan, Perth: the first century of the burgh, *Trans. Perthshire Society of Natural Science* (Special Issue 1973), 30-50 at 39-40.

26. R. C. Reid, The Caput of Annandale or the Curse of St Malachy, *Dumfriesshire Trans.*, 3rd series, 32 (1953-4), 155-66.

27. Macfarlane, *Geographical Coll.* 2, 109.

28. Daniel Defoe, *A tour through the whole island of Great Britain* (1724-6, 1968 reprint) 2, 765; T. D. Lauder, *An Account of the Great Floods of August 1829 in the Province of Moray* (1830, 3rd edn. 1873); D. Nairne, *Memorable Floods in the Highlands during the Nineteenth Century* (1895).

29. H. R. G. Inglis, The roads and bridges in the early history of Scotland, *PSAS*, 47 (1912-13), 303-33 at 322-4; *The Chronicle of Perth* (1831), 22.

30. *The New Statistical Account of Scotland* (1845), 10 (Perthshire), 812n; G. D. Hay and G. Stell, The Old Bridge, Bridge of Earn: a posthumous account, in A. Fenton and G. Stell, eds., *Loads and Roads in Scotland and beyond* (1984), 92-104.

31. M. Wood *et al*, *Extracts from the records of the burgh of Edinburgh, 1655-1665*, 54; M. Wood, All the statelie buildings of . . . Thomas Robertson, *Book of the Old Edinburgh Club*, 24 (1942), 126-51.

32. S(cottish) B(urgh) R(ecord) S(ociety), *Extracts from the records of the burgh of Glasgow, 1691-1717*, 12-13, 24.

33. SBRS, *Extracts from the records of the burgh of Edinburgh, 1573-1589*, 3.

34. G. Stell, Scottish Burgh Houses, 1560-1707, in A. T. Simpson and S. Stevenson, eds., *Town Houses and Structures in Medieval Scotland* (1980), 1-31 at 7 and refs cited.

35. SBRS, *Glasgow Burgh Recs, 1663-1690*, 229, 255.

36. R. Renwick, ed., *Extracts from the Records of the Royal Burgh of Lanark* (1893), 73.

37. *SBRS Miscellany*, 13 (1881), 49-157.

38. H. B. Mackintosh, *Elgin Past and Present* (1914), 60, 68.

39. F. Bond, *An Introduction to English Church Architecture* (1913) 2, 875-6.

40. H. M. Paton *et al*, eds., *Accounts of the Masters of Works*, 1, 1529-1615 (1957), 311.

41. J. Ferguson, *Linlithgow Palace; its history and traditions* (1910), 185-6, 330.

42. *The Gentleman's Magazine*, 12 (1742), 545.

43. N(ational) L(ibrary of) S(cotland), Hutton Collection correspondence, Advocates Manuscripts 29. 4. 2(xi), f.263r.

44. RCAHMS, *Inventory of Roxburghshire* (1956), 1, No. 414; H. (Lord) Cockburn, *Circuit Journeys* (1888, 1983 edn.), 57.

45. W. D. Simpson, *Duffus Castle* (Official Guide 1951, 1968 reprint); *idem*, The Castles of Duffus, Rait and Morton Reconsidered, *PSAS*, 91 (1958-9), 10-14 at 13-14.

46. Simpson, *Duffus Castle*, 3.

47. SBRS, *Glasgow Burgh Recs, 1630-1662*, 229ff; *ibid., 1663-1690*, 243ff; see also A. Gibb, *Glasgow, the making of a city* (1983), 25-9, 46-8.

48. R. Chambers, *Fires in Edinburgh* (1824), 11-29.

49. J. Dennistoun, ed., *Coltness Collections, 1608-1840* (1842) 2, 48-9.

50. SBRS, *Edinburgh Burgh Recs, 1573-1589*, 446.

51. H. Armet, Notes on rebuilding in Edinburgh in the last quarter of the seventeenth century, *Book of the Old Edinburgh Club*, 29 (1956), 111-42; Stell, *op. cit.* (1980), 30 n. 64.

52. Gibb, *op. cit.*, 27, 46, 48.

53. A. H. Millar, ed., *Glamis Papers: the 'Book of Record'* (Scottish History Society 1st series, 9, 1890), 34.

54. Royal Commission on Historical Manuscripts, Series 1, II Second Report (1871), Appendix, Duke of Sutherland (Dunrobin MSS), 180. The Kalendar of Fearn is now lodged in the National Library of Scotland, Deposit 314. 18.

55. SBRS, *Glasgow Burgh Recs, 1573-1642*, 224; *ibid., 1663-1690*, 243ff.

56. W. MacGill, *Old Ross-shire and Scotland* (1909), No. 42; *Origines Parochiales Scotiae* (Bannatyne Club, 1850-55) 2 (2), 524; Hugh Miller, *My Schools and Schoolmasters* (1854), 167-8, 172; D. Gregory, *History of the Western Highlands and Isles of Scotland* (1881 edn., reprinted 1975), 302-3.

57. R. Nicholson, *Scotland, the later Middle Ages* (1974), 204-5, 207-8.

58. *Registrum Episcopatus Moraviensis* (Bannatyne Club, 1837), No. 303.

59. J. Stuart *et al*, eds., *The Exchequer Rolls of Scotland* (1878-1908) 3 (1379-1406), 276, 316, 348, 376, 403, 430; *ibid.*, 4 (1406-36), 68-9, 173.

60. J. S. Richardson and H. B. Mackintosh, *Elgin Cathedral* (Official Guide 1980), 9.

61. D. MacGibbon and T. Ross, *The Ecclesiastical Architecture of Scotland* (1896-7) 2, 122.

62. [B. C. Skinner], *Pluscarden Abbey* (1981), 3 [not paginated].

63. 'The Old Cicerone of Elgin Cathedral' [J. Shanks], *Elgin and a Guide to Elgin Cathedral* (1866), 193.

64. *Ibid.*, prologue; Mackintosh, *op. cit.* (1914), 285-9; Cockburn, *op. cit.*, 9, 165.

65. Goodall, ed., *Chron. Bower* 1, 364, 375; RCAHMS, *Inventory of Fife* (1933), No. 455 at p. 231. The account by Gervase of Canterbury of the burning of Canterbury Cathedral in 1174 and its subsequent repair provides a detailed and instructive comparison, W. Stubbs, ed., *Gervase of Canterbury: Historical Works* (Rolls Series 73, 1879-80) 1, 1-6. See also the account of the fire at Barnwell Priory church in 1287 in J. W. Clark, ed., *The Observances . . . of . . . Barnwell* (1897), xix, cited by Durkan, *op. cit.*, 89n.

66. Durkan, *op. cit.*

67. RCAHMS, *Inventory of Roxburghshire* (1956), 2, No. 567 at 267-8.

68. F. J. H. Skene, ed., *Liber Pluscardensis* (1877-80) 1, 371; 2, 280; RCAHMS, *Inventory of West Lothian* (1929), Nos. 352, 356.

69. W. C. Dickinson, G. Donaldson and I. A. Milne, eds., *A Source Book of Scottish History*, 2, 1424-1567 (1958 edn.), 133-5.

70. Jean Froissart in P. H. Brown, *Early Travellers in Scotland* (1891), 12. Cf. D. H. Gordon, Fire and the Sword: The Technique of Destruction, *Antiquity*, 27 (1953), 149-52.

71. For the effects of invasions on the sizes of monastic communities see M. Dilworth, The Border Abbeys in the Sixteenth Century, *Records of the Scottish Church History Society*, 21, part 3 (1983), 233-47.

72. Cf. J. Morton, *The Monastic Annals of Teviotdale* (1832), 10-11, and I. B. Cowan and D. E. Easson, *Medieval Religious Houses, Scotland* (1976), 92.

73. J. Bain, ed., *Calendar of Documents relating to Scotland* (1881-8), 2, No. 969; 3, No. 112.

74. RCAHMS, *Inventory of Roxburghshire* (1956), 1, No. 414 at p. 196.

75. *Ibid.*

76. *State Papers during the Reign of Henry the Eighth* (Record Commissioners, 1-11, 1830-52), 5, Correspondence relating to Scotland, part 4, 515, cited in RCAHMS, *Inventory of Roxburghshire* (1956), 1, No. 504 at 240.

77. A. Theiner, ed., *Vetera Monumenta Hibernorum et Scotorum Historiam Illustrantia* (1864), 527, cited in RCAHMS, *Inventory of Roxburghshire* (1956), 1, No. 504 at 240-1.

78. J. S. Richardson, M. Wood and C. J. Tabraham, *Melrose Abbey* (Official Guide 1981), 40, and RCAHMS, *Inventory of Roxburghshire* (1956), 2, No. 567 at 268.

79. A. O. Anderson, ed., *Early Sources of Scottish History, 500 to 1286* (1922) 2, 476.

80. Bain, ed., *Cal. Docs. Scot.*, 4, No. 1825.

81. B. H. St. J. O'Neil, *Caerlaverock Castle* (Official Guide), 8-9.

82. M. Toynbee, King James II of Scotland: Artillery and Fortification, *The Stewarts*, 11 (1962), 157-62.

83. G. Buchanan (transl. J. Aikman), *The History of Scotland* (1827-9), 2, 159; T. Thomson, ed., *The Auchinleck Chronicle, ane Schort Memoriale of the Scottis Corniklis for Addicioun* (1819-1877), 54.

84. J. Pinkerton, *The History of Scotland from the Accession of the House of Stuart to Mary, with Appendixes of Original Papers* (1797) 1, 486-8.

85. MacGill, *Old Ross-shire*, No. 677; see also *Origines Parochiales* 2 (2), 441-3.

86. *Chron. Auchinleck*, 53.

87. G. G. Smith, ed., *The Book of Islay* (1895), 240-8; RCAHMS, *Inventory of Argyll*, 5 (1984), No. 403.

88. D. MacGibbon and T. Ross, *The Castellated and Domestic Architecture of Scotland* (1887-92) 4, 64.

89. NLS Advocates MS 29. 4. 2. (xi), f.225; A. A. Tait, The Protectorate Citadels of Scotland, *Architectural History*, 8 (1965), 9-24 at 13-15.

90. M. Livingston *et al*, eds., *Registrum Secreti Sigilli Regum Scottorum* (1908-   ), 6 (1567-74), No. 1653.

91. Cowan and Easson, *op. cit.*, 27-9.

92. McRoberts, *op. cit.*, 171.

93. Defoe, *op. cit.* 2, 711.

Tenements: the Industrial Legacy

Peter Robinson

[The author's paper, Tenements: A Pre-Industrial Urban Tradition (*ROSC* 1984, 52-64), explored some of the motives for flat living in Scotland up to 1750. This paper continues and concludes the story over the period of urban expansion and industrial success from 1750 until 1918.]

Progressive agricultural improvements and the beginnings of industrialisation greatly increased the wealth of Scotland from the mid-eighteenth century onwards. Textiles, iron, coal and, latterly, ship-building and engineering involved development that led to a dramatic shift from the land to the towns. Increased wealth stimulated urban building of all kinds and, through time, moved the commercial emphasis of Scotland from the Forth to the Clyde. The effect was to transform an established pre-industrial urban tenement tradition from a minority building form into a dominant one; initially as the prospering middle classes built bigger and better flats, and later as mass housing for an industrial proletariat.

Not a little of the first flush of wealth from agricultural improvements and industrial success found its way to Edinburgh, stimulating suburban expansion on the south side and later providing a driving force for the municipally inspired Craig New Town of 1767. Almost inevitably there was a short-lived reaction to the congestion of the Ancient Royalty and to the entrenched flat tradition as the 'London model' of terraced house caught the imagination of the wealthier classes in Argyle and George Squares, but on the south side the tenement was never seriously challenged as development edged down old field roads and new streets. The terraced house, however, gained an initial hold to the north, only to be supplanted later when a growing proportion of New Town expansion was devoted exclusively to flats. This was particularly so in streets with a north-south axis even in the Craig New Town, such as Hanover, Frederick and Castle Streets.

The proportion of flats also increased westward along Queen Street and by degrees northwards down the hill beyond Queen Street Gardens in what would have been relatively remote suburban fringes of the day.

Suburban expansion was a clear reaction by the better-off to the congestion and dangers of the Old Town, and the way of life it represented; not least to persistent collapses of overcrowded and unhealthy lands.[1] The increasing proportion of suburban tenements might, therefore, be seen as something of a contradiction, but a metamorphosis was under way. Far from abandoning the tenement, the middle classes were experimenting with the flat idiom in new and exciting ways and transforming an essentially medieval building form into something that was culturally and socially acceptable. Over the period 1775 to 1825 the purpose-built middle-class tenement became larger and more elegant. A main-door flat in Castle Street could have as many as twelve rooms on three floors, and in Moray Place, Heriot Row and Great King Street flats were integrated into the design of great palace facades.

The closing years of the eighteenth century and the first of the nineteenth were a period of vigorous experiment and considerable refinement, and Edinburgh's example of elegant town expansion was copied widely, as were the flats. Glasgow, Dundee, Aberdeen, Perth, Greenock and elsewhere all pursued their own variations of both, and these in turn provided inspiration and models for later developments. Georgian good manners dictated that the turnpike stair, where it remained, should be discreetly hidden at the back of the building. The turnpike lingered on in Glasgow and Dundee well into the nineteenth century to become the hallmark of the 'plattie' in the latter, although it was virtually abandoned in Edinburgh in favour of straight stairs and half-landings. The Castle Street tenement (Fig. 1) shows the distinctive Edinburgh three-door con-

1. Nos. 39-43 Castle Street, Edinburgh: built in 1794 as four flats: two main door flats (nos. 39 and 43) and two upper flats (nos. 41 upper left and right). Sir Walter Scott owned and occupied no. 39 from 1802-1826. The centre door (no. 41) gives access to the common stair at the front of the building.

figuration of main-door flat, stair and main-door flat so typical of the period. The main-door flat (No. 39 Castle Street) should also be one of the better known, given its direct associations with Sir Walter Scott.

Overcrowding and Disease

Rich and poor had enjoyed a close and familiar relationship in the 130 acres of the Ancient Royalty. It was one that had been galvanised by common hardship. The narrow turnpike stairs had amounted to vertical streets with a gradation of classes living within the same building. In later days the very highest and lowest flats were, it seems, 'possessed by artificers, while the gentry and better sort of people dwelt in fifth and sixth stories'.[2] Rents varied considerably even within the same structure and they were all generally low. When incomes were meagre, life was plain.[3] Some of this flavour lingered on to impress at least one American visitor who was prompted to write humorously of the Old Town in the early 1830s:

> You may call on a friend of note, and discover him
> With a shoemaker under, a staymaker over him.
> My dwelling begins with a periwig maker:
> I'm under a corncutter, over a baker;
> Above, the chiropodist; cookery too;
> O'er that is a Laundress — o'er is a Jew:
> A painter and tailor divide the eighth flat,
> And a dancing academy thrives over that![4]

When the rich left the old town centres of Glasgow and Edinburgh for the fashionable suburbs, their places were taken up by successive waves of poorer incomers. The effect, however, was decidedly unpleasant. Further subdivisions of the older 'lands' (tenements) occurred, and the great social divide developed between the old and the new, cutting right across the old familiar relationships. Squalor of a truly horrific kind took over as the incomers, often from rural areas and unaccustomed to the disciplines of high-density life, crowded into the ancient and decaying lands. First-hand accounts of the historic cores of Glasgow and Edinburgh pointed to unspeakably degrading conditions for many. When William Chambers reported on the Ancient Royalty to the Poor Law Commissioners in 1840, he was driven to write: 'Society, in the densely peopled closes which I have alluded to, has sunk to something indescribably vile and abject. Human beings are living in a state worse than brutes'.[5]

Catastrophic collapses continued in the heart of the capital. As late as November 1861, thirty-five people died and many more were injured when a tenement at the head of Chalmer's Close fell without warning.[6] This tragedy was guaranteed a place in Edinburgh's folklore when a boy trapped in the debris shouted to his rescuers: 'Heave awa' chaps, I'm no deid yet!' The quotation survives above Paisley Close as a testament to the dead and injured. A more enduring memorial was the attention this collapse focused on conditions in the High Street, ultimately leading to the appointment in 1862 of Dr. (later Sir) Henry Duncan Littlejohn, the City's first Medical Officer of Health.

Municipal reaction was generally slow and concentrated on matters of sanitation, overcrowding and health. The notorious 'ticketing' of small houses in Glasgow, dating from the mid-1860s, was a particularly degrading attempt to regulate overcrowding. Under this system houses of three rooms or less, and less than 2,000 cubic feet in volume, were measured and their capacity inscribed on a metal ticket fixed to the front door. Capacity was worked out as the number of occupants over eight years old, allowed at the rate of 300 cubic feet per person. By the early 1880s one-seventh of the total population of Glasgow, about 75,000 people, lived under these conditions.[7]

New streets in Edinburgh, including Victoria Street at the West Bow and the later Blackfriars and St Mary's Streets and others, were inspired by municipal initiative, but their effect generally was harmful to those at the bottom end of the housing ladder. Such schemes played a part in removing ghetto areas by a process of displacement which exacerbated overcrowding at a time when cheap accommodation for rent was in increasingly short supply. Quite simply a combination of general improvements and commercial intrusion was forcing a steadily increasing working population into a diminishing number of decayed and subdivided lands, so driving up the price of house room. In 1829 the Improvement Commissioners swept away an area of the West Bow, and between 1830 and 1841 railway improvements systematically cleared the back of the Canongate and Abbey Hill, while vacant spaces in the centre were converted to industrial and commercial use or developed with public buildings.[8] Much the same was happening in Dundee, and in Glasgow the coming of the railways had a similar effect in the High Street area.

Philanthropic Reaction
There was a certain sympathy for the plight of the poor, even if the overwhelming majority of the better-off were content to view the ghettos from a comfortable distance. 'We had often wondered', said one observer, 'how the Lowland Scotch mechanic retained his virtue and his courage, when so many malign influences are at work, whose tendency is to destroy both'.[9] It is interesting to note that overcrowding was not confined to the older areas. William Chambers was able to point in 1840 to a house in Jamaica Street in Edinburgh New Town 'which a few years ago contained, and probably still contains, 150 persons'.[10] This was, literally, on the doorstep of some of the most fashionable houses in the city, where no doubt the threat of cholera would have helped to focus the mind. It was small wonder that well-meaning and idealistic gestures by the better-off were generally hostile to that model of poverty represented by the overcrowded and squalid lands, just as the middle classes had themselves sought radical change some eighty years before.

There were many experiments in artisan housing. Of some interest are the Pilrig Model Dwellings, started in 1852 as a semi-philanthropic venture on cheap land midway between Leith and Edinburgh on ground owned by Mr Balfour of Pilrig. They were a deliberate attempt to try something different, and they were described at the time as occupying 'a kind of intermediate character between the town and country house'.[11] The cottage flat solution chosen was not, of course, new. It represented a return to smaller burgh practice, but an essential difference was that each house had its own front door and a small garden, and the houses were so arranged that the upper and lower floors were approached from opposite sides of the building. The flats were small, but most had an internal WC. It was an arrangement that was refined in the later 1850s at Rosebank Cottages, now clearly visible from the Western Approach Road. Here the flats were approached from opposite sides of the building, but unlike the Pilrig example, access to the upper flats was from a shared external stair and balcony.[12] This general arrangement was borrowed in turn in 1861 by the Edinburgh Co-operative Building Company for the well-known and widely copied 'Colonies' development beside the Water of Leith (Fig. 2).[13]

Although similar in appearance to Rosebank, the Colonies were conceived as an experiment in home ownership for the artisan classes rather than as a scheme for rental, so adding a quite new dimension to the drive for better housing. It was an initiative emulated with less success in Dundee in the Blyth Street and City Road area some three years later where the houses were also of the cottage flat type.[14] It is interesting to record that neither experiment was successful in promoting home ownership among the class for whom it was primarily intended. Quite simply, a majority of working people led lives too insecure to contemplate such a step.[15] However, the building form survived and thrived in Edinburgh to become a popular local variant of the cottage flat theme.

2. The Edinburgh Colonies. The upper flats each of two storeys are reached from the stairs, in this instance 16-30 Dunrobin Place. The lower single-storey flats, that is 1-15 Dunrobin Place, are reached from the other side of the building. Note the similarity of this arrangement to pre-industrial and small burgh practice. R. C. L. Miller.

The Shopocracy

Well-meaning as the philanthropic experiments were, there was little chance that any could succeed in making a substantial impact on the quite intractable problem of accommodating an urban working force. It was a point that was recognised fully by the remarkable Committee of the Working Classes of Edinburgh, set up in July 1858. Their view was blunt: 'The most enthusiastic philanthropist will one day tire of building houses for the working classes when he discovers that such investments are unremunerative; and that, after all, the people whom he intends to benefit were unconscious of the good intention'.[16] They were critical of a number of local philanthropic experiments, and their examination of real options came down firmly in favour of the traditional four-storey tenement financed by private capital and built for rent. The reasons they gave for what might seem to be an unimaginative conclusion revealed a depth of local prejudice in favour of what was described as 'the Scottish system of building':

> There can be no doubt that a Scotchman is quite as wedded to his flats as an Englishman to his floors. All the arguments for common stairs go for nothing in the eyes of a native of Edinburgh . . . His ideas of the importance of his native country are always enhanced by his comparison of the substantial Scotch structures of stone with the slight buildings of brick which grow up around Manchester and Birmingham . . . it is not for them to recommend any radical reform in the manners and customs of their country . . . where ground is scarce and feu duties are high — the Scottish system possesses the advantage in points of economy, in durability, in substantial appearance, in warmth, and capacity for standing tear and wear, there can be no comparison whatsoever.[17]

The model plan put forward by the Committee (Fig. 3) shows a conventional four-storey arrangement with four back-to-back 'room and kitchen' houses to each landing, each in turn equipped with a pantry and WC. The plan appears to have been an amalgam of ideas based on successful local practice, and it was an arrangement that was to be widely adopted over the next forty years in the City. Once again it suggests that long-standing local practice and habit were dominant forces in dictating housing form, and this is not a difficult theme to demonstrate over a period of dramatic urban expansion, when taken together with the equally powerful motivating forces of speculation and investment.

There is no question that, at least over the period 1851-1914, investment in property was familiar to the small saver looking for a safe income: 'the shopocracy', in the language of the day. These were the shopkeepers and others interested in a steady and enduring income: people who could be equated in present-day terms with the building society investor. The details have been researched some time ago in a long essay on working-class housing in Glasgow.[18] The point of crucial importance is that neither speculation, nor investment in housing for a steady income, favours innovation. The small investor was, and remains, innately conservative in his choices, and his actions would reinforce whatever local prejudices prevailed.

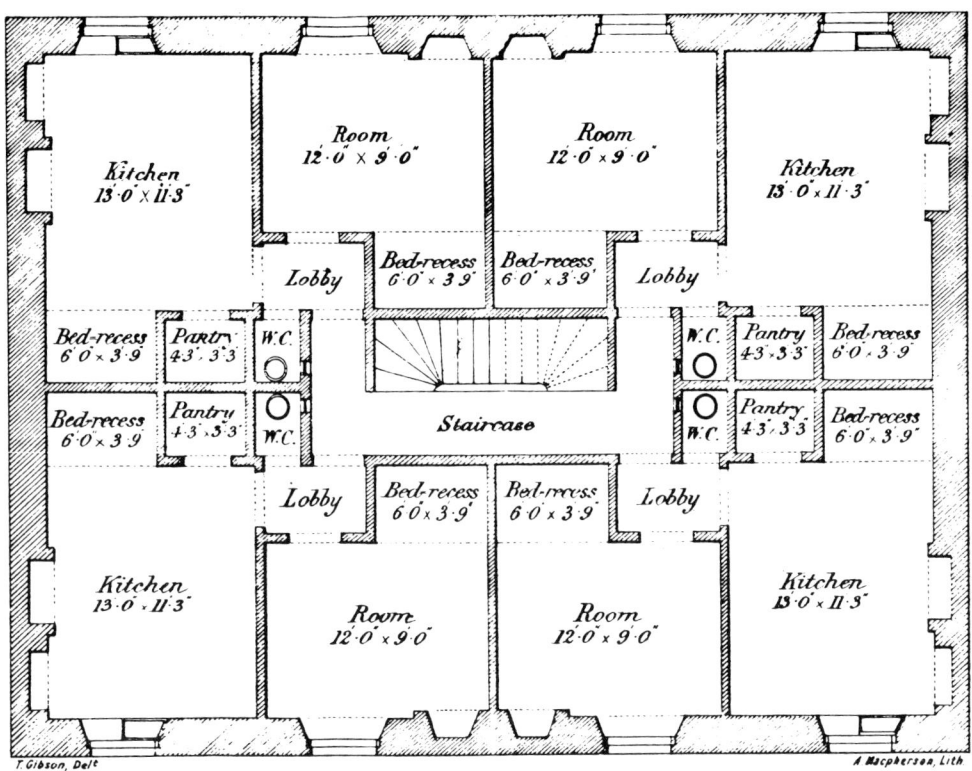

REPORT ON

HOUSES FOR THE WORKING CLASSES

OF EDINBURGH.

Plan of all Floors above Ground Floor

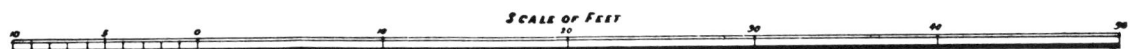

SCALE OF FEET

3. Model Plan from the Report of a Committee of the Working Classes of Edinburgh, etc., 1860. The arrangement shows four room and kitchen houses to each of four floors. The probable cost of such a tenement 58 feet by 38 feet was estimated by the Committee at £1,350. The rent of 16 houses at £7.10.0 came to £120 pa, less £26 feu duty. Factorage, repairs, taxes and insurance gave an annual profit of £94, or a rate of interest of 7 per cent per annum.

The effect was that plans which had shown signs of local success were refined and repeated, and this is precisely what happened to the Edinburgh 'model plan' in areas like Polwarth, Gorgie/Dalry and Easter Road in later years. Figs. 4-5 show a typical Dean of Guild submission based on a refinement of the model plan for a pair of tenements containing together sixteen room and kitchen houses in the Polwarth area. Elsewhere, just as in Edinburgh, successful local practice and more up-market middle-class designs were being increasingly adapted to satisfy the new demands of an industrial working force.

Other powerful influences were also reinforcing successful local practice. The rate of interest on flat building, the 'bond rate', was lower than for terraced development, because the risk of empties was much reduced.[19] Typical financing would involve the borrowing of something like two-thirds of the cost of a working-class tenement containing around a dozen houses for rent. This would produce a return of 5-7%

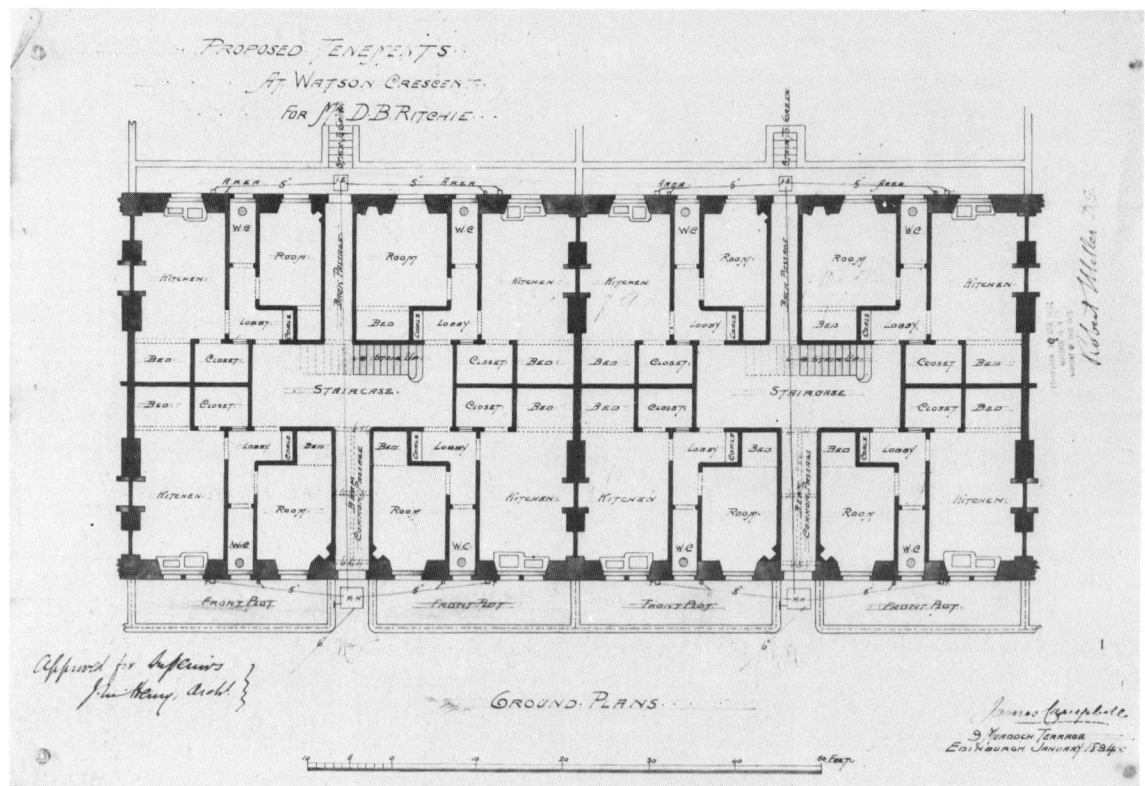

4.   Typical Dean of Guild Lining for two working class tenements in Polwarth, Edinburgh, dated January 1894. The annual rents are just visible in pencil on the print, ranging from £9.11.0 to £10.5.0 for a ground-floor room and kitchen with inside WC.

per annum as a minimum after all risks and maintenance were covered.[20] The conventional wisdom of the day was that while the prevailing rate of interest dictated the tempo of building, the level of feu duty dictated the density. The Scottish feuing system created what amounted to a self-fulfilling prophecy operating through the mechanisms of potential value. Congestion bred congestion as adjacent land values reflected the possibility of an equivalent density of development. It was a process that was reinforced in areas such as Bruntsfield in Edinburgh by the need to buy substantial recently built detached properties to assemble land in the right location for development. The 1918 Royal Commission on Housing in Scotland was able to report:

> When industrial activity became pronounced in the middle of the last century, towns began to expand rapidly, and it was found by owners of ground that a great deal of money could be made by such owners in selling or feuing their ground for housing purposes.

With the example of housing people in tenements before them, their calculations were naturally based upon what was the utmost number of people who could be housed on a given area, so that from the total earnings of the people so housed on that area the largest possible sum could be extracted as cost of ground in the shape of ground rent. This practice has developed, and it has become practically universal in large towns to build on the intensive system.[21]

Victorian Suburb

The tenement became the preferred development solution for a substantial portion of the Scottish housing market in the last fifty years of the nineteenth century in situations where sites were scarce and land values were high. Detached villas and terraced development catered for the top end of the new building market and the tenement for the rest. Local prejudices created a great variety of flat types, largely catering for middle-class and artisan need, giving each city and town a distinctive 'feel'. The Glasgow,

5. Front elevation as designed for the flats in Fig. 4.

Edinburgh, Dundee and Aberdeen stereotypes referred to in ROSC 1984 were all variations of what was basically a four-storey theme, as were preferred Paisley, Rutherglen and Greenock solutions, while burghs like Arbroath, Bathgate and Kirkcaldy developed their own versions of the cottage flat type. All over Scotland local pressures appear to have been at work refining and confirming particular local forms within well-defined housing markets, which helped to make the period 1850 to about 1905 the great era of flat building. Construction of tenements (Fig. 6) would have been a routine affair, and executed with speed, efficiency and a large measure of standardisation. There could be considerable density of development of a typical working-class street block (Fig. 7), such as might have been built at the turn of the century in Glasgow or Paisley.

Victorian tenement developments were a simple and direct response to demand. This applied as much to the planning of the suburb with its public buildings, open spaces, shopping patterns and communications, as to the basic organisation of the flat unit itself. The one-room house, the 'single-end', was simply a kitchen. It represented the bottom end of a market that could typically extend to four rooms and kitchen, or more for middle-class occupation. The National Trust's tenement at 145 Buccleuch Street, Glasgow is a good example of a better sort of house with bathroom and hot water (Fig. 8). The Victorian tenement suburb was a more spacious affair than its Georgian equivalent, even though different classes were still living in close proximity by modern standards. Professor MacMillan's 1960s description of the nineteenth-century Woodlands development, just to the north of Charing Cross in Glasgow, strikes a familiar note when compared with life on a turnpike stair in the overcrowded Ancient Royalty two centuries earlier:

6. Building tenements in Yoker, Glasgow in the 1890s. The window arrangement on this back elevation suggests that these were relatively large flats, at least two rooms and kitchen. University of Strathclyde Department of Engineering.

. . . social stratification in Glasgow occurs, not only East and West as in most cities, but also vertically. Poorer class tenements tend to be found on the flat, frequently behind the main roads; with better class tenements with gardens starting up the hill slopes and terraced houses and villas on the hilltops.[22]

By 1900 it was the newly built suburbs of single-ends and room and kitchens that were attracting working populations away from the congested inner areas of subdivided lands. The new suburbs were, in effect, a formalised response to overcrowding through purpose-built subdivision, although many families in these cramped circumstances still found it necessary to take lodgers to help pay the rent. Thus the over-crowding often remained, being merely displaced from the town centre to the suburban boundary. It was the tenement world many people remember with some affection, even if it was a harsh and mechanistic introduction to city life for a majority of the con-tinuing flow of urban incomers. The extent to which

congestion and overcrowding played their part in moulding the special qualities we identify with the urbanised Scot, and especially the Glaswegian, must remain a matter for speculation. This is something we seem only instinctively to understand. To a large extent the tenements *were* the cities, and above all Glasgow.

The Failure of Speculation

The private investor lost interest in the lower end of the housing market after about 1904 through a combination of circumstances which led to a some-what paradoxical situation of both overcrowding and over-building.

Rent rises in the 1890s and low interest rates had encouraged speculation in house building, and a surplus of flats developed at a time when demand was falling off. At the bottom end of the market tenants were showing themselves to be unable, or unwilling, to pay for house room. Interest rates and the standards

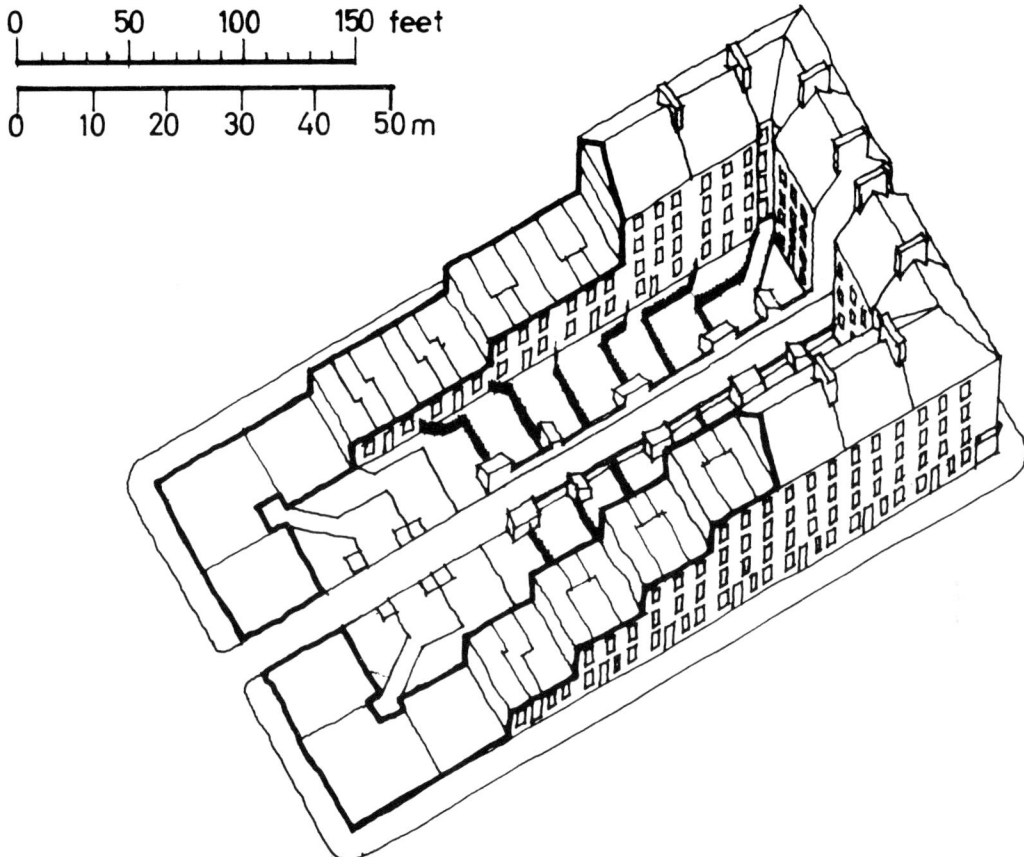

7. Diagram of a typical Glasgow or Paisley street block of room and kitchen and single-end houses of a type common c.1900, showing the high density of development. If there were twelve houses to a close, then this block would contain 264 houses.

demanded by local authorities were also rising, just as the tax burden on the landlord was increasing.[23] The subdivision of older houses continued, as did new buildings for salaried employees, at least until 1914, but with the introduction of rent control in 1915 the private rented market was dead. The lack of profitability ensured the perpetuation of poor conditions for many years and made state intervention inevitable.[24]

The effect of control was to fix rental income from property for nearly forty years, and it was an effect that was exacerbated by the Scottish rating system because this imposed an element of the rate burden on the landlord. As rate payments increased with both the cost of living and inflation, so the net return to the landlord from his property diminished. It was a cycle that led inevitably to decay and, not infrequently, to abandonment. Baird, writing in 1954, observed:

> When other factors, such as increases in taxation and the cost of repairs, were already operating to reduce the return on house property — sometimes to a very low or even negative figure — the additional burden (of rates) has obviously been an extremely serious one.[25]

Liability for owners' rates ceased in 1956, and even then rents were expected to be reduced accordingly.[26] It is not difficult to explain the dilapidated condition of many of the surviving tenements when this situation is taken together with a legacy of generally low rents. These circumstances help to account for the odd phenomenon in the late 1940s and early 1950s of title deeds for tenement properties changing hands over a drink, often for little more than the price of a packet of cigarettes. Baird again:

8. Typical Glasgow kitchen, forming the core of every tenement house in the City. This illustration comes from what in the 1890s would be a better than averagely equipped house of two rooms, kitchen and bathroom, with a built-in hot water system. 145 Buccleuch Street. National Trust for Scotland.

Between 1 January 1946 and 31 January 1953, 268 tenement properties in Glasgow comprising 3569 houses were offered free by their owners to the City Council. By January 1953 owners of a further 67 tenement properties comprising 1806 houses had intimated to the City Assessor that they had ceased to collect rents and it is certain that many more had ceased to do so without giving such intimation.[27]

The Industrial Legacy

Speculation had left a legacy of great richness and variety, so that by the turn of the present century tenements were occupied by a wide social spectrum in every corner of Scotland. For the middle classes flat life could be spacious and comfortable, but it was the small and ill-equipped house types occupied by the working classes, dominated by the surviving over-crowded lands and congested newer areas, that caught the official eye.

The housing of the working classes in the United Kingdom as a whole had come under scrutiny in the mid-1880s with the appointment of the Dilke Commission, reporting in 1885. The Scottish element of this report was a slim affair and took a generally complacent view of the abilities of the four cities to cope with their problems.[28] A further committee appointed by the Chancellor of the Exchequer in 1912 looked at, among other things, 'the nature and working of the existing ownerships, tenancy, and taxation and rating of land and buildings in urban districts and the surrounding neighbourhoods and their effect on industry and the conditions of life'. It resulted in the report *Scottish Land, Rural and Urban*, published in 1914[29], which in timing and content overlapped with the appointment of the second and more important Royal Commission on Housing in 1912. This latter Commission was to be an exclusively Scottish investigation. It was prompted by the persistence of poor housing throughout the country, and it remains the first and only large-scale Parliamentary enquiry devoted exclusively to housing conditions in Scotland. The final report was delayed by the War and was not published until 1918.[30]

The Report and minutes of evidence of the 1918 Royal Commission on Housing are important social documents, giving us a snapshot image of the way the working population in Scotland lived on the eve of municipal intervention. As regards the tenement it provides a summary of the position at the end of the most intensive period of private sector flat building, as well as offering a rudimentary but helpful classification of building forms. There is also a well-argued case for and against the tenement form of building vis-à-vis English practice. The Report had an effect on subsequent municipal building activity and house forms in the inter-war period. This can be traced through the accompanying Special Report, setting out plan types which were to become familiar in the following twenty years.[31]

The Commissioners' underlying philosophy of thinning out the cities found expression in a long-term process that has continued with the New Towns and overspill agreements of the 1950s and 1960s and is arguably not yet complete.

Isolated 'up market' private sector building for rent continued in the 1920s and 1930s, in areas like Hyndland in Glasgow and Learmonth in Edinburgh on much the same pattern as before the 1914-18 war, but in the 1920s the private sector became increasingly preoccupied with building semi-detached and bungalow developments largely for owner occupation. Thereafter it was left to municipal landlords to carry on building flats for rent, although private-sector conversions and 'making down' did, of course, continue unabated. It effectively ended a four-hundred-year period of development and refinement.

The earlier discussion about the origins of a Scottish flat tradition suggested that our stereotyped images of the tenement may have their beginnings as much in a basic need for security in a poor and unsettled country as in crowding. One might speculate that the 'two booths and loft' model of urban dwelling, such as that described in the Canongate in 1490, was a common starting point which underwent a process of subdivision and refinement in a pre-industrial period, with the extent of subdivision depending on local circumstances. Clearly, crowding in at least parts of old Edinburgh, forced upward development and subdivision on prestige frontages to an extent that would have been unnecessary in a smaller burgh where occupation by two households on two floors might represent the full extent of making down. Eventually subdivision alone appears to have ceased to be acceptable at least on the Edinburgh High Street, and purpose-built structures started to appear. The massive seventeenth-century mansion flats of Parliament Close and Mylne's Court were the product of intensive crowding, while it is likely that the smaller-scale cottage flat of smaller burghs derived from simple subdivision and economy.

Once particular building forms became established in the minds of local peer groups over a long interval of time, an innate conservatism appears to have taken over until middle-class prosperity and town expansion provided the climate for a crucial period of inventiveness and refinement at the close of the eighteenth century. These Georgian models were then adapted and greatly multiplied in a later period of intense land speculation. Latterly, precedent and habit were enshrined in statute and underlined by the force of law, so leading to a final geographical diffusion that has left few corners of Scotland without some evidence of flatted development. Steen Eiler Rasmussen refers to a similar process of continuity and refinement in describing the development of a continental European flat tradition; and, in the industrial period at least, Scotland would seem to fit closely into the model he describes.[32]

Municipal Postscript

In the strictest sense 1918 or thereabouts might be regarded as the end of the story, but if one takes the view that our tenement tradition is as much about the power of habit as a particular building type, then it is worth closing with a brief glimpse at the progress of council house building over the past sixty years or so with special reference to Glasgow.

Scotland had been forced into public housing programmes after 1918, like many continental countries and England, although unlike England municipal action provided another opportunity for a new and idealistic departure from the tenement tradition. But once again the powerful forces of custom appear to have ensured that it was a short-lived reaction. History was repeating itself, by following the same path back to local orthodoxy as we found in the middle-class

Georgian suburbs and in the later market reaction to Victorian philanthropic ventures.

Initially, 'general needs' council housing in Scotland followed the English pattern of cottages, or semi-detached houses, but when slum-clearance programmes began in the mid-1920s, local authorities showed a distinct preference for flats. Three-storey walkups of a type recommended by the 1918 Royal Commission[33] allowed higher densities than were possible with cottages or semi-detached houses, and it was a trend that continued. Between 1919 and 1946 over half of all the houses built by the City of Glasgow were flats.[34] The typical three-storey council tenement of that period was found almost everywhere in the City.

The formalisation of planning and the designation of Glasgow's green belt after the Second World War presented the City with a land shortage problem which led in turn to an increasing proportion of flats being built on greenfield sites on the urban fringe. It was the period of Drumchapel, Castlemilk and Easterhouse, all developed during the 1950s. A resumption of the slum-clearance programmes in the mid-1950s intensified this land shortage, as less than half the number of houses demolished in the older inner city areas could be replaced on the same sites simply because each new house was built to generally higher standards. Inevitably the response was to build at ever increasing densities, ultimately leading to the emergence of the familiar multi-storey flats in the 1960s which now form such a conspicuous part of Glasgow's skyline.[35]

If the green belt and post-war land shortages in Glasgow are taken as a substitute for the Flodden Wall, and the status of the 'second city of the Empire' as a surrogate for the pride and self-interest of the seventeenth-century Edinburgh merchant, then there is more than a hint in this somewhat over-simplified account of events that a combination of planning policies and civic pride was recreating the very conditions that had led to the refinement and intensification of a tenement tradition in Edinburgh three and a half centuries earlier. Was it really the pressure to keep Glasgow as a city of one million people within the confined boundaries of the green belt that was forcing a policy to build high?

Acknowledgements

I would like to acknowledge the considerable help and advice given by Dr. Makey, Edinburgh City Archivist, in the preparation of these papers and to Dr. Frank Walker and David Walker for their most helpful comments. The research was supported by the Royal Incorporation of Architects in Scotland through the Thomas Ross Bursary 1977 and by a Royal Institute of British Architects Research Award 1981.

References

1. A gable collapse may have affected the timing of the Proposals pamphlet of 1752 as this passage from the Advertisement suggests:

'The narrow limits of the royalty of Edinburgh, and the want of certain public buildings and other useful and ornamental accommodations in the city, have long been regretted. An opportunity of remedying these inconveniences was often wished for, and Providence has now furnished a very fair one. In September last the side-wall of a building of six stories high, in which several reputable families lived, gave way all of a sudden . . . This melancholy accident occasioned a general survey to be made of the old houses; and such as were insufficient were pulled down; so that several of the principal parts of the town were laid in ruins — nor was this favourable opportunity let slip'. Quoted in A. J. Youngson, *The Making of Classical Edinburgh 1750-1840* (Edinburgh 1966), 3.

2. *Minor Antiquities* (Edinburgh 1833), 58.

3. Henry Grey Graham, *The Social Life of Scotland in the Eighteenth Century* (London 1909). See Chapter 3, Town Life — Edinburgh, 81-126.

4. *Philadelphia American Courier*, quoted in John Heiton, *The Castes of Edinburgh* (Edinburgh 1833), 225.

5. Wm. Chambers, *Report on the Sanitary State of the Residences of the Poorer Classes in the Old Town of Edinburgh* (Edinburgh 1840), 3.

6. 26th November 1861.

7. John Butt, Working Class Housing in Glasgow, 1851-1914, in Stanley A. Chapman, ed., *The History of Working Class Housing — A Symposium* (Newton Abbot 1971), 68.

8. *Report of a Committee of the Working Classes of Edinburgh on the Present Overcrowded and Uncomfortable State of Their Dwelling Houses, with an Introduction and Notes by Alexander Macpherson, Secretary of the Committee* (Edinburgh 1860), 12.

9. Quoted in John Heiton, *op. cit.*, 228-229.

10. Wm. Chambers, *op. cit.*, 1.

11. *Report of a Committee of the Working Classes, etc., op. cit.*, 16; and see also 'Report of the Visiting Sub-Committee', 23-24.

12. Rosebank Cottages were designed by Alexander McGregor, apparently under the instruction of (later Sir) James Gowans, the railway contractor turned architect and later Lord Dean of Guild of the City of Edinburgh. Alexander McGregor, when he subsequently gave evidence to the Royal Commission on Housing 1885, described the underlying philosophy behind the design. The full reference of that part of the Report applying to Scotland is C4409, *Second Report of Her Majesty's Commissioners for Inquiring into the Housing of the Working Classes — Scotland, 1885* (The Dilke Commission. The first report related to England and Wales).

13. The Edinburgh Co-operative Building Co. Ltd. was registered on 25 May 1861. See *Transactions*, National Association for the Promotion of Social Science, 1863, 627.

14. The Blyth Street houses survive, but the Dundee Working Men's Housing Association was a financial failure. There is passing reference in David Walker, *The Architecture of Dundee*, in S. J. Jones, ed., *Dundee and District*, British Association for the Advancement of Science, undated, 295; and more fully in Enid Gauldie, *Cruel Habitations, A History of Working-Class Housing, 1780-1918* (London 1974), 203-204.

15. This general point of home ownership *vis-à-vis* rent is discussed at some length in the *Report of a Committee of the Working Classes etc.*, *op. cit.*, 18-20.

16. The committee was set up on 15 July 1858 after a public meeting in Buccleuch Street Hall.

17. *Ibid.*, 16-17.

18. See John Butt, Working Class Housing in Glasgow, *op. cit.*

19. Cd. 8731, *Royal Commission on Housing in Scotland, Report etc.*, para. 484, 62.

20. *Scottish Land, The Report of the Scottish Land Enquiry Committee* (London 1914). See Chapter XXIV, pp. 325-331; and see also Sir James Gowans, *Model Dwelling Houses with a Description of a Model Tenement* (Edinburgh 1886), 5-6.

21. Cd. 8731, *op. cit.*, para. 1612, 245.

22. See Macmillan's brief analysis of the Woodlands area of Glasgow. A. Macmillan, Two Notes on Glasgow, *Glasgow Institute of Architects Yearbook, 1967*.

23. These points are made in a quotation from Glasgow City Archives, Glasgow Municipal Commission Minutes, 305-10, in John Butt, Working Class Housing in Glasgow, 1851-1914, in Stanley A. Chapman, ed., *op. cit.*, 73.

24. Analysis of Rent Control, Scottish Record Office, DD6/606, quoted in I. H. Adams, *The Making of Urban Scotland* (London 1978), 170.

25. Robert Baird, Housing, in A. K. Cairncross, ed., *The Scottish Economy* (Cambridge 1954), 205.

26. See *Valuation and Rating (Scotland) Act 1956*, Part II, Rating, Section 16.

27. Robert Baird, *op. cit.*, 206.

28. C4409, *The Second Report of Her Majesty's Commissioners for Inquiring into the Housing of the Working Classes: Scotland*, HMSO 1885.

29. *Scottish Land, The Report of the Scottish Land Enquiry Committee* (London 1914).

30. Cd. 8731, *Royal Commission on Housing in Scotland*, HMSO 1918. The Commissioners were appointed on 30th October 1912 to inquire 'into the Housing of the Industrial Population of Scotland, rural and urban . . . and to report what legislative or administrative action is in their opinion desirable to remedy existing defects'.

31. Cd. 8760, Royal Commission on Housing in Scotland, *Special Report, on The Design, Construction and Materials of Various Types of Small Dwelling Houses in Scotland*, HMSO 1917.

32. Steen Eiler Rasmussen, *Towns and Buildings* (Liverpool 1951). See 'Land and Speculation', 172-182.

33. Cd. 8731, *op. cit.*, para. 537, 70.

34. A. G. Jury, *Housing Centenary, A Review of Municipal Housing in Glasgow from 1866-1966*, The Corporation of the City of Glasgow, 1966, Table XVIII, p. 45. See also *Farewell to the Single End: A History of Glasgow Corporation Housing, 1866-1975*, The City of Glasgow District Council, 1975.

35. The circumstances leading to building at higher densities in Glasgow in the post-war period are studied in Roger Smith, Multi-Dwelling Building in Scotland, 1750-1970: A Study Based on Housing in the Clyde Valley, in Anthony Sutcliffe, ed., *Multi-Storey Living, The British Working Class Experience* (London 1974), see 223-231.

An Early Sixteenth-Century French Architectural Source for the Palace of Falkland

Dana Bentley-Cranch

The Royal Palace of Falkland,[1] in the County of Fife, has long been considered the most important example of early French Renaissance architecture in Scotland. No precise architectural source in France has ever been suggested; it has been variously assumed that Scotland's King James V, during his visit to France in 1536-37, observed buildings in France in a general way and decided to emulate them, that James's two French wives influenced his building plans, and that some details may have been copied from Renaissance buildings in England. I believe, however, that a specific source may be found in two residences built for one of the most outstanding men of the French Renaissance, Florimond Robertet: his town house, the Hôtel d'Alluye, in Blois, and, near the same town, his Château at Bury in which James V actually stayed during his visit to France.

Florimond Robertet (?-29 November 1527) was a civil servant who served three Kings of France, Charles VIII, Louis XII and François Ier, as secretary, counsellor, treasurer and Secretary of State to become the most powerful man in France. His influence, both political and cultural, was immense and far-reaching.[2] Following the example of his father, Jean Robertet, civil servant and poet,[3] he spared time from his political duties to cultivate the acquaintance of men of letters and to act as patron to artists and poets. On his death in 1527, Clément Marot, the leading French Renaissance poet, was inspired to write in his honour one of his best works, in the form of a 'mourning poem', *La Déploration de Florimond Robertet*.[4] In 1494 Florimond Robertet accompanied Charles VIII on the first of the French campaigns in Italy. The demands of war and politics did not prevent both King and secretary from closely observing all aspects of Italian

art and culture. Writing from Naples to the Duke of Bourbon, in a letter countersigned by Robertet, Charles enthusiastically declared his intention of setting Italian painters to work in his Château at Amboise.[5] Charles' 'Italian additions' at Amboise were superficial and in the nature of decorations imposed upon a medieval foundation; Florimond

1. The Hôtel d'Alluye, street side. Photo: Author.

2. The Hôtel d'Alluye, courtyard. Photo: Author.

Robertet, on the other hand, with a deeper understanding of Italian art, was to succeed in fusing Italian and Gothic Elements into a new French style, and to be one of the first to introduce this early Renaissance style in France.

The Hôtel d'Alluye[6] in the Rue St. Honoré, a narrow street in the centre of Blois, was one of the first town houses to be built in the early French Renaissance style and may even have been the first, since building was probably started about 1498 and completed by 1508.[7] Although the street front is not entirely successful because of the relatively small site of the house, the crowding due to the attached neighbouring houses, and the narrowness of the Rue St. Honoré which prevents the observer from obtaining a clear frontal view, it is nevertheless an impressive façade (Fig. 1). Bricks and stone are combined in an unusual chequerboard effect, the regularity of which is impaired by the asymmetrical placing of windows, elaborately sculptured with a variety of motifs, among them dolphins, initials, coats-of-arms, grotesques and angels' heads. Below a pierced balustrade large gargoyles project horizontally. From the very steeply

gabled roof rise high decorated chimneys and, at irregular intervals, four beautifully sculptured dormer windows. The main entrance, through a wide Gothic arch flanked by classical pillars, leads straight from the street to the inner courtyard, around the sides of which are arranged the principal rooms. Although Italian influence predominates in the classical simplicity of the arcaded galleries of the ground- and first-floor frontages around the courtyard (Fig. 2), it combines easily with the Gothic arches, the ornate sculptured decorations, the steep gables and dormer windows above a pierced balustrade of dolphins to give a pleasing mixture of elements. An interesting Italianate detail is the set of twelve medallions portraying the Twelve Caesars where the profile heads, in pairs facing each other, are arranged on the string-course between the ground and first floors. The heads, sculptured in high relief, are enclosed in garlands of leaves, flowers and fruits. Florimond Robertet was possibly one of the first Frenchmen to incorporate 'Caesar medallions' into a French building; that he was responsible for introducing an extension of this motif, that of depicting contemporary personages in the same

3. The Hôtel d'Alluye. Medallion of Cardinal Georges d'Amboise. Photo: Author.

format, is certain. To his Twelve Caesars, Robertet added a thirteenth portraying his patron, friend, fellow-minister and fellow-enthusiast for Italian art, Cardinal Georges d'Amboise (Fig. 3).[8] This extension, bizarre though it may appear nowadays, was perfectly logical in the early French Renaissance concept.

After Florimond Robertet's death in 1527, the Hôtel d'Alluye remained in the Robertet family only until 1606. Passing through several hands, the property was acquired in 1865 by an insurance society, the Mutuelle Générale d'Assurances, who carefully restored the building and made of it their administrative headquarters.

Unlike the Hôtel d'Alluye, continuously occupied and now in a high state of preservation, Florimond Robertet's country residence, his Château at Bury, passed out of the Robertet family in 1604, subsequently fell into decay and today consists of a few scattered ruins.[9] Fortunately, however, the architect

Du Cerceau included Bury in the second volume of his survey of important buildings in France published in 1579, and his plans permit a reconstruction of the Château (Fig. 4).[10] The site, acquired by Robertet on the 2nd of January 1511,[11] lies about ten kilometres from Blois on a small hill overlooking the hamlet of Bury. Completely walled round, the site was divided into four rectangles; two were laid out in formal gardens, one contained the domestic offices, stables, etc., and the fourth was the house proper in the form of buildings grouped around a courtyard. The encircling wall, the towers at each corner, the moat and the drawbridge entrance guarded by two smaller towers, give a medieval and defensive appearance to the exterior, an appearance completely belied by the interior. The entrance wall conceals, on the inside, not the engines of war, but an arcaded cloister for pleasant promenades, and the two wings, with lesser rooms and a gallery, lead to the principal part of the house, the fourth side of the square, whose centre rises not in a fortified turret but in a frivolous and ornate pavilion situated directly opposite the drawbridge entrance. The elegance and novelty of this lay-out are echoed in the decorations of the three façades; very flat pilasters and strong horizontal string-courses define each storey, marking out the surface in a symmetrical chequerboard pattern. Above these façades in the steep gables of the roof are dormer windows, still medieval in form but decorated, as at the Hôtel d'Alluye, in the new style with elaborately sculptured dolphins and candelabra. Building at Bury, begun in 1511, probably continued until about 1524,[12] but some part of the château may have been completed by 1515, since one of the fragments of sculpture found among the ruins of Bury bore the letter L, initial of King Louis XII who died on the 1st of January 1515.[13]

When James V of Scotland visited France in 1536, the first phase of Renaissance building was over and a second phase had begun. In the first phase, the next two important châteaux to be built, after Bury, were Chenonceau, between 1515 and 1526, and Azay-le-Rideau, between 1518 and 1529. Chenonceau was originally conceived as a simple square block, with a turret at each corner and a corridor through the middle (the extension across the River Cher was a later addition); Azay-le-Rideau was built on the L-shaped plan, a plan well-known and in use in Scotland from the fifteenth century. These houses were built for rich *bourgeois* financiers; royal building in the first phase

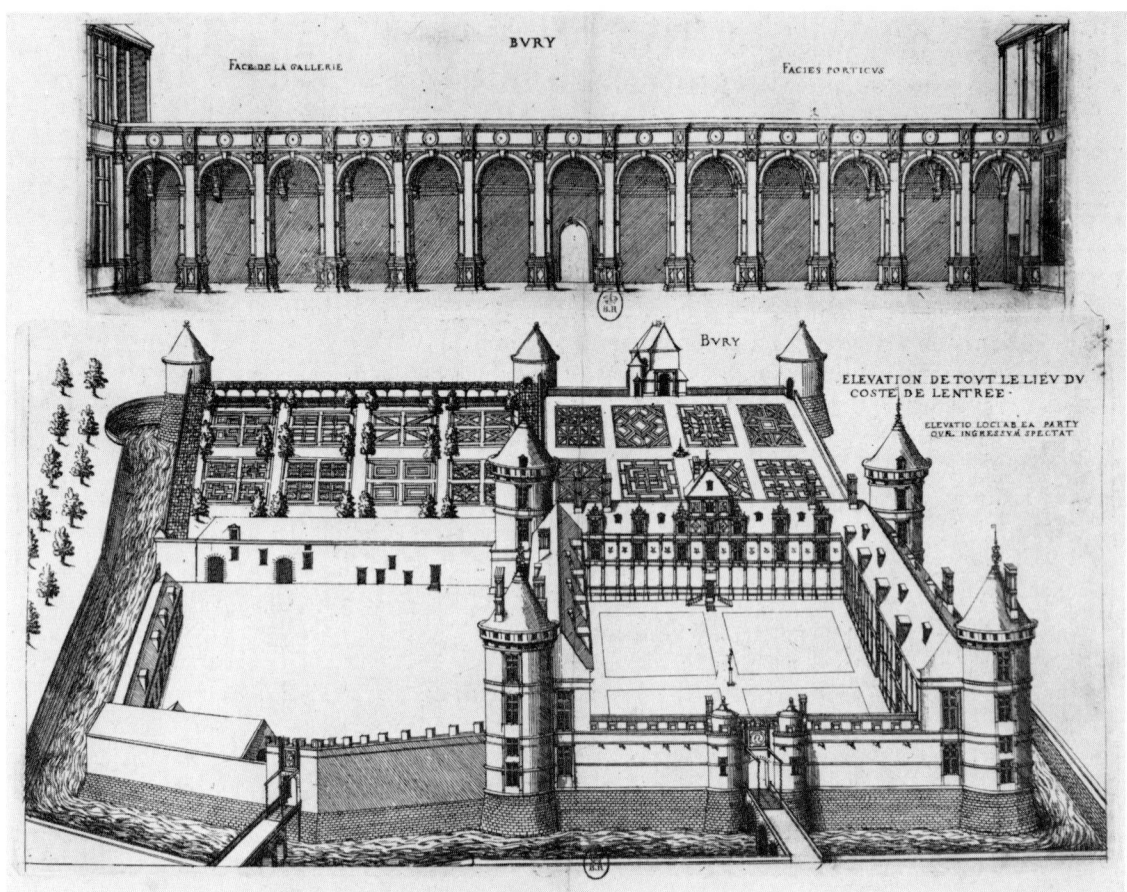

4. Du Cerceau's plan of the Château of Bury, 1579. Bibliothèque Nationale, Paris.

was confined to the château of Blois, where François Ier, between 1515 and 1524, added a wing constructed on existing foundations, and to Chambord, started in the first phase but overlapping with the second. The plans for Chambord were drawn up in 1519; building was interrupted from 1524-1527 by the Italian Wars and the captivity of François Ier, and the main part of the château, designed as a square block with corner turrets, was not roofed over until 1537. The second phase of Renaissance building began about 1528 after the return of François Ier from captivity and manifested itself mainly in a proliferation of Royal châteaux around Paris. Of these, the Château de Madrid (today non-existent) in the Bois de Boulogne was started in 1528, and variants of its plan — two square blocks linked by corridors — were later used for three more royal residences: St. Germain, La Muette de St. Germain (both built between 1539-

1549) and Challuau.[14] Alterations and additions to transform the medieval castle of Fontainebleau were also started in 1528 by François Ier, and work went on continuously until his death in 1547.

James V landed at Dieppe on the 10th of September 1536, visited Saint-Quentin and proceeded to Lyons to meet François Ier, and to be betrothed to his daughter Madeleine, in mid-October. The two Kings and the French Court then journeyed back across France to reach Paris on the 29th of December.[15] The Court's itinerary was: Tarare, Roanne, La Palisse, Moulins, Bourges, Amboise, Châtellerault, Loches, Blois, Amboise, Bury, Blois, Chamerolles, Fontainebleau, Paris.[16] James therefore actually stayed at Bury, with François Ier and the French Court, for a visit lasting from the 19th to the 23rd of November. That Bury should have been chosen to house the royal party is not surprising: the Robertet family had retained the favour of François Ier after the death in 1527 of Florimond (his two sons had taken over their father's functions and occupied important Government posts),[17] and the Court had already stayed there in March 1529 and in October-November 1530,[18] the latter visit an important one, being part of the first Royal Progress of Eleanor, François Ier's newly married second wife, on her way to Paris for her coronation. Bury, thus honoured in 1530, was still so outstanding, even in 1536, as to be almost a 'required visit' for a distinguished visitor and especially for a monarch as interested in architecture as James later proved himself to be. For similar reasons James may well have been shown the Hôtel d'Alluye in Blois, a town which figures twice in the itinerary for visits between the 13th and 16th of November and again between the 23rd of November and the beginning of December, and where the contract for the marriage between James and François Ier's daughter Madeleine was signed on the 26th of November.

Were James's two French wives, firstly Madeleine, and secondly Marie de Guise, Duchesse de Longueville, familiar with the new building in France and particularly with the Hôtel d'Alluye and the Château of Bury, and did they influence his taste in architecture? As regards the first question, Madeleine, born on the 10th of August 1520 and thus 16 at the time of her marriage to the 24-year-old James V on the 1st of January 1537,[19] may have been in the habit of travelling with her father's Court as it progressed around France; if so, she would have seen all the royal châteaux, would have resided on many occasions in Blois, would actually have stayed at Bury in 1529 and 1530, and may even have been there on earlier occasions although perhaps at too tender an age to observe architectural details.[20] In respect of the year 1536, it is reasonable to assume that Madeleine was already in Lyons with the royal party when James arrived,[21] and subsequently accompanied her father and fiancé on their Royal Progress across France and thus stayed with them at Bury. Madeleine certainly must have been present in Blois on the 26th of November for the signing of her marriage contract, which took place immediately after the visit to Bury. As regards the second question, although Madeleine may have been able, on this Progress, to view nearly all the new building in France with her fiancé and participate in his appreciation, her influence in his subsequent building activities must have been neg-

ligible, since she died on the 2nd of July 1537 barely two months after her arrival in Scotland.

Marie de Guise, who became James's second wife by proxy in May 1538 and arrived in Scotland in the following month, had spent much of her early life at the French Court. She was presented, at the age of 15, in Paris in March 1531 on the occasion of the coronation of François Ier's second wife, Eleanor. Thereafter, according to her biographer,[22] she probably divided her time until her first marriage in 1534 to the Duc de Longueville between her own family and the French Court, and after marriage between her husband's châteaux at Amiens, Rouen and Châteaudun and the Court.[23] It can therefore be assumed that she took part in some of the Royal Progresses around France and became familiar with the new building. Whether she knew Bury and the Hôtel d'Alluye, and whether she was in the royal party staying at Bury for the two official 'distinguished-foreigners' visits (i.e. that of Queen Eleanor in October-November 1530 and that of James V in November 1536) cannot be stated with certainty.[24] It is undeniable, however, that from about 1528 an interest in architecture had become so fashionable as to be almost obligatory for members of the French Court, and that the frenzy of building among courtiers was so widespread as to be satirised by the leading Court poet.[25] Marie's influence on James's taste in building is difficult to assess. That she had shared the current French interest in architecture is obvious from her request to her mother to send French masons to Scotland.[26] But these masons, six in number, did not arrive in Scotland until the summer of 1539[27] when the alterations to Falkland Palace had already been planned and even partially completed, since a portion bears the date '1537'.[28] Although Marie certainly contributed to the renovations at the other royal palaces of Stirling and Linlithgow, it would appear that the credit for 'Renaissance Falkland' should go entirely to James V.

From the twelfth century onward the little town of Falkland had a royal castle, but this was either demolished or gradually allowed to decay when the Stuart Kings started to build the present Palace around a courtyard at some little distance from the old castle. During the reign of James II (reigned 1437-1460) the buildings along the north side of the courtyard, the North Range, were constructed. In about 1501 James IV began to build the ranges on the east

5. The Palace of Falkland, South Range and part of ruined East Range, from courtyard. Drawn by R. W. Billings, 1845-52; engraved by G. B. Smith. Royal Commission on Ancient Monuments, Scotland, FID/96/33.

and south sides of the courtyard. When James IV was killed at the Battle of Flodden in 1513, his son James V succeeded to the throne at the age of one year and work at Falkland ceased. In 1537, after his return from France, James V started on the alterations and additions to his father's work which were to make of the Palace of Falkland 'a display of early-Renaissance architecture without parallel in the British Isles', as one modern scholar has observed,[29] and the work at Falkland continued until James V's premature death in 1542 at the age of 30 put an end to building. Today all that remains of the North Range is the foundations,[30] the East Range is roofless and partly in ruins, and only the South Range has survived intact.[31] The extent of James V's contribution can be assessed from the state of the Palace as it is today, supplemented by a mid-nineteenth-century drawing by R. W. Billings (Fig. 5).[32]

The entrance to the Palace is the Great Gate-House,

situated at the west end of the South Range; its two massive round towers, battlements and barred windows give an impression of warlike defence, an impression strengthened by the late Scottish Gothic aspect of the five huge stone buttresses on the street side of the South Range. When one passes through the Gate-House into the courtyard, however, these warlike elements disappear; James transformed the façades of the South (Fig. 6) and East Ranges, replacing the heavy buttresses by very flat pilasters topped by slender columns, symmetrically spaced out and interspersed by a frieze of circular stone sculptured medallions. At each corner of the courtyard is placed a small tower with conical roof. In the steep roofs of the South Range very tall chimneys and decorated dormer windows are placed at irregular intervals.

When James V started work on the Palace at Falkland in 1537[33] he was, unlike Florimond Robertet

6. The Palace of Falkland, South Range, showing medallions. Royal Commission on Ancient Monuments, Scotland, F/227.

who constructed his château at Bury as an entity on hitherto unoccupied ground, faced with the hard task of converting an existing building of heavy and forbidding aspect to the pleasing elegance of the early French Renaissance style. That he managed this so successfully is of course in part due to his own taste and energy; but it is also due to the fact that, while staying at Bury, he was able to examine carefully the one building in France which externally most closely resembled his own Falkland and subsequently to copy it. The medieval and defensive exterior aspect of Bury is a deception which conceals the new-style interior. Whether this was entirely intentional on the part of Robertet can never be known; the surprise and delight of the visitor once over the drawbridge and through the gate-house must however have been complete. It is exactly this same shock of surprise and pleasure which James V achieved at Falkland, not by anachronistically building a medieval exterior, but by leaving what was already there and entirely altering the aspect of his

courtyard. Of all the buildings which James saw in France — both during the Royal Progress with François Ier, and later in the four months he and Madeleine spent in France after their marriage[34] — and which all contained elements of the new style, Bury is the only one to contain them all: the contrasting exterior and interior, the courtyard plan surrounded by ranges of buildings, the symmetrical façades with very flat pilasters, the medallion friezes, the steep roofs and decorated dormers.[35] In addition, the Hôtel d'Alluye, although on a much smaller scale than Bury, has very much the same plan of buildings ranged round a courtyard (which provokes the same surprise when the visitor enters from the narrow street), and especially the Hôtel d'Alluye has its medallions. Du Cerceau's print shows that medallions were placed above the arcades at Bury to decorate the interior of the entrance wall; who or what they depict cannot be seen, nor are the details of their sculptured surrounds apparent. The medallions at the Hôtel

7. The Palace of Falkland, South Range, showing medallions 4, 5, 6 and 7. Royal Commission on Ancient Monuments, Scotland, F/238.

d'Alluye, however, still in good condition today, may have served as models for James V. There were twenty medallions at Falkland, ten on the East Range and ten on the South Range, arranged in pairs. The ravages of time have nearly obliterated those on the East Range.[36] Those on the South Range have fared better, and some show all their original beauty and elegance (Fig. 7).[37] From these it would appear that all the medallions were enclosed in ornate garlands of entwined flowers, fruit and leaves sculptured in high relief, as are those at the Hôtel d'Alluye. The subjects, however, are not the Twelve Caesars but are more in the style of Robertet's 'Thirteenth Caesar',[38] and are either members of the Scottish Court, heroes and heroines of mythology, or perhaps members of the Court in the guise of gods and heroes of antiquity in a fashion which was becoming popular in France at the time of James's visit.[39]

By 1537 medallions had appeared on buildings in England; the earliest were probably those introduced in 1521 by Cardinal Wolsey to decorate his Hampton Court Palace. The assumption could therefore be made that English medallions inspired those at Falkland, but there is no evidence to substantiate this theory. James V never visited England, and his uneasy relations with his uncle, King Henry VIII, were not conducive to fruitful cultural borrowings. James's model of a Renaissance Prince was his father-in-law, François Ier, and French influence, already in evidence during the early part of James V's reign, became predominant at the Scottish Court after his French visit. The medallions at the Hôtel d'Alluye may indeed have been the source not only for the Falkland medallions, but also for those at Hampton Court Palace. Cardinal Wolsey and Florimond Robertet, political counterparts for several years, met in 1520 at the Field of the Cloth of Gold; although it is not possible to ascertain whether Wolsey visited the Hôtel d'Alluye, it is nevertheless the case that it was after this meeting that medallions were added to Hampton Court Palace.[40]

The influence of Florimond Robertet in the field of architecture was far-reaching; in France the Italian architect Sebastiano Serlio probably used the plan of Bury to construct for the Cardinal of Ferrara the house at Fontainebleau known as 'Le Grande Ferrare', which subsequently became the model for the French town house for over a century,[41] and a staircase in the courtyard at Bury was probably the model for a similar staircase built in 1531 in the Cour d'Ovale at the Château of Fountainebleau.[42] In England the first influence of Bury would seem to have been on Sutton Place in Surrey. Sir Richard Weston, favourite of Henry VIII and twice ambassador to France, visited the Loire valley in 1519 during his embassy. In 1521 he started building Sutton Place; the original plan must have been an almost exact copy of Bury, with its externally imposing gatehouse range, opening to reveal the internal courtyard, the principal rooms opposite the entrance gate, and the elegant, sophisticated and symmetrical wall-decoration of horizontal string-courses and vertical pilasters.[43] Although today the gatehouse range at Sutton Place has completely disappeared, leaving only three sides to the courtyard, an equivalent (though larger) gatehouse range can be found at Layer Marney Hall in Essex, built by the first Baron Marney shortly before his death in 1523.[44] The Layer Marney gatehouse range (the only part of the house ever completed) is so similar to the lost Sutton

Place gatehouse range that the common source of Bury seems inevitable.

Robertet's influence, reaching as far as Falkland, perpetuates the visit to France of Scotland's Renaissance King in one of the most beautiful early Renaissance buildings in Scotland.

References

1. In 1952 the Hereditary Constable, Captain and Keeper of Falkland Palace, Major Michael Crichton-Stuart, M.C., M.A., appointed the National Trust for Scotland to the position of Deputy Keeper. I wish to thank the present Hereditary Constable, Captain and Keeper, Mr Ninian Crichton-Stuart, and the Head Guide of Falkland Palace, Miss Jemma Cordery, for their courtesy and assistance.

For the history of Falkland up to the present day and a Guide to the Palace, see *The Royal Palace of Falkland* by Sir Iain Moncrieffe of that Ilk, and *The Palace of Falkland, a Self-Guided Tour*, by Major Michael Crichton-Stuart, both published by the National Trust for Scotland.

2. See C. A. Mayer and D. Bentley-Cranch, *Florimond Robertet: Italianisme et Renaissance française*, in *Mélanges à la mémoire de Franco Simone*, t.IV (Geneva 1983), 135-149, and R. Scheurer and A. Lapeyre, *Les Notaires et Secrétaires du Roi sous les règnes de Louis XI, Charles VIII et Louis XII (1461-1515)* (Paris, Bibliothèque Nationale, 1978), 2 vols., vol. I, no. 589.

3. On Jean Robertet, see M. Zsuppan, *An Early Example of the Renaissance Themes of Immortality and Divine Inspiration: The Work of Jean Robertet*, Bibliothèque d'Humanisme et Renaissance, t.XXVIII, 1966, pp. 553-563; *Jean Robertet's Life and Career: A Reassessment*, Bibliothèque d'Humanisme et Renaissance, t.XXXI, 1969, 333-342, and *Jean Robertet, Oeuvres* (Geneva 1970); and C. A. Mayer and D. Bentley-Cranch, *Florimond Robertet: Italianisme et Renaissance française, art. cit.*

4. See *Clément Marot, Oeuvres complètes*, critical edition by C. A. Mayer, 6 vols. (London, Paris, Geneva, 1958-1980), Vol. III, *Oeuvres lyriques*, no. VI, and C. A. Mayer, *Clément Marot* (Paris 1972), 151-163.

5. See P. Pélicier, *Lettres de Charles VIII, roi de France*, Société de l'histoire de France, 1898-1905, 5 vols., Vol. IV, lettre DCCCLXI, 28 mars 1495: 'Avec ce j'ay trouvé en ce pays des meilleurs peintres; je vous en enverray pour faire d'aussi beaux planchers qu'il est possible. Les planchers de Beauce, de Lyon et d'autres lieux de France ne sont en riens approuchans de beaulté et richesse ceulx d'icy; c'est pourquoy je m'en fourniray et les meneray avecques moy pour en faire à Amboise'.

6. The title of Baron d'Alluye was conferred upon Florimond Robertet in 1510.

7. Cf. A. Blunt, *Art and Architecture in France, 1500-1700* (London 1953, reprinted 1957), 13.

8. Georges d'Amboise started rebuilding his Château at Gaillon in 1501; when he died in 1510 important Italianate additions had been superimposed on earlier foundations. See A. Blunt, *Art and Architecture in France, 1500-1700, op. cit.*, 6-8.

9. The site of Bury is private property; the present owners occupy a dwelling constructed around one of the ruined towers.

10. J. Androuet Du Cerceau, *Les plus excellents bastimens de France*, 2 vols. (Paris, Vol. I, 1576, Vol. II, 1579). See A. Blunt, *op. cit.*, 8.

11. For the price of 4000 *écus d'or* (Archives de Loir-et-Cher, E. Titres du comté de Rostaing: Bury et Molineuf): see H. de la Vallière, *Bury en Blaisois*, Revue de Loir-et-Cher, August, October, November, 1889, 83, 106, 117.

12. A grant from the Crown for additions and embellishments to Bury is recorded however for 1526: 'Dons pour l'agrandissement du château de Bury', *Catalogue des Actes de François Ier* (Paris, 1887), 10 vols., Vol. VII, 135, no. 23886.

13. See P. Lesuer, *Le Château de Bury et Fra Giocondo*, Gazette des Beaux-Arts, XII, 3e période, 1925, 337-357.

14. Of these three, only St. Germain has survived in much altered form. See A. Blunt, *Art and Architecture in France, 1500-1700, op. cit.*, 23-26.

15. See R. J. Knecht, *Francis I* (Cambridge 1982), p. 285, and C. Bingham, *James V, King of Scots* (London 1971), 118-122.

16. *Catalogue des Actes de François Ier, op. cit.*, Vol. VIII, *Itinéraires*.

17. See *Clément Marot, Oeuvres complètes, ed. cit.*, Vol. III, *Oeuvres lyriques*, no. VI, *La Déploration de Florimond Robertet*, 151.

18. *Catalogue des Actes de François Ier, op. cit.*, Vol. VIII, *Itinéraires*. Bury was also visited by the French Court in 1534 and 1545.

19. An event celebrated by the poet Clément Marot in a wedding-poem, *Chant nuptial du Roy d'Escoce & de Madame Magdalene Premiere Fille de France*, (*Clément Marot, Oeuvres complètes, ed. cit.*, Vol. III, *Oeuvres lyriques*, No. LXXXVI, Epithalame II).

20. In a letter to Florimond Robertet of 1526, François Ier mentions previous visits to Bury with his wife, mother and children, and looks forward to more such visits in the future: '... château de Bury auquel nous, nostre très chère et très aimée dame et mère et nos très chers et très aimez enfans, nous sommes quelque temps venuz et recréez et espérons cy après quelquefois venir et recréez' (cf. H. de la Vallière, *art. cit.*).

21. French and Scottish contemporary accounts give romantic details of the meeting between James and Madeleine while omitting any mention of where they met

(see P. de Bourdeille, Abbé de Brantôme, *Oeuvre complètes*, ed. L. Lalanne, 11 vols., 1864-82, Vol. 8, *Des Dames*, 127-8, and Robert Lindsay of Pitscottie, *Historie and Cronicles of Scotland, 1437-1575*, Scottish Text Society, 1899-1911, 3 vols., Vol. I, 361-3). Madeleine's presence in Lyons is confirmed, however, by the existence of her portrait by Corneille de Lyons. This painter worked exclusively in Lyons (see D. Bentley-Cranch, *A Portrait of Clément Marot by Corneille de Lyons*, Bibliothèque d'Humanisme et Renaissance, t.XXV, 1963, 174-77), and Madeleine must therefore have sat to him for her portrait during one of the visits of the French Court to that town. In the portrait (now in the Château of Blois, with a copy at the Château of Versailles) the Princess appears to be about 16, her age in 1536. During that year the Court, exceptionally, visited Lyons briefly in every month up to and including October except September (see *Catalogue des Actes de François Ier, op. cit.*, Vol. VIII, *Itinéraires*). Madeleine's portrait is most likely to have been painted during the October visit to mark her betrothal to James V.

It is probable that Corneille de Lyons painted James at the same time. A portrait attributed to this artist (now in the Collection of the National Trust at Polesden Lacey) depicting a handsome young man with reddish hair, blue eyes, thin face, pale complexion and wearing what appears to be the chain and medallion of the Ordre de Saint-Michel (an honour bestowed on James V by François Ier early in 1536) bears on the back of the panel the inscription in an old hand: 'Le roi âgé 25'. Although the iconography of James V consists mainly of rather stereotyped images conforming to a common pattern portraying the idea of kingship rather than personality (cf. the wedding portrait of James and Marie de Guise at Hardwick Hall, reproduced in R. K. Marshall, *Mary of Guise* (London 1977), opp. 48), there is a likeness between the features in such images and the portrait in question. The portrait also tallies quite closely with contemporary descriptions of James V (cf. R. K. Marshall, *Mary of Guise, op. cit.*, 41). As regards the inscription, no other European king, apart from James V, would have been 25 years old when painted in the costume of the mid-30s as shown in this portrait.

Corneille de Lyon also painted Marie de Guise (Scottish National Portrait Gallery). This trio of portraits of the young Scottish king and his two wives, portrayed by a painter whose ability to catch a likeness was highly praised by his contemporaries, forms an interesting iconographical addition to the history of the reign.

22. Dr. R. K. Marshall, whose help I gratefully acknowledge.

23. R. K. Marshall, *Mary of Guise, op. cit.*, 32-37.

24. Marie was present at the coronation of Eleanor (see above, p. 89), and she and her husband were among the guests at the wedding of James V and Madeleine; see R. K. Marshall, *op. cit.*, 33 and 38.

25. In a witty and elegant poem in which he asks François Ier for money, Clément Marot pretends that he has spent a lot on building castles for himself (a plea which the king must often have heard from his courtiers) and makes this complaint ridiculous and pretentious by saying that he has built at obviously imaginery villages which bear his own name, 'Clément' and 'Marot':

Car puis ung peu j'ay basti à Clement
Là où j'ay faict ung grand desboursement,
Et à Marot, qui est ung peu plus loing.

(*Clément Marot, Oeuvres complètes, ed. cit.*, Vol. I, *Les Epîtres*, no. XXV, *Au Roy, pour avoir esté desrobé*, vv. 115-117).

26. R. K. Marshall, *op. cit.*, 75-76.

27. *Ibid.*, and *Accounts of the Lord High Treasurer of Scotland, 1473-1566*, ed. T. Dickson and Sir James Balfour Paul, 11 vols., 1877-1916, Vol. VII, 184. A Frenchman, Nicholas Roy, appointed to the post of Master Mason, worked at Falkland between 1539 and 1541 (*Accounts of the Masters of Works for building and repairing Royal Palaces and Castles, Vol. I, 1529-1615*, ed. H. M. Paton (Edinburgh 1957), xxxiii-iv, and C. Bingham, *op. cit.*, 169).

28. See below, note 33.

29. M. Girouard, Falkland Palace, Fife, in *Country Life*, August 27 1959, 118-121 and September 3 1959, 178-181.

30. Beautifully converted into a rose garden. The North Range was destroyed by fire in 1654 following the occupation of the Palace by Cromwell's troops.

31. Some subsidiary buildings at a short distance from the Palace, the Royal Stables and Tennis Court, are still in existence. The fourth, or West, side of the courtyard originally consisted mainly of stables and domestic offices; today these have disappeared, and a wall partially closes off the courtyard from the adjoining orchard.

32. 1845-52; engraved by G. B. Smith.

33. The date 1537 is inscribed on one pilaster on the East Range.

34. James and Madeleine were married on the 1st of January 1537 and set sail for Scotland in May. Where they spent the intervening four months is not certain; part or all of the time they may have been with the French Court which in January was in Paris and St. Germain, in February in St. Germain, Chantilly, Villers-Cotterês and Compiègne, and in March and April was centred on François Ier's headquarters at Hedin whence he conducted his northern campaign against Charles V (*Catalogue des Actes de François Ier, op. cit.*, Vol. VIII, *Itinéraires*).

35. James may have adapted two further features from Bury for Falkland. Du Cerceau's ground-plan shows the existence of a long gallery or corridor in one wing; if the adjoining rooms opened into this corridor instead of, as was usual, into each other, domestic comfort would have been much improved. There is a similar corridor arrangement in the South Range at Falkland. The pavilion opposite the

entrance gate at Bury, according to Du Cerceau, contained the principal rooms, presumably used for royal guests. The Cross-House at Falkland, situated above the East Range and, like Bury's pavilion, having views both into the inner courtyard and to the garden outside, although originally constructed for James IV, was completely refurbished by James V to provide royal apartments for himself and his queen.

36. East Range Medallions (from left to right):

1st pair; Medallion 1: profile of man turned to right.

Medallion 2: profile of man turned to left (i.e. the two heads face each other).

2nd pair; Medallion 3: profile of man turned to right, peaked cap on head.

Medallion 4: almost all obliterated.

3rd pair; Medallion 5: profile of man turned to right, perhaps a peaked cap on head.

Medallion 6: completely obliterated, only the position marked by square base.

4th pair; Medallion 7: almost all obliterated.

Medallion 8: almost all obliterated except for a portion at the foot which might be part of an arm extending over the surround.

5th pair; Medallion 9: almost all obliterated except for a slight vestige of the head.

Medallion 10: almost all obliterated.

37. South Range Medallions (from left to right):

1st pair; Medallion 1: man, almost full-face, bearded, crown or turban on head, details of garland clear, good condition.

Medallion 2: face, part of head and lower part of garland almost obliterated, not possible to distinguish whether man or woman, possibly full-face position.

2nd pair; Medallion 3: woman, turned three-quarters to right, wavy hair, details of garland clear, good conditions.

Medallion 4: man, full face, short hair, details of garland clear, good condition.

3rd pair; Medallion 5: man, turned three-quarters to right, apparently dressed in armour, casque or helmet on head, details of garland clear, good condition.

Medallion 6: might be man or woman, either long hair or looped head-dress, dress opened at neck, turned three-quarters to left, details of garland very clear, very good condition.

4th pair; Medallion 7: man, turned three-quarters to right, thin face, dress not clear but giving the effect of a Roman toga, details of garland clear, good condition.

Medallion 8: woman, almost full-face turned slightly to left, longish hair, dress unclear, part of garland obliterated, fair condition.

5th pair; Medallion 9: not clear whether man or woman, turned three-quarters to right, dress unclear, almost all obliterated, poor condition.

Medallion 10: not clear whether man or woman, almost all obliterated except left side of garland.

38. See above, p. 87.

39. Among other examples, a popular drawing of the time depicted François Ier simultaneously as Minerva, Mars, Diana, Love and Mercury, thus attributing to him the qualities of each deity (Bibliothèque Nationale, Cabinet des Estampes, Na 255. Rés). His daughter, Marguerite de France, later Duchesse de Savoie, is shown as Minerva in an enamel portrait (now in the Wallace Collection, London). On this fashion and its links with Renaissance poets see D. Bentley-Cranch, L'iconographie de Marguerite de Savoie, in *Culture et pouvoir au temps de l'Humanisme et de la Renaissance, Actes du Congrès Marguerite de Savoie, Annecy, Chambery, Turin, 1974* (Geneva-Paris 1978), 243-256 et Planches I-XXIV.

40. See C. A. Mayer and D. Bentley-Cranch, *Florimond Robertet: Italianisme et Renaissance française, art. cit.*, n. 32.

41. See A. Blunt, *op. cit.*, 38-44.

42. See *Ibid.*, 26-28. The staircase has a double flight of steps, bridging an arch, leading to a single flight which enters the building at first-floor level.

43. See J. Quentin Hughes and Norbert Lynton, *Renaissance Architecture*, Vol. IV of *Simpson's History of Architectural Development*, 1962, 216-7 and pp. 297-9, and in the Catalogue of the Exhibition, *The Renaissance at Sutton Place*, May-September 1983, published by the Sutton Place Heritage Trust, the article by M. Howard, Sutton Place and Early Tudor Architecture, 23-32.

44. See M. Howard, *art. cit.*, 27-28.

A Project in Experimental Archaeology: Avasjö 1982

Caroline R Wickham-Jones, P Ann Clarke and Andrew Barlow

Introduction

In August 1982 a small project in experimental archaeology was initiated by Tomas Johansson of the Institutet for Forhistorisk Teknologi, Östersund, Sweden. The participants were Lars Forsberg and Ellinor Sydberg from Umeå, and Andrew Barlow, Ann Clarke and Caroline Wickham-Jones from the National Museum of Antiquities of Scotland, Edinburgh. The aim of the experiment was to introduce laboratory-based archaeologists to the potential of intensive field-based work. Various solutions to technical problems indicated by prehistoric material were examined in a forested environment.

Method

For one week the group lived by activities appropriate to a hunter/fisher/gatherer economy. In many particulars these activities sought to replicate those derived by inference from the local archaeological record. They were supplemented by others recorded amongst the methods of environmental exploitation used by recent subsistence economies in that zone, notably the Lapps.

Food was procured partly from the surrounding area (berries, fungi, lichens, fish, etc.), and partly from outside sources. A reindeer carcass was obtained and butchered, and this provided a large part of the diet which was supplemented with modern provisions such as bread, cheese and apples. A Lapp tent was used to provide shelter at night, and modern sleeping bags and recording equipment were taken.

The Site and Situation

The experiment took place on the eastern shore of Lille Avasjö lake about two and a half kilometres to the east of Avasjö village in the Åsele commune, Västerbotten (Fig. 1). This area, the southern tip of Lappland, is characterised by extensive stony moraines and numerous lakes. Tree cover is continuous except where clearance has taken place for settlement, hydro-electric power or agriculture. The forest is of mixed birch and pine and represents about fifty years of growth. Like most Swedish woodland it has been managed and cropped, and the distribution of plant and animal species is not representative of a natural woodland. During the project the group visited an area of unmanaged, relict forest at Rödberget (Fig. 1), where there are taller, larger trees, denser undergrowth and a greater abundance of dead wood.

Similar projects have been carried out by Johansson throughout the last ten years, and it was largely knowledge of his expertise that brought the group together in Sweden. In addition, unlike Britain, Sweden today still has areas capable of supporting such work in relative seclusion. Johansson selected the site within an area with which he was familiar. As well as providing several basic resources such as water, wood and dry ground, access was relatively easy, although the isolated nature of the area meant that there was little outside interference. The stretch of lake shore had been used by Johansson once before for a similar week-long experiment using two people.

Once at the site, locations had to be selected for the erection of the tent, and setting of hearths. These were not easy to find. The previous well-positioned hearth was therefore re-used and the tent was located a short distance to the north in a suitably flat, mossy clearing. Adjacent to the hearth was a large boulder that had doubled as both hearth and bed in the earlier experiment. This time a concave face provided a suitable position against which to smoke meat (Fig. 2).

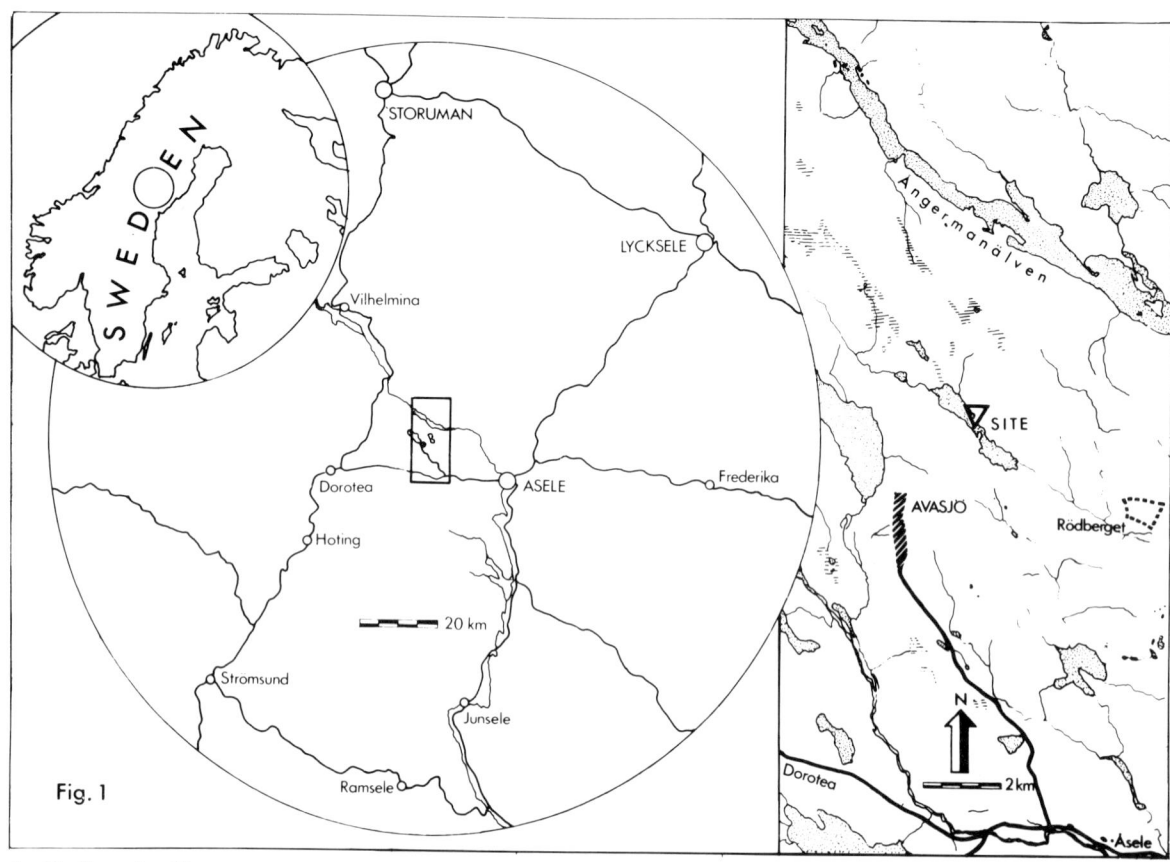

1. Site Location Map.

Diary

Day 1: Equipment was carried to the site, necessitating several trips by boat across the lake. A relatively flat, mossy clearing was selected in which to erect the tent, and poles were collected from the surrounding forest. Once the tent was up, a small cobble hearth was built inside. Around this, spruce branches were laid to provide some insulation from the damp moss below. Fishing gorges of juniper, made with quartzite flakes, were attached to birch rods by lines of twine, birch root, or sinew. These were used to catch roach and perch which were then used to bait juniper pike hooks. Towards the end of the day, fire was made with a bow drill (Fig. 3).

Day 2: Birch was stripped from the trees, peeled and folded into a series of watertight containers sealed with resin when necessary. In the afternoon the reindeer carcass was collected, skinned and butchered, using quartzite flakes. A small amount (c. 2.5kg) of meat was set to cook between sheets of birch bark in a pit lined with hot stones and insulated with sphagnum. Some of the meat was hung to roast over the fire and the rest put in a smoke house built of a framework of poles laid against a concave-sided boulder. A supply of rotted birch was collected and stripped to provide fuel for the smoking.

Day 3: The reindeer skin was strung out between two suitably placed pine trees, and scrapers of bone and quartzite were made. During scraping it was found that much of the subcutaneous fat could be removed by the hands alone. The tendency of the sharper quartzite scrapers to cut into the skin made the bone tool more suitable for most of the closer work. The reindeer head was opened and the antlers were removed and stripped of their velvet. Groove and splinter technique was used to detach a spall which was then shaped into a double-edged harpoon head and ground down upon a quartzite flagstone. Local red slate was also worked, first by grooving with a sharp flake and by light chipping with a soft hammer

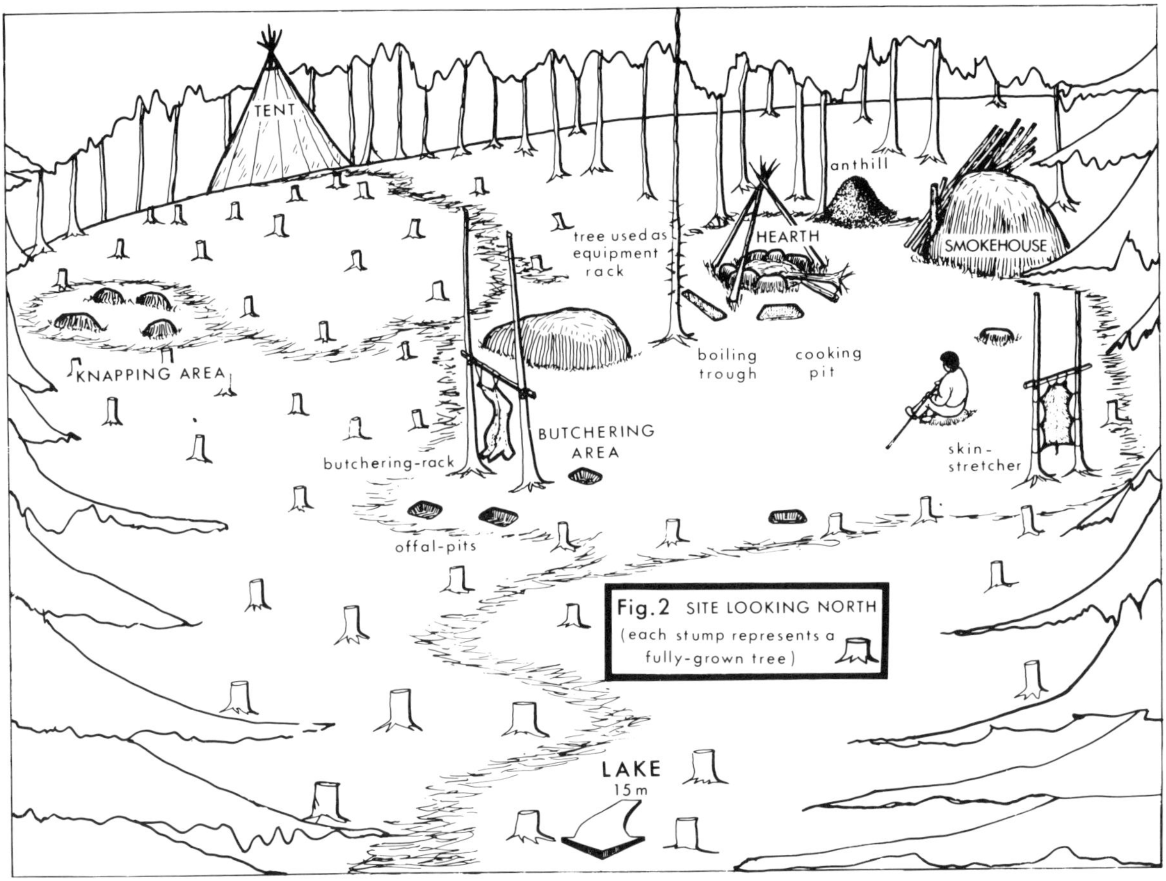

TENT

tree used as
equipment
rack

anthill

HEARTH

SMOKEHOUSE

KNAPPING AREA

boiling
trough

cooking
pit

skin-
stretcher

butchering-rack

BUTCHERING
AREA

offal-pits

Fig.2 SITE LOOKING NORTH
(each stump represents a
fully-grown tree)

LAKE
15 m

2. Site Looking North.

3. Making Fire.

to produce a blank, and then by grinding. Knives and points could be easily produced, but were found to have soft, friable edges.

Day 4: The group walked to an area of unmanaged, relict woodland, Rödberget, about five kilometres to the south-east. On the way branches of juniper suitable for bow-making were collected. Once there, as well as examining the woodland, brief attempts at shooting a home-made, composite bow were made. It was raining heavily so that, upon returning to the camp, a fire was lit inside the tent and everyone gathered inside. Although most of the time was spent living and working around the outside hearth, the tent, when used, proved surprisingly roomy.

Day 5: Work commenced upon stripping the juniper boughs for bow-making, and a straight, thin piece of birch was selected to make an arrow shaft. This was peeled and scraped with a concave quartzite edge. Experiments with the working of slate and with skin scraping continued. A suitable shaft for the antler harpoon head was selected and was first bound on with sinew and then sealed with resin. A different cooking method was tried. A large birchbark trough was sunk into the ground and filled with water and meat. Hot stones were dropped in and the whole sealed with more bark and covered with sphagnum. The stones boiled the water within seconds and the meat was cooked in about half an hour.

Day 6: Work on the bows, arrow shaft, slate grinding and skin scraping continued. A new technique of quartzite knapping, holding the blank against a wooden support, was tried. In the evening flat bread was baked upon heated slabs by the fire.

Day 7: The material goods pertaining to and resulting from the week were collected and, in accordance with local custom, the hearth area was generally tidied. The tent was dismantled, the canvas folded and the poles laid aside. An elk skin, spoiled by the rain, was slung over a branch and water poured over all of the hearths. As on arrival, several trips were necessary to ferry and transport the equipment away.

Although the main occupations of the project have been set out above, some tasks were carried out intermittently throughout the week. The most time-consuming were collecting firewood and stripping birch logs for the smoke house. The fires consumed a huge amount of wood, and even when large, slower-burning tar stumps of pine and spruce were collected, there always seemed to be a need for more wood.

Water also had to be brought to the site from a short distance, and its transport too involved much time.

Stone knapping was an important activity although carried out less frequently than timber collecting. Tools were made primarily of local, fine-quality quartzite but flint, chert and jasper were also used. They were made on a very *ad hoc* basis as old pieces blunted or different working edges were required. For most tasks raw flakes provided adequate, sharp edges, and little artificial shaping by retouch was carried out. Occasionally, retouch was used to resharpen an edge. Knapping took place on most days but the number of tools used and the amount of debris present at the end of the week was very low.

Fishing, involving the preparation of gorges or hooks, lines and rods, also took place at intervals, and the one activity which never seemed to cease was eating. Local berries were not abundant but there were enough to be collected on any trip away from the central living area, from where they soon disappeared. Likewise, there were edible fungi and lichens dotted around the forest floor. The smoked meat provided a constant supply of food, supplemented by a few fish and individually varying amounts of imported items. Although no one ever felt outrageously hungry, even during the first two days when no outside food was eaten, no one was ever completely satisfied either, so that a constant input of small amounts of energy seemed to be the answer.

Remains

During the week the site polarised into several areas (Fig. 2). The tent area was used for sleeping and storage. To the south was the hearth, around which most daily activities concentrated. This included the smoke house, butchery area and skin-scraping frame. Between the two a knapping area had originally been selected but was used only sporadically, much stone tool manufacture taking place in the more congenial atmosphere of the hearth. To the west lay the shore of the lake, used along its length for fishing, but a demarcation arose between that part used for the collection of drinking water to the north, and that part used for the cleaning of fish, etc., to the south.

At the end of the week, after clearance, little could be seen of the tent stance apart from its hearth, an adjacent stack of poles and the discarded elk skin. Around the main hearth area the hearth, cooking tripod and pits and smoke house remained. No structural features had existed elsewhere. Although the bone and antler tools were removed, many of the stone flakes remained, scattered across the site as they had been discarded or lost. Of the butchering site, little remained except pits with the discarded part of the carcass. Various birch bark containers, fishing rods and gorges, etc. were also abandoned.

Results

Of the six participants, only two were experienced in such work. Consequently, it was found that there was so much to learn, with activities to be observed if not participated in, that controlled experiment was not possible. For that, a group greatly experienced in life in such a situation would be necessary. It can be argued that each individual activity could be carried out and controlled within a laboratory or other isolated setting. Indeed, for such work in a laboratory, specialists in only one, relevant field are necessary. However, the advantage of putting tasks into a context such as that at Avasjö is that it is then possible to see techniques running together into a more dynamic situation. When the participants also live within that context, then the situation can last for days rather than hours and attention can be focused upon aspects of the work that might otherwise be ignored. Although laboratory-based experiment has its advantages, so too does freer-flowing work where, for example, certain practical realities, otherwise masked by the isolation of the task, may be revealed. Ideally, experiments in prehistoric technology should be conducted in as wide a variety of situations as possible.

Although it was not carefully controlled, certain general points did emerge from the project. The techniques and lifestyle practised were those of a hunter/gatherer/fisher group, but many of these points are felt to be relevant to later prehistory also. During the week the most obvious point to emerge was the wide range of local resources available to satisfy many daily requirements. For the purposes of the following discussion the use of these resources has been divided into artifactual and consumable use. Also, it is important to notice that the lists involved are not intended to be conclusive, but rather to provide examples of range. At no time does this article pretend to be a practical guide to the do-it-yourself prehistoric life.

Artifacts

In a forested or wooded environment many needs are

supplied by the trees themselves. Straight poles can be collected to provide frames for tents, cooking, smoking and drying, and they are also useful as fishing rods, bows, arrows and fire-making equipment. Containers of various sizes and shapes, fishing gorges and hooks, and soft insulated flooring are all easily made from wood, and wood by-products such as birch bark, willow and other roots, tinder and resin play an important part.

Other artifactual needs may largely be fulfilled by the use of two more resources, animals and stone. Bone, antler and horn can be derived from most forms of animal life and provide hard materials. Although these will have different properties according to the source, such variation can be used to the benefit of the tasks involved. Animals also provide many other materials, like sinew, guts and hides. Hides fulfil many needs, for clothing, shelter or containers, but they also produce problems. It has been estimated that a single Eskimo family uses between forty and fifty reindeer skins per year.[1] Such consumption represents a considerable amount of hunting, skinning and drying, etc., and the preparation of such hides is not easy. They must be stretched and dried quickly after scraping, and if they are used without tanning, then further soaking when in use will not only stiffen them, but also, if they are not carefully redried, the hair will drop out. In any wet climate the initial drying and preparation and further curing of items of skin must have been a major task.

Stone can be used in two ways, either as it is found or after flaking. Natural stones and pebbles of various shapes, sizes and hardnesses are everywhere and have many uses. Flakeable stones, however, are not so common, so that although there were many possible varieties besides flint, they may well have had to be imported. Basic flaking can provide sharp edges for cutting, and blunter edges for scraping, whittling, etc., often on the same tool. Unretouched edges blunt easily, however, and must be reworked or the tool replaced. Abundance of raw material, intensity of the task in hand and proximity to the nearest knapping area will all help to determine which course is pursued. Retouching work is also useful because it can provide an edge of specific, predetermined properties for any particular task and it can be used to provide tools of a specific shape, for example for hafting. The role of stone tools may vary greatly on different sites. They may be used simply as a primary tool kit to manufacture artifacts from other materials, or they may themselves be transformed into daily tools such as drill bits or arrowheads.

Consumable Use

i Fire: Although fire can also be used as an artifact, to harden or sharpen tools, it is dealt with here as a process which consumes available resources. The production of fire with, for example, a bow drill is a skilled task which has its own problems. The components of the maker's kit, for instance, must be completely dry in order to function. Once suitable pieces have been assembled, they assume some degree of importance and must be looked after and transported with care. Fire is central to the life of a community and, once started, it must be watched and fed. The collection of firewood becomes an important task and has two major aspects, quality and quantity.

a) Quality. Many different qualities of wood exist in any forest, each of which has different uses. For a smoke-house fire, for example, smoke-producing, rotten birch logs, stripped of their bark to lessen the tar content of the smoke, are the most suitable. For a general fire, however, slow-burning tar stumps of fir may be preferred to last through the night, or smaller dry logs to produce a great heat, perhaps for cooking.

b) Quantity. Fires may vary greatly in size but they all consume wood constantly, and the task of collecting it must involve a sizeable proportion of any group's time. Such trips, however, are not completely unrewarding in other ways. They may, for example, provide important opportunities for the reconnaisance of new areas or the monitoring of well-known ones. In this way valuable experience may also be offered to the young for whom the collection of timber is a common task.

Dead wood, however, is not an infinite resource. At Avasjö, although the site had been used only once before, for a similar week-long project involving two fires, by the end of the 1982 experiment much of the suitable material had been gathered from within easy reach of the living area. Once all the timber is used, it could be several decades before enough dead wood is regenerated to support further fires. Natural forest contains more dead timber than managed woodland, but it does seem that the exhaustion of timber for burning would play an important part in dictating site abandonment.

ii Food: Many food requirements can be satisfied within the locality of a site as vegetable matter is collected and wildlife taken. With a diet that is less varied than that of today, however, large quantities of the staple items are necessary to provide essential nutrition. Within four days the bulk of the reindeer was consumed by five people. In a community of any size, hunting for game such as this must involve a considerable input of time and energy throughout the year. Although animals can, of course, be killed and butchered in large numbers, there are the ensuing problems of transporting and preserving large quantities of meat. In addition to biological preservation for later consumption, preservation from predators is also necessary, for which structures of various types, often leaving little archaeological trace, must be built.

Shelter

Another basic requirement of any community is shelter. This may be provided in many ways, from using natural features to the construction of various types and complexities of structure. The form of shelter is affected by many things, such as the mobility and size of the group, likely permanence of the site, climate and terrain. Within any one area there may be few sites where conditions are exactly suitable for the erection of shelter. This is obviously important for a mobile group that wishes to return to an area time after time but which has exhausted supplies of dead wood, food, etc. around one particular site.

Transport

Whether communities are nomadic or not, transportation is an important part of any society, and its role is often underestimated in studies of prehistory. Although the great variety of ways in which needs may be fulfilled from the surrounding environment have been stressed, there remain many items that would require transportation. For any one group the movement involved may be divided into two major types: maintenance trips and peripatetic trips. Individual communities may place more or less emphasis on either type.

Maintenance trips involve the collection of goods integral to the life of the community such as food and stone. The length and duration of the trips involved can vary greatly, as can the number of people present. In some cases those going on the journey may be procuring the goods themselves, in which case the carriage of suitable equipment is also necessary. If, on the other hand, trade or barter is involved, then the relevant exchange medium must be taken. In most cases the cargo will be heavier on the homeward trip. Where the carcasses of large animals are involved, the movement of such a dead weight over rough ground is not easy, even when trussed upon a carrying pole. If butchery takes place away from the settlement the carriage of many, often awkward, smaller items may be no easier. The advantages of off-site butchery must be determined by many factors, such as the size and number of animals and the amount of the carcass normally exploited. In order to prevent the meat souring, butchery and preservation at the kill site would be a necessity where the journey back was long or the weather warm.[2]

Peripatetic trips involve the movement of the whole community to a new settlement. In some cases the group size may increase or decrease at the new site according to the time of year, type of environment to be exploited, and so on. Such trips may occur with varying frequency. Some communities may move many times a year, others only once in a generation. The problems involved with any transportation will vary greatly with the individuals concerned. The material culture, as well as the climate and environment, will dictate how much is to be moved and just how easy that movement is.

Travelling conditions vary from season to season just as they do in different terrains, and the presence or absence of pack animals and equipment such as boats and sledges will affect transport greatly. In this context, the alterations that have taken place in the nature of the countryside with the onset and development of agriculture must be noted. Not only have areas of dense woodland been opened up, but water courses have been altered, and the clearance of stones and boulders to form fields has lent an unnaturally level and smooth appearance to the ground itself.

General Conclusions

Throughout the project stone tools played a relatively minor part. Even though flakes may be fashioned — as they were not during the experiment — into more complex pieces such as arrowheads, etc., there is still a wealth of perishable material culture to be accounted for. Although they were doubtless important to daily life, the relative importance of stone knapping within any prehistoric site has apparently been over-emphasised by the accident of preservation. Today, with more sophisticated analyses possible, the importance of flaked stone lies not only in its survival, but also in the fact that it can suggest some of the aspects of material culture which have long since disappeared.

The relative unimportance of stone knapping during the project served to emphasise the great variety of other tasks necessary. The group attempted a few of these tasks only, but the need for a constant preoccupation with preparing and daily mending of items of wood, bone or skin, for instance, was clear. In addition, any fire needs regular attention, and there is always food, fuel and water to be collected. It is likely that most members of a community would have a degree of skill in most tasks, but complete individual self-sufficiency is unlikely. There are also communal tasks such as fire tending or the care of shelters, and the importance of job division by age should not be overlooked.

Finally, the project affirmed the influence of the environment upon any settlement or society. This may be studied at different levels of magnitude, and previous work has concentrated upon either the micro-fossils of the environment such as pollen or snails, or upon macro-environmental studies of whole areas or climates. In between, however, there is a stratified set of individual environments, for example around a single hearth, individual tent or travelling band. The environment examined will vary according to its reference point: 'The environment can only be defined relative to the subject whose environment it is, be it a single individual, a local or regional population, or an entire species. It does not therefore exist as a system but rather as a set of possibilities'.[3]

Influences such as the availability of firewood, level ground, etc., have already been noted, and the role of such specific factors in any individual environment is great. Different people and societies respond to environmental stimuli in many different ways, however, so that any comparison or reconstruction between apparently similar loci must be undertaken with care. Not only are minute variations such as terrain or rainfall to be taken into account, but also the possibility of idiosyncratic reactions to such variations must not be forgotten.

This final point takes us back to the problem of living reconstructions of prehistoric life today. We have tried to show that when undertaken and used with care, such experiment can be most useful. In addition to the interest of applying theory in the field, it stimulates a broader approach to archaeological material that can be of benefit.

Acknowledgements

The participants from Edinburgh thank the Russell Trust, the Society of Antiquaries of Scotland, the Prehistoric Society and the National Museum of Antiquities of Scotland, all of whom gave generous grants to help defray the costs of the exercise.

References

1. K. Knutsson, Skrapor och Skrapning, in *Tor* 1975-77, 19-62.

2. G. C. Frison, *Prehistoric Hunters of the High Plains* (New York 1978).

3. T. Ingold, The Hunter and his Spear: Notes on the Cultural Mediation of Social and Ecological Systems, in A. Sheridan and G. Bailey, eds., *Economic Archaeology* 1981, 119-30 (= Brit. Archaeol. Rep. S96).

Post-Medieval Pots and Potters at Throsk in Stirlingshire

David H Caldwell and Valerie E Dean

Continuing fieldwork at Throsk, a few miles to the east of Stirling, on the south bank of the River Forth, has revealed substantial remains of a post-medieval pottery industry. A previous interim report[1] published some of the typical products of the Throsk kilns, and the opportunity is taken here of giving a more complete picture of them. The pottery is all earthenware, normally covered with a green to brown lead glaze. The fabric tends to be reddish-brown in appearance although the jugs, probably the commonest type, have a reduced grey fabric under their green glaze. The level of technical skill in turning these vessels compares unfavourably with earlier medieval pots. The Throsk pots are often thick-walled and clumsy with extensive knife-trimming.

Since the nineteenth century whole vessels have been recovered from Throsk and the neighbouring lands of Bandeath, Drypow and Cockspow, and have ended up in the collections of the National Museums in Edinburgh and the Smith Institute in Stirling. The archaeological evidence for the actual manufacture of these pots in this locality consists of substantial

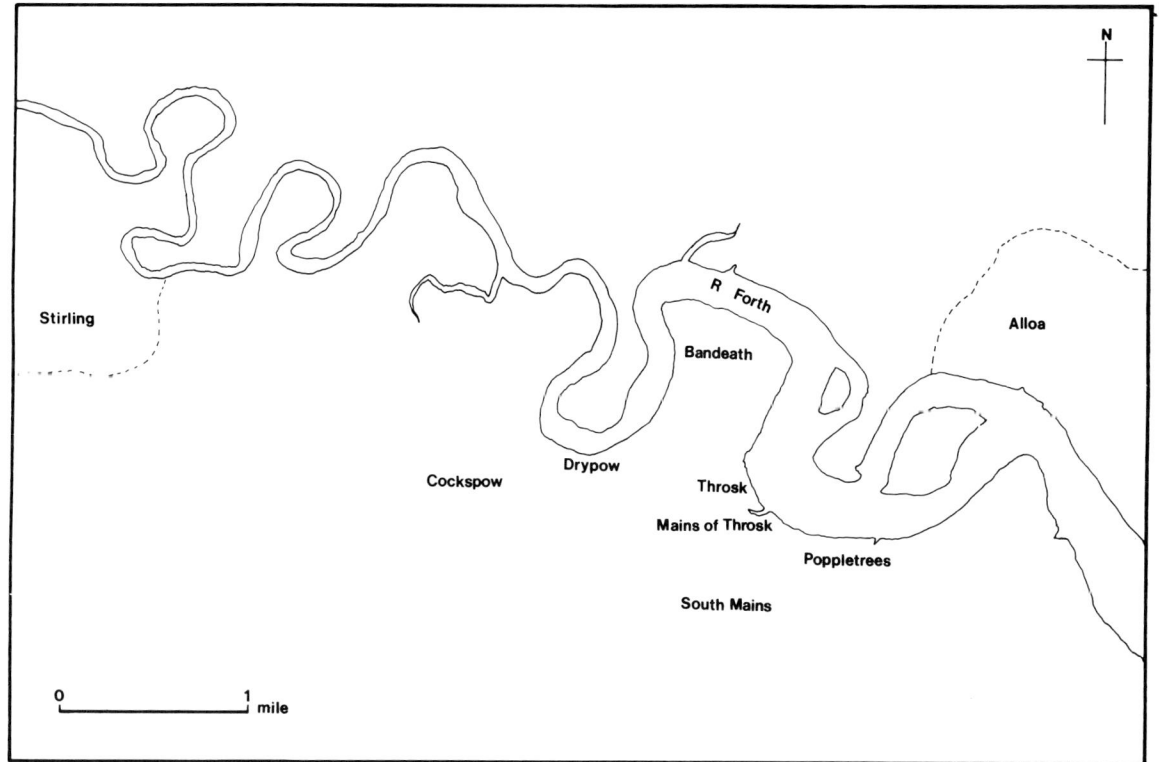

1. Sketch map showing sites where potters are known to have worked or where pottery has been discovered.

2. A typical example of a Throsk jug, discarded by the potters since it has split open in the kiln. Height 0.325m. A/1895.

spreads of sherds brought to the surface by ploughing. Many of them are clearly from vessels which broke or became misshapen in the process of manufacture, and also included are kiln supports, bricks and pieces of daub from the kiln walls.

Some of this material appears to have been used by local farmers to improve drainage. The lands about Throsk are typical flat, carse lands, now almost entirely stripped of their covering of peat. The blue-grey carse clay immediately under the plough soil is pock-marked with deep mossy holes into which pottery, including virtually intact vessels, has been dropped. This observation is based not just on small-scale excavation but the experience of Mr Arbuckle and his father, the farmers of South Mains Farm. It is unlikely that this kiln waste would have been carted any great distance, and in at least one case a substantial surface spread of sherds appears to have been ploughed up from a pottery dump which may have accumulated next to one of the kilns. The process of reclaiming the carse lands about Throsk for agricultural purposes has presumably been going on piecemeal over a period of several hundred years. For instance some of the neighbouring land at Dunmore was only cleared in the last quarter of the eighteenth century[2] and there are still areas of moss round about. The lands of Throsk, Bandeath, Poppletrees and Cockspow, all in the barony of Cowie, belonged before the Reformation to the Abbey of Cambuskenneth, but their full agricultural potential may not have been realised before the mid-sixteenth century when they

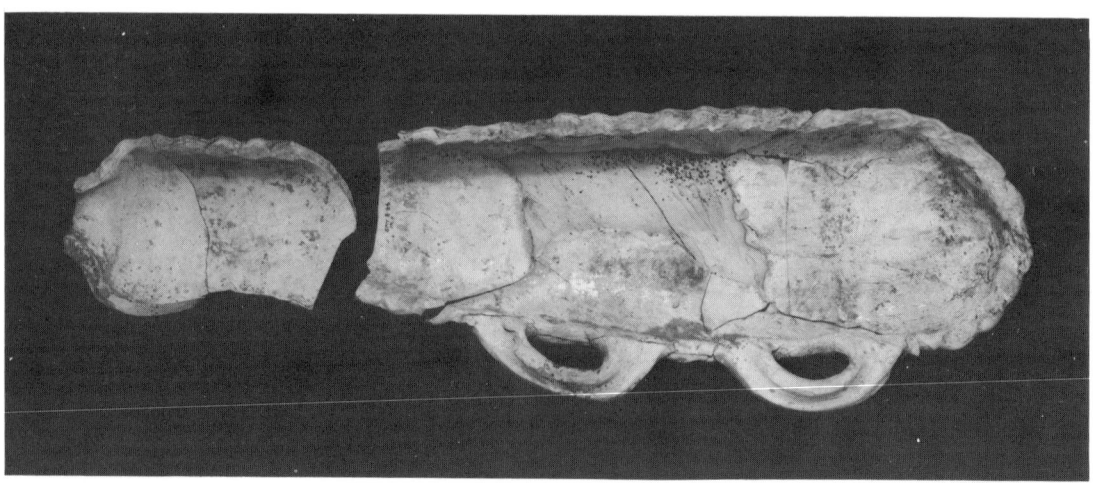

3. Two pieces from dripping-pans. Lengths 0.46m and 0.195m. A/1896.

were feued out, Throsk to the sitting tenant, John Abercromby, the rest to the Earl of Mar.[3]

It may well be that the origins of the pottery industry at Throsk owe not a little to the difficulty of making a living from farming on the initially limited, reclaimed land. A problem at the moment is knowing when, exactly, the industry started. On a stylistic basis some of the pottery, particularly jugs with frilly bases in imitation of German stoneware, might date to the sixteenth century, but the documentary evidence can at present only be stretched back as far as 1644 with the commencement of baptismal records for the parish of St Ninians in which all the lands mentioned above (except Dunmore) lie. A William, an Alexander and a John Pollock, all adults, occur in the first two years of this register[4] and can be shown from later records, principally their testaments, to have been potters or piggers, the latter word being derived from the usual Scots term for an earthenware vessel, a pig.

Throughout the rest of the seventeenth century and the first quarter of the eighteenth century a total of twelve potters or piggers can so far be identified, six Pollocks (sometimes rendered as Poog), two Christies and two Matsons, and one Abercromby and one Buchan, all living at Throsk apart from John Matson, potter in Cockspow, and John Christie, pigger in Poppletrees.[5] This research, however, is still in its early stages and we expect that more potters may be teased out from the documents.

Of these twelve, at least four are known to have been adults in the 1640s and '50s. In 1694, out of thirty-eight tenants listed on the Laird of Balgownie's lands in St Ninians Parish (Throsk and Poppletrees), four are apparently men who describe themselves elsewhere as potters or piggers.[6]

It is clear from testaments that pot-making was not a full-time activity, perhaps only indulged in during the winter. The inventories of the possessions of Alexander Pollock, pigger in Throsk, who died in 1671, and of John Pollock, pigger in Throsk, who died in 1674, mention cows, horses, sheep and corn, but no clay, pots or tools are itemised, and, of course, the testaments deal only with the deceased's movables in any case.[7]

By the sixteenth century pot-making to satisfy local needs was already well established in the Stirling area. There is the archaeological evidence for fifteenth-century production at Stenhouse near Falkirk,[8] and there is the documentary evidence for a pottery at St Ninians itself in the sixteenth century, and for a pigmaker in Stirling in 1521 and a potter in 1613.[9] The nearby place name of Pottirow of Touch is also suggestive.

If the industry at Throsk is the successor of these earlier ones, with potters moving from them to Throsk, one of the main gains must surely have been easy access to the River Forth and thereby to much of Scotland. It is not at present clear how large an area the Throsk potters were serving. Pottery which can be matched at Throsk turns up on occupation sites all over Scotland, and it is hoped that programmes of scientific analysis — thin sectioning and neutron activation — will help establish what quantity is from Throsk or kilns elsewhere.

4. (a) Large jugs, varying in height from about 0.25m to 0.35m seem to be the commonest type produced at Throsk. They normally have a band of wavy-line incised decoration on their shoulders and are completely covered with green glaze on the outside.

(b) 'Ointment pot' of red fabric, glazed inside. See fig. 31 of the previous interim report for the base of a similar jar.

(c) Stopper, the top crudely formed and dabbed with brown glaze. The potter's finger marks are clearly visible all over it. This is the only such piece discovered so far and it may have been made to fit in the neck of small jugs like (d).

(d) Small narrow necked jug in reduced grey fabric covered in green glaze.

(e) Jug with frilly base, perhaps in imitation of imported stone ware. It is glazed light green both inside and out.

(f) Small jug in red fabric with patchy brownish green glaze on its exterior.

(g) Bowl, red fabric, glazed inside only.

(h) Dish, red fabric, glazed inside only.

(i) Chamber pot (?), light brown fabric, glazed inside only. These appear to be amongst the commoner types.

(j) Pot-lid, reddish brown fabric, glazed on upper surfaces only.

(k) Pirlie pig (money box), red fabric, brown glaze almost entirely flaked off.

(l) Kiln stands, like miniature cooling towers, occur in large numbers. Many are splashed with glaze and fire-darkened.

(m) Skillets with fold-over handles are also common. They are normally in reddish brown fabric with brown glazed insides, and vary in size from about 0.16 to 0.23m diameter at the rim.

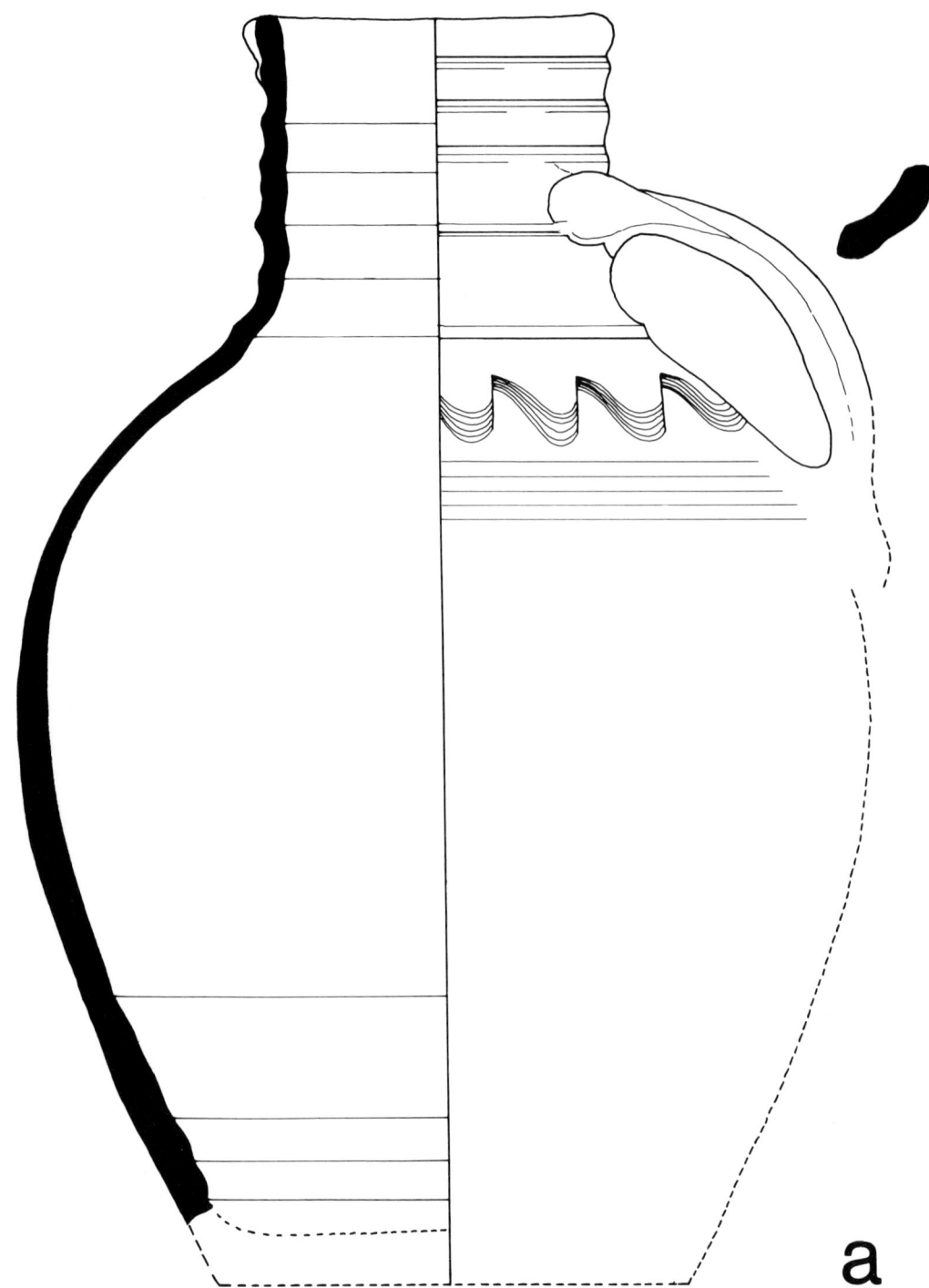

Note to Fig. 4: all drawings are reproduced at ½ scale and all pieces of pottery are in the National Museums of Scotland except for the small jug (f) which is in a private collection. The drawings are by V. E. Dean.

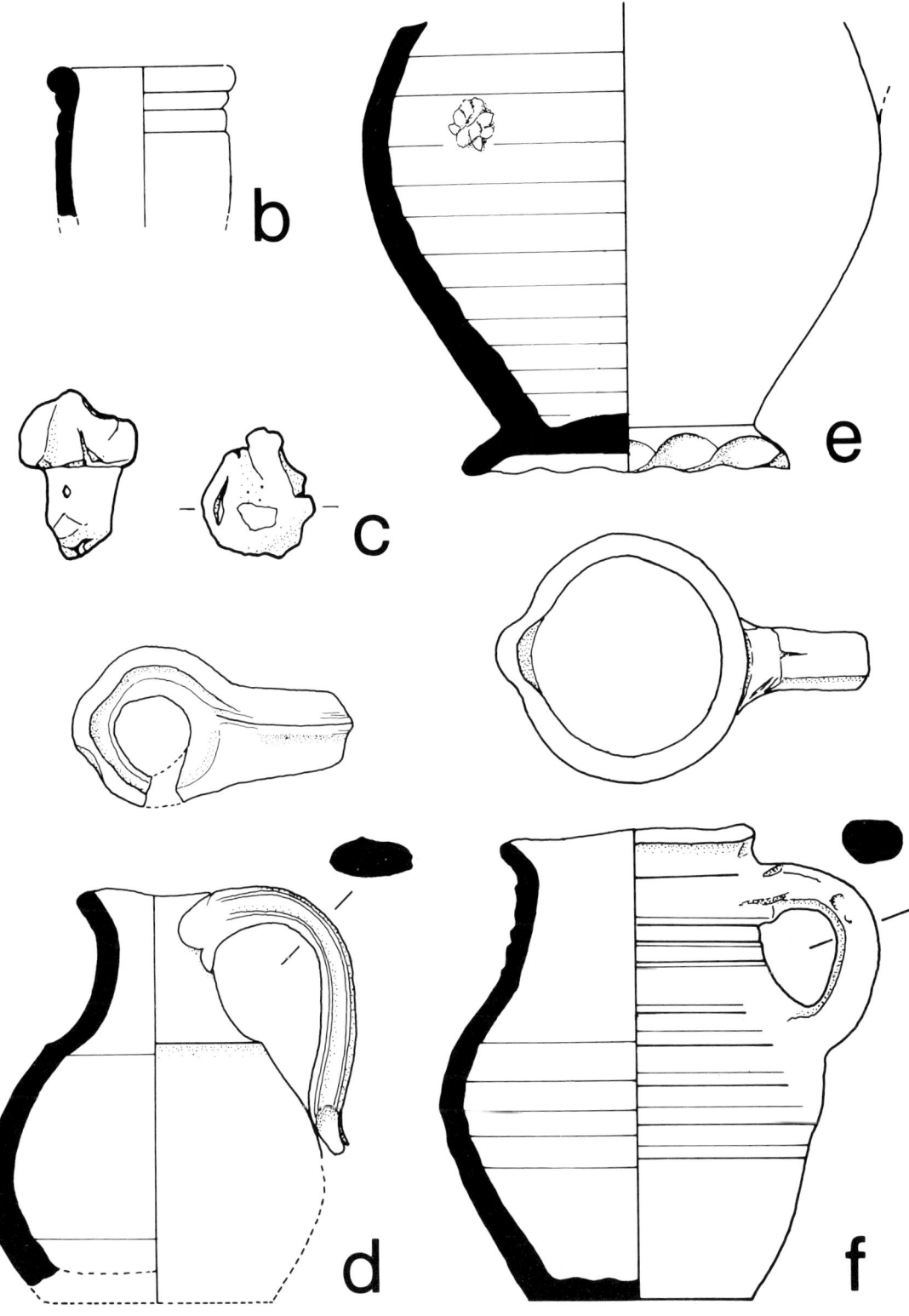

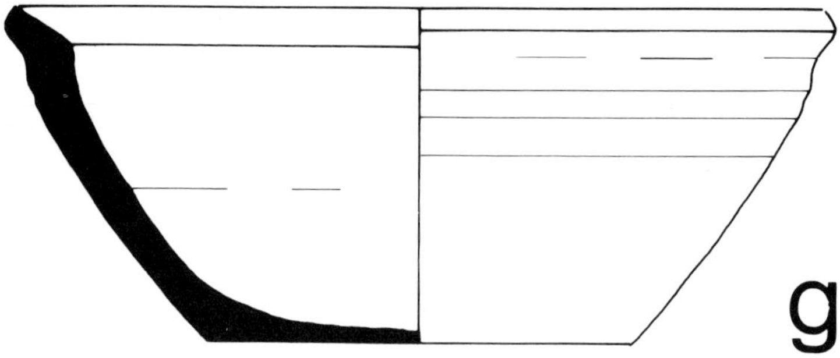

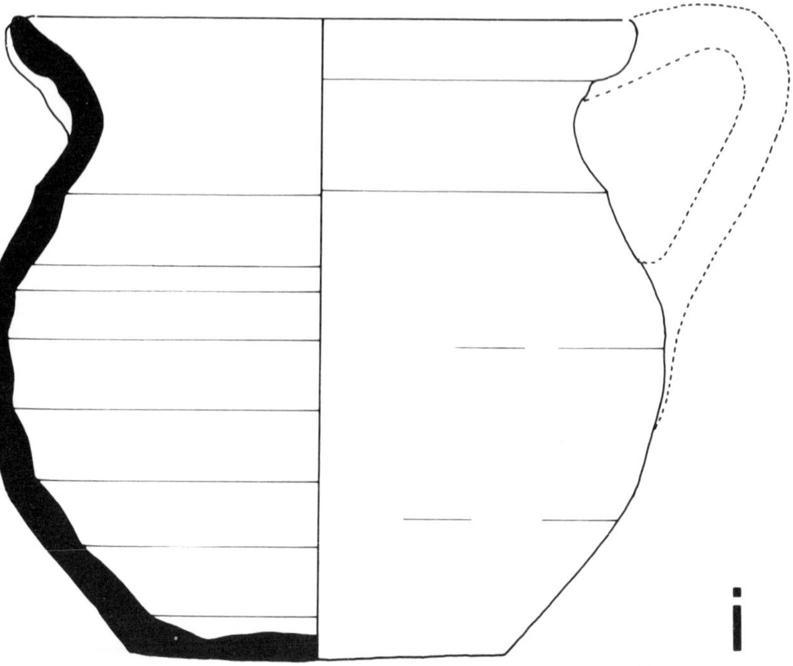

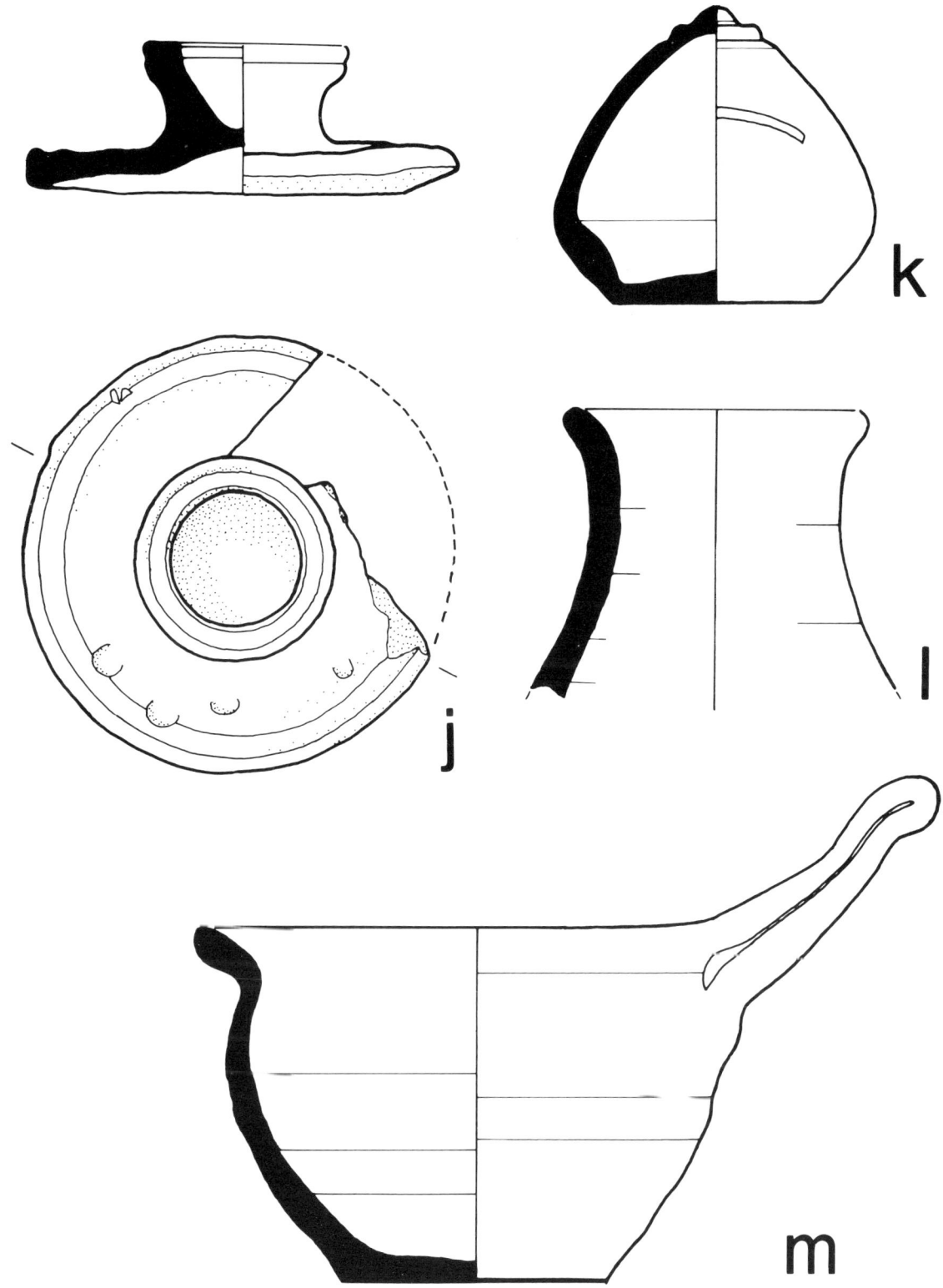

Acknowledgements

We are most grateful to Mr Arbuckle of South Mains for his support and interest and also those who helped with the work, including R. M. Carmichael, J. Strobridge, I. McDowall, R. Caldwell, K. Mitchell and S. Wingrove.

References

1. D. H. Caldwell and V. Dean, The Post-Medieval Pottery Industry at Throsk, Stirlingshire, in *Scottish Pottery Historical Review*, 6 (1981), 21-27.

2. J. Sinclair, ed., *The Statistical Account of Scotland*, III (Edinburgh 1792), 487.

3. *Registrum Magni Sigilli (1580-93)*, no. 1292; Scottish Record Office GD 124/1 nos. 976, 982, 999.

4. New Register House OPR 488/1 *passim*.

5. Information on most of these is derived essentially from the St Ninian's parish register (OPR 488) and the *Stirling Register of Testaments* (Scottish Record Society), 1904. For Henry Abercromby, see A. W. C. Hallen, Abercromby Family in Stirlingshire, in *The Scottish Antiquary*, 10 (1896), 68; and for James Buchan, Hallen, A. W. C., Dame Erskine's Account-Book, in *The Scottish Antiquary*, 9 (1895), 107.

6. The 1694 information is derived from the list of hearths (for tax purposes) of St Ninians Parish in the Scottish Record Office, E69/22.

7. Scottish Record Office CC 21/5/8 nos. 110, 452.

8. The pottery from archaeological excavations at Stenhouse is in the collections of Falkirk Museum and the National Museums, Edinburgh, and is in the process of being written up for publication by G. Haggarty.

9. *Extracts from the Records of the Royal Burgh of Stirling AD 1519-1666* (Glasgow 1887), 10; Scottish Record Office B 66/25 nos. 119, 135, 137, 185, 231.

Dr I F Grant (1887-1983): The Highland Folk Museum and a Bibliography of her Written Works

Hugh Cheape

It is not my intention here to sketch out a biography of Dr Elsie Grant; it might be fairly claimed that this rates a book to itself and, considering her character and achievements during a long life, it is a task that will certainly be undertaken by a forthcoming generation. Dr Grant was an enthusiastic and prolific writer and, besides more than a dozen major books, she published many articles and pamphlets which are not now available and which consequently may not be familiar in the future. All these publications are important and worth placing on record. She herself was modest about her success as a writer and had not listed or recorded her publications; indeed such was her output that she never tried to recall all her written and published works. It is fitting that an attempt be made to do this now as a tribute and mark of respect by those who knew her.

It would be impertinent to rehearse the experiences of Dr Grant's childhood or her early career in any detail, although in conversation over several years she returned frequently to reflect on circumstances which were to affect her life and work significantly. It seems desirable to place some elements of these conversations on record while the memory of them persists, in the belief that they throw light on some of the inspiration behind Dr Grant's lifelong interest in Highland history and also on the founding of *Am Fasgadh*, the Highland Folk Museum.

Dr Grant was born in Edinburgh on 21 July 1887 and was brought up in London and in the Highlands. Her parents went to India when she was still young, leaving her in the care of her grandfather when he was Governor of Chelsea Hospital and a member of Queen Victoria's Household, and then in the care of an unmarried aunt to whom she was very attached and to

whom she owed much in the way of informal and social education. Of formal education as we understand it today, she had little. She was educated privately and she educated herself by her wits and intelligence. Her stream of writings was of course an academic as well as a popular success and she was always quietly pleased that she should be so happily sharing the company of scholars and leaders of society all of whom had probably raised themselves on the

1. Miss I. F. Grant on receiving her Honorary Degree of LL.D. from the University of Edinburgh in 1948.

basis of a full and formal education at school and university.

An advantage of being in London as a little girl was that Dr Grant was taken frequently to the big London museums. She described how on the occasions when she was taken to the British Museum, she was inspired by the sight of the Elgin Marbles and the Museum's collections of Greek and Roman sculpture. This was Dr Grant's earliest memory of museums, but it was not her formative one. She often recounted the experience of a trip with her mother to Stockholm and Oslo and her amazement and fascination with the folk museums there. The two pioneering projects at Skansen in Sweden and at Lillehammer in Norway included formal museum collections and display in the conventional sense and also the ambitious element of open-air collections of buildings and their contents. Dr Grant brought back to this country a vision of a museum for the Highlands which would preserve its fast-disappearing material culture and also its traditions and values.

The Swedish Nordiska Museum, founded in 1873 by the energetic scholar and patriot Artur Hazelius, has exercised a lasting influence on successive generations of museum curators as well as on Dr Grant. The crisis which had inspired Hazelius in his project was the destruction of local, regional and national characteristics of language and ways of life. The 'industrial revolution' was at its height in the Sweden of the 1870s, but it coincided more or less with the fullest flood of nineteenth-century romanticism so that the attention of contemporary historians, poets and novelists was caught and held by the very real danger of the obliteration of a national culture.

The other half of the Nordiska Museum is the large open-air museum, Skansen, founded in 1891 on a hill on the edge of Stockholm. It became the example and pattern of all open-air museums, consisting of buildings brought lock, stock and barrel from different localities and re-erected on the seventy-five acre site. Dr Grant spoke of her admiration for Hazelius' work, and she herself pioneered this type of enterprise in Britain. When *Am Fasgadh* was established at its permanent home in Kingussie, she reconstructed four buildings entirely with her own resources and had ambitions to do more.

The Nordiska Museum was founded in response to the popular sense of the need to preserve what would soon be lost and also to the strong spirit of pan-Scandinavianism then prevailing. In the view of Hazelius and his contemporaries, the true source of Swedish traditional culture was in the peasant communities. National art and culture were equated with peasant or folk culture and were to be interpreted and exemplified in 'folk museums'. The core of the Museum was therefore the 'Department of Peasant Culture'. Dr Grant fully appreciated the value of the folk museum movement and described how she set her sights on doing in the Highlands what the far-sighted European nations had done for their respective cultures. Later, when her plans began to mature, she wrote:

> In this great European movement Great Britain has hitherto had little share. The only attempts that have been made to make 'folk life' collections have been on a small scale, and there is nothing at all comparable to the open-air museums of the continent. The Highlands have had an age-old civilization, beautiful and unique, and an opportunity will be presented to them to be the pioneers in Great Britain in forming a collection illustrative of the life of the past. Will it not be a strange thing and a tragic one if the Gaels . . . do not do as much as the Swedes, the Dutch, the Tyrolese, the other peoples of Europe, to ensure that an adequate record of the old ways of life of their people is kept for the generations to come?[1]

The use of inverted commas for 'folk life' was deliberate, being an expression of Dr Grant's belief that the term was not necessarily generally applicable or not applicable in the Highlands and Islands in the sense in which it was certainly generally understood. In 1912, she had visited the Rijksmuseum in Amsterdam and had been most impressed with the costume gallery in the basement of the Museum. This was a display of 'Dutch Peasant Clothes'. The Rijksmuseum was then one of the few institutions in Europe which studied and presented 'peasant culture'. The impressions stayed with her, but she also experienced a growing feeling that the display of 'folk culture' in a Highland museum was not an altogether satisfactory concept. It was of course difficult to find the right term for a museum of wide-ranging social history; it required a name which people could understand, but Dr Grant was concerned that the prevailing understanding of 'folk' was that it described a primitive or 'peasant' culture of an unsophisticated country people. She wanted a Highland museum to tell the story of the life and work of the people of the Highlands and Islands.

Dr Grant's thesis was that this was no 'peasant' culture but an ancient and an aristocratic culture. Highland society, though hierarchical, was well integrated and adhered to the values of an aristocracy whose values had a long pedigree. These values were adopted, imitated and reflected on by all levels of society as, for example, Gaelic song and story clearly indicated. Every member of the Highland community looked to an aristocratic and heroic past and understood its conventions and metaphors. It was a justly proud reflection of Dr Grant's, for example, that her own great grandfather, William Mackintosh of Balnespick, was the subject of an Ossianic ballad, that is, a traditional Gaelic elegy in which the subject was cast in the mould of a Fingalian hero. The poem opens in conventional style:

'S coimeas mise do dh'Oisean
'Bhiodh ag innse mar a thachair do'n Fhéinn

[I am like Ossian
Who would be telling of the Fingalians . . .][2]

Thus the ideals of a warrior Gaelic aristocracy of the early centuries A.D. were regarded as the standards to which manhood should still conform.

The material culture of recent generations demonstrated this noble inheritance. The furniture and plenishings of the house of the chief and the laird were adopted and emulated by the tacksman. The latter did not consider sending to the Capital for the items which he admired; he employed local men to copy the styles of the laird for himself and, in their turn, the local men copied the styles for their own homes. Dr Grant returned frequently to this theme and described its different strands in her written work.

Dr Grant used to observe, and it is probably often still true of public attitudes today, that when she was young, everybody's picture of a museum was of a museum of archaeology, a museum of prehistoric artefacts. Alternatively, people assumed that museums were concerned only with rarities or freaks. When she founded her own museum therefore, she knew that she was going against the general notion of a museum and also drawing a distinction between a Scandinavian 'folk museum' and a Highland 'folk museum'. She was, as she colourfully described

herself, 'just cussed', and her determination to forge ahead and develop a folk museum was, she said, 'sheer cussedness'. She had to demonstrate that the ethos of the folk museum was quite different from the generally accepted picture of a museum and concerned itself not with the rare and the curious but with the familiar and the workaday, with the life of a people with an ancient and aristocratic culture.

The springboard for a Highland 'folk museum' was created in 1930. Dr Grant initiated and organised the 1930 *Highland Exhibition* which was held in Inverness Town Hall from 4 August to 20 September that year. The exhibition included a wide selection of Highland and Island material from prehistoric to modern times covering a wide spectrum of themes from the relics of primitive belief to the techniques of contemporary transport and communications. The largest category of material was subsumed under the heading of 'Folk Life' in which it was possible to illustrate the particular identity of Highland history and artefacts and to emphasise the regional variation evident in a country as small as Scotland in a period when the distinctive regional characteristics of language and culture were declining into the universal mundanity of modern industrialised society.

The *Highland Exhibition* was an important step in the realisation of plans for a Highland Folk Museum. Dr Grant, as one of the prime movers and organisers of the Exhibition, hoped that it would grow into a Highland Folk Museum, and at the opening ceremony and in the accompanying literature she spelled out in unequivocal terms that the opportunity of preserving a past which was then slipping away fast beyond recall was the unquestionable duty of that generation, that this was 'the last chance', and that the shining example of the Scandinavian countries was there to emulate. She owned that there was plenty of ready interest in the Exhibition and that it generated new interest — it had about 20,000 visitors in seven weeks — but, at the same time and unfortunately, nothing came of it. The material, over 2,100 exhibits, that had been accumulated and was recorded in the published 136-page Catalogue was returned apart from some items which were purchased, but the resulting legacy of interest and goodwill meant that when the Highland Folk Museum was established, some of this same material found a permanent home there.

The value of such catalogues grows as the years

2. The sword, anvil and cooking pot of Donald Fraser, the Blacksmith of Moy, borrowed for the Highland Exhibition in 1930. The Smith, known as *Caiptin nan Coig*, the Captain of the Five, surprised and routed with four companions the column of troops on their night march from Inverness to Moy in an attempt to capture the Prince in February 1746.

pass, so the fact that over half a century has passed since the Exhibition enhances the value of the Catalogue rather than diminishes it. Not only is the *Highland Exhibition* Catalogue a tribute to Dr Grant's own efforts and industry but it is also a record of a unique accumulation of Highland and Island material culture. Many of the pieces were researched and provenanced items from museum collections such as the Anthropological Museum in Marischal College, Aberdeen, the Smith Institute, Stirling, and local burgh museums such as Elgin and Banff. Many of the pieces were lent by individuals throughout the Highlands and Islands who knew at first hand how the pieces were made or used. Dr Grant always lamented the subsequent disappearance of one object which was in the Exhibition and which she felt would have been a most valued addition to the collections of the Highland Folk Museum. Mr John Williamson lent a large wooden plough for the agriculture section of the displays. It was a plough that had been built for ox draught for the breaking up of waste land and old pasture on the farm of Cradlehall by Inverness. In the years following the Exhibition, it disappeared without trace, and although we have a graphic record of it, its loss is still keenly felt.

Dr Grant had been disappointed by the failure of the 1930 Exhibition to create a national folk museum, but she did not abandon her plan. Having received a

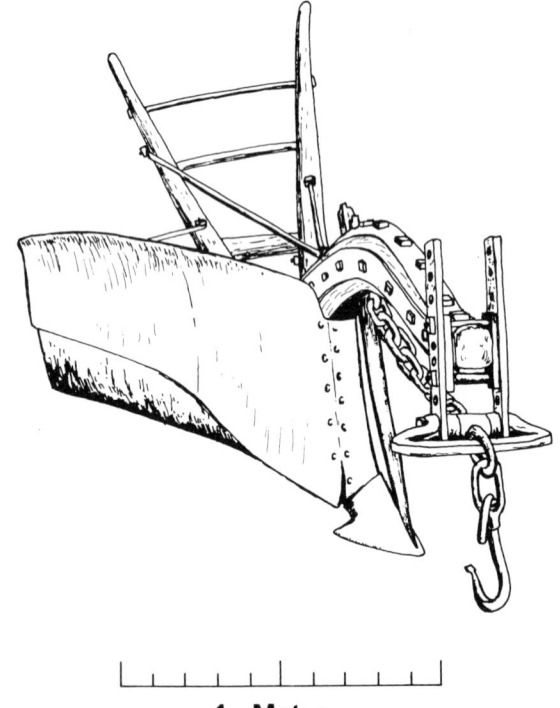

1   Metre

3. Large wooden plough built for draught by oxen and used on the farm of Cradlehall, Inverness. This was borrowed for the Highland Exhibition in 1930 and subsequently disappeared. (Drawn from a photograph by Colin Hendry, National Museums.)

legacy from her aunt, she decided that she now had the resources to do the job herself. Her experiences with the *Highland Exhibition* with its large General and Executive Committees had persuaded her that the advantages of running a museum with a committee might well be outweighed by the disadvantages of so doing. In fact she described how disagreement and acrimony before the Exhibition had threatened its success, and that Sir Alexander MacEwen, the Convener of the Executive Committee, had taken a firm stance and saved the day. She had learnt what might be said to be a general maxim: that a folk museum can really only be created and run by one person and that the vision and enterprise necessary for such an ambition could only be individual to be effective.

Dr Grant herself was due to go to Egypt when she saw the advertisement for a church on Iona. This was the redundant United Free Church, and Dr Grant contacted her lawyer to get a report on the building's roof. It was checked, approved and purchased, and in 1935 the Highland Folk Museum was set up on Iona. Hers was the bold and independent plan for which we in Scotland must be eternally grateful. We should also reflect, as she herself would from time to time gently hint, that it was not to our nation's credit that the torch which she lit with such conviction and inspiration was not taken up. She believed that, with the example of Skansen and Lillehammer available to us, the Highland Folk Museum would, in the fullness of time, become a National Museum. That was a very fair belief, and it goes without saying that the collections of *Am Fasgadh* are of national importance and of the status of national treasure. Dr Grant used to comment wryly that she had never expected to be stuck with it!

After three or four years on Iona, the collection was beginning to outgrow the U.F. Church building. Dr Grant saw that the island was not the right place for a museum of that type, and her own ambitions for it were becoming difficult to realise. It was so placed that people could not readily visit it in one day from their home or hotel. The Hebridean location, the charm and the ancient religious associations were not enough for an enterprise of that scope. A national folk museum movement showed no signs of developing, and Dr Grant felt that a mainland location would be a prerequisite for this to happen. She began to look for a different site and saw another church building at Laggan in upper Badenoch. She acquired it while recognising that the move there would be an interim measure only.

Dr Grant vividly described the move from Iona early in 1939 as a ghastly experience. The collection was packed by a removals firm but the weather deteriorated and Atlantic storms battering the island kept her waiting for three weeks. When eventually the collection was safely delivered to Laggan, a new threat appeared. The 1939-45 War had broken out and the County Council was considering the requisition of the church at Laggan as a store for the furniture and belongings of evacuees. Dr Grant wrote around desperately to gather support for her cause, and recounted movingly how she realised when the cause was won and the collection would be safe. She had looked for other sites for the Museum and examined one near Oban, one near Nairn, and properties near Grantown-on-Spey, a location which she would have preferred, but she found them all very expensive. She looked at the old Slaughter House and a mill at Kingussie before she acquired the house and three acres of Pitmain Lodge. Here at last was a central location on the A9 trunk road, and room to expand. The Highland Folk Museum moved there in 1944 and opened to the public on 1 June.

After fifty years of existence for *Am Fasgadh* and the growing awareness in the profession of the difficulties and complexities of running institutions for public consumption, we recognise and can better appreciate the single-minded effort and determination of Dr Grant in her enterprise. She herself referred to the creation of a Highland Folk Museum succinctly — that everyone said that it should be done and nobody was doing it, so she did it herself. We should also recognise that she was running *Am Fasgadh* by herself and meeting all the expenses herself. She received very little in the way of public support. The story of the creation and development of *Am Fasgadh* has been written by Dr Grant herself, and is at present in typescript form. Dr Grant gave up the Museum in 1954 for a well-earned retirement which she occupied industriously with her writing. The Museum property and the collections were purchased by the Pilgrim Trust which then presented them to the four Scottish Universities of St Andrews, Glasgow, Aberdeen and Edinburgh.[3] Dr Grant was awarded the MBE in 1959 and was made an Honorary member of the Scottish Country Life Museums Trust in 1977.

E

INTERIOR INVERNESS-SHIRE COTTAGE, THE HIGHLAND FOLK MUSEUM. KINGUSSIE. 8·276.

4. Interior and hearth of the Mainland Inverness-shire type of Highland house which Dr. Grant had constructed at the Highland Folk Museum in 1945.

The sequel to the early years has been described by the Curator, Mr Ross Noble, but on several occasions Dr Grant returned in conversation to two incidents in her experiences of collecting for *Am Fasgadh* in the late 1930s. They are both significant for the light they throw on the process of collecting for a museum and the knowledge and understanding of what a museum might be. When on a collecting 'foray' in Mull, she saw an old house near Bunessan on the Ross of Mull and it appeared to be deserted. She asked in the local shop to whom it belonged, and she was told that it was an old man in Glasgow who was unlikely to be coming back to the island again. Dr Grant explained her errand and asked whom she could contact for permission to find materials for the Museum. After a long rigmarole, she gathered that the old man had two nephews who could be contacted, and the shop-keeper agreed to get a message to them. Dr Grant subsequently went to some trouble the following year to go back to visit the same spot, and to her horror found the house empty and unroofed and the doors and windows removed. She went back to the local shop and asked what had happened to the house, and had the shopkeeper passed on her message? Yes, he

had passed on her message, but the two nephews had meanwhile unroofed the house and destroyed the contents. Naturally Dr Grant was crestfallen, and the shopkeeper, touched by her obvious disappointment, inquired if he might be able to find her something else. Yes indeed, was her quick reply, and he asked her if she would be interested in a potato dish. She said that that was just what she was looking for. He then produced it, but reluctantly, because, as he explained, he thought that she was too much of a lady and that such an ordinary object would not be at all suitable for a lady. This was of course a rare and fortunate find, a dish with wooden sides and basketwork base in which potatoes were served, the water draining off through the base into a handful of fodder which thus made a more tasty bite for the cow.

Dr Grant described vividly another of her ex-periences, and clearly the incident had burned itself into her memory and touched her deeply. For her work of collecting she was given an introduction to the district nurse in Tarbert, Harris. She knew that a local contact like this ensured introductions to other local families. The nurse directed Dr Grant to an old house in Tarbert where they had old things which the nurse was sure that they would probably let her have. When Dr Grant visited the house, the woman who answered the door had a look of desperation in her face. It transpired that inside her daughter lay very ill with diabetes. The woman was badly in need of money to buy the right food for her invalid daughter. She produced one or two items for Dr Grant, a staved milk coggie for example, and it was evident that she would have liked as much money as possible for these things. Dr Grant recognised the need and desperation, and made an offer. The woman was clearly relieved and gave Dr Grant heartfelt thanks. Dr Grant in her turn was glad to give the money and felt that she had really been of some help to this woman in her plight. She felt sure that she took the blessing of this woman back to *Am Fasgadh*.

It was clear from many conversations that the writing of her first book, *Everyday Life on an Old Highland Farm*, was a labour of love and an inspiration for Dr Grant. It generated a specialist knowledge which fed her later writings and the creation of the Highland Folk Museum. Dr Grant's uncle, Col. George Mackintosh, lent her the farm account book of her great great great grandfather, William Mackintosh of Balnespick, to make what she wanted of it. The material in the manuscript described the activities on the farm of Dunachton in the parish of Alvie in Badenoch between 1769 and 1782, but after the lapse of 150 years was not easy to understand and in places obscure. Knowing the locality of Dunachton and Alvie parish well, she was able to trace out the details in the manuscript on the ground. She became aware that some of these details were still self-evident, that much more had obviously disappeared and that more was disappearing in her own day. Dr Grant remembered vividly how an eighteenth-century stone drain was exposed by twentieth-century tile draining on the land of Dunachton. By coincidence, the old drain was dug up when she was herself researching the book in the early 1920s and she has described the incident elsewhere in print.[4]

Other historical detail was revealed in traditional knowledge surviving in the locality. She was friendly with a retired farmer in the area, Mr Duncan Davidson, and her conversations with him about farming in days gone by and the old language of farming fired her imagination and illuminated some of the obscure language of the account book. She has recently recorded in print her indebtedness to Mr Davidson.[5] Mr Davidson's great grandfather had been a tenant of 'old Dunachton', and figures in William Mackintosh's farm account book. When the Mackintosh tack on Dunachton in Strath Spey expired, the Davidsons had moved to Balnespick in Strathdearn with the laird's family. This may be taken as demonstrating a particular attachment between laird and tenant. Dr Grant herself was aware that to describe the strength of the old relationship between laird and tenant was distinctly unfashionable in historical research and writing. She would pose the fair question as to how common this relationship might have been and would suggest that if the tenant moved with the laird, this might be taken as an indication of the strength of attachment between laird and tenant. There could of course be other more substantial reasons for tenants moving, but Dr Grant used this evidence for the not unreasonable proposition that 'the lairds were not all monstrous as a class'.

Dr Grant described with a twinkle that as a member of the Free Church, Mr Davidson disapproved of old stories. Dr Grant loved to recall that in times long since passed, the old zest for storytelling meant that the first question asked after introductory compliments when meeting might be whether any Ossianic lore could be recited — *Am bheil dad agad air an Fhéinn?*[6] If the answer was in the affirmative, the whole community would foregather to listen to the stories. With the traditional enthusiasm, Dr Grant had asked him if he, Mr Davidson, had stories of the Fianna, but he had declined the question. Place names in the Eastern and Central Highlands such as Dun Yardill at Inverfarigaig on the south side of Loch Ness suggest that these stories had once exercised their magic in these parts. 'Dun Yardill' is the anglicised spelling of *Dun Dhearduil*, 'the Fort of Deirdre', and Dr Grant was certain that the stories of Deirdre and Cuchullin and the later Fingalian stories of Oisean and Fionn MacCumhail were localised in the Highlands; the Fenian host after all was said to lie in Tomnahurich in Inverness. She felt that Mr Davidson would have been familiar with stories about the Fianna, but that for very good reasons of his own he would not tell them and she did not press him. As a strict and devout Seceder, he had said with obvious deliberation: 'It would not be profitable to talk about these'.

Mr Davidson was, however, interested in the old ways and doubtless enjoyed talking about them, readily recalling the life of the community which he had known as a boy. For Dr Grant's purposes it was certainly more profitable to talk about these. The work of herding which is described in the farm account book bulked large in the life of the unenclosed communities. It was commonly a job for the children, and Mr Davidson was of a generation of children that had been sent out to herd beasts. He remembered it as pleasant, no doubt if and when the weather was fine, but also boring and irksome. The Education Act of 1872 made attendance at school compulsory, and its enforcement meant the decline in the use of children for herding and, incidentally, the spread of wire fencing as farmers were forced to find alternative methods of controlling beasts.

Mr Davidson explained traditional terms such as *tathing* to Dr Grant. This was the word used to describe poinding or folding of cattle to increase the fertility of selected areas of ground, a practice that had been carried on in Kingussie within the memory of those living in the early twentieth century. On land divided into infield and outfield, *tathing* was used to restore some fertility to the outfield prior to cropping with oats or bere. By having this described at first hand, Dr Grant gained an insight into the old-style farming which was characteristic of the husbandry of Dunachton in the mid-eighteenth century as evidenced by the manuscript account book.

Old tools and implements were also passing into obscurity and could also be explained by Mr Davidson. Dr Grant always quoted *caibe làir* as an example. This was the Gaelic name for a flauchter or turfing spade which was used for skinning the turf from the soil for opening peat banks, building turf walls or for roofing buildings. It was important to register and record such a word not only because the tool and the term were passing into oblivion but also because of its use in the locality. By the early twentieth century, Gaelic was beginning to pass out of use in the Central Highlands, to the extent now that knowledge of the use of the flauchter spade and the Gaelic term *caibe làir* sixty years ago might seem surprising. Who in the area today would know what the *caibe làir* was and how it was used? Dr Grant collected several of these spades for *Am Fasgadh* and used to comment that it must have been commonly used until relatively recently judging by the numbers of spade blades which could still be picked up.[7]

At the age of 61, Elsie Grant's achievements were given formal recognition in the award of an honorary degree, the degree of Doctor of Laws, by the University of Edinburgh. The laureation address delivered on that occasion in Edinburgh should be quoted in full to allow us to reflect on the contemporary perspective on Dr Grant's success during the inter-war years and on her later career still to come in 1948. Academia naturally gave priority then to her major publications although this is the common denominator of so many of these awards. But the uniqueness of her achievement is reflected in the fact that the major part of the address is given over to her museum work.

University of Edinburgh
The Hon. Degree of LL.D.
Laureation Address 2nd July 1948
Miss Isabel Frances Grant

Miss Grant's *Social and Economic Development of Scotland before 1603* was a pioneer work. Later writers may criticise it here and there, but it is significant that those who criticise are also content to use. This work had been preceded by her *Everyday Life on an Old Highland Farm, 1769-1787*; it was succeeded by her volumes of *Everyday Life in Old Scotland*. In the former Miss Grant reconstructed the daily life of the people on a Speyside farm in Inverness-shire; in the latter, she strove to depict the everyday life of the people of Scotland from the earliest times to the nineteenth century. Both works contain a wealth of material and information. But Miss Grant was not content to rest there. The printed word and the illustration was not enough. She set herself next to the task of saving and preserving old implements, old domestic utensils, old furniture — anything that revealed the life of times past — and hence grew up her well-known Museum.

At *Am Fasgadh* we can study with her guidance the ancient Scottish traditions of spinning and weaving, the development of agriculture from its primitive state and the local arts and crafts, not forgetting those of the kitchen. And we can learn better there than elsewhere, and with more sense of reality; for not only is the collection the largest of its kind in Scotland, private or public, but there a beginning has been made of placing things in their proper setting. For under the trees, stand the Black House of the Outer Isles, with the 'clack' mill and the Soay sheep beside it, and the earlier and the more recent Speyside cottages, complete in the likeness of bygone days, waiting, as it were, for the return of their former inhabitants.

In our admiration for such a Museum, we must not forget that it has been created by Miss Grant single-handed and from her own resources.

Services to learning such as these merit a doctor's gown, and in the name of the Senatus Academicus, I ask you to confer upon Miss Grant, the Degree of Doctor of Laws.

5. Laden dresser and shelves in a fisherman's house on the Kincardineshire coast in the 1920s. Dr. Grant drew particular inspiration from the fishing community of Muchalls beside which she and her family lived for a time.

THE WRITTEN AND PUBLISHED WORK OF
DR. I. F. GRANT MBE TO 1985:

1921　An Old Scottish Handicraft Industry, in *Scottish Historical Review* Vol. 18 (1921), 277-289.

An account of the knitted stocking and worsteds industry in the north-east of Scotland from the second half of the seventeenth century until approximately 1920.

1922　The Survival of the Small Unit in Industry, in *The Economic Journal* Vol. 32:128 (1922), 489-505.

An Old-time Scots Fisher-wedding, in *The Country Heart* No. 7 (July-September 1922), 259-260.

The wedding of Margaret Christie and Alexander Johnstone which took place about 1854 was described by the former in her widowhood to Dr Grant who turned the account into this article. The account is no more specific than to say that the couple lived in an East Coast fishing village. In fact the events took place in Muchalls in the parish of Fetteresso, Kincardineshire, between Stonehaven and Aberdeen. Dr Grant's father, Col. Grant, had retired from the Army and taken a lease of Muchalls Castle, and Dr Grant herself met and conversed with an older generation of fisher folk. Another fact which is not mentioned in this article but which undoubtedly made an impression on the author was the unbroken tradition of adherence to the Episcopalian Church which was characteristic of many of the East Coast fishing villages. Dr Grant described the intense feeling of pride with which fisher families preserved the memory of service in the rectory or of family descent from those who had been held up in creels and sculls for baptism by interned non-juring Episcopalian ministers in the Tolbooth of Stonehaven. Dr Grant lamented the fact that no research had been carried out on the East Coast Episcopalian line-fishing communities. She frequently used to describe in conversation the furniture and plenishings of the fishermen's houses in these communities when there were twenty or more thriving fishing villages between Aberdeen and Montrose.

1923　The Glen of the Bruachaig, in *Industrial Peace* Vol. 11 (1923), 142-144.

A description of a deserted settlement in a glen of the East Central Highlands. Dr Grant excelled at reconstructing the past of Highland communities which were subtly different from the archetypes of popular history or imagination such as the Highland village of the West Coast or Hebrides. For example, she never underestimated the extent and effect of the 'Clearances', but she always emphasised that, taking the Highlands as a whole, the picture was much more complex than the assumption of straightforward mass eviction. Here she touches on a point which she has developed elsewhere in suggesting that a deserted settlement was not 'cleared' but was literally priced out of existence in the course of the nineteenth century: 'Sixty years ago [i.e. 1860s] it went out of cultivation, when Scotch agriculture felt the staggering blows of the abolition of corn duties and the competition of the corn lands of the New World'.

1924　*Everyday Life on an Old Highland Farm 1769-1782* (Longmans Green and Co., London 1924), 292pp.

Dr Grant's first book and a 'milestone' as she described it in her own self-education. It includes with analytical text the carefully edited farm accounts of William Mackintosh of Balnespick. The accounts describe the methods of pre-improvement agriculture, of infield and outfield and arable land held in runrig on the farm of Dunachton in Badenoch. Balnespick was the tacksman or leaseholder of Mackintosh, and he farmed the land with joint-tenants and sub-tenants. In this area which is now so sparsely populated, Dunachton itself supported at least 240 people on holdings which varied from farms of over sixty acres to crofts of under three acres. The tacksman has been sternly treated by the contemporary eighteenth-century pen and by latter-day historians, but Dr Grant's study has served to demonstrate that not all tacksmen were bad and that clearly definable virtues flowed from a benevolent paternalism.

The Income of Tenants on a Scotch Openfield Farm in the Eighteenth Century, in *The Economic Journal* Vol. 34:133 (1924), 83-89.

The Development of a Highland Estate, in *The Estate Magazine* Vol. 24:11 (1924), 823-828.

A study of the transition from pre-improvement agriculture to an enclosed farm or modern agricultural holding on the estate of Newton in Kirkhill parish on the Beauly Firth, six miles west of Inverness. The study uses a rent roll of 1749-1754 and an estate map of 1786, and sets the specific information against the generalising information of the Statistical Accounts. A useful detail which the map exemplifies is the creation in the late eighteenth century of a cottar population which provided seasonal labour for the farms, worked small allotments of land and plied a trade, in this case as weavers.

Lion Street, in *The Town Crier* No. 38 (June 1924), 6. Childhood memories of Brompton Road, London.

1925　Highland Rural Industries, in *The Edinburgh Review* Vol. 241 (1925), 167-184.

1926　*A Candle in the Hills* (Hodder and Stoughton, London [1926]), 319pp.

A futuristic novel of a Britain under totalitarian rule in which counter-revolution is inspired and led by a single woman. The loyalist rising begins in the Highlands. The story reflects the contemporary currents of social and economic unease such as the Russian Revolution and at home the decline in heavy industries, rising unemployment and the General Strike.

The Social Effects of the Agricultural Reforms and Enclosure Movement in Aberdeenshire, in *The Economic Journal: Economic History* Vol. 1 (1926), 89-116.

Published as a supplement to *The Economic Journal*. The Journal was edited by John Maynard Keynes for thirty-two years from 1912. Dr Grant worked as a researcher for Keynes, and it gave her great pleasure to publish in his Journal and especially to have two supplements to her name. This article offers an analysis of the descriptions, statistics and comparisons in the 'Old' and 'New' Statistical Accounts for Aberdeenshire.

The Highland Openfield System, in *Geographical Teacher* 13 (1926), 480-488.

1928 Some Accounts of Individual Highland Sporting Estates, in *The Economic Journal: Economic History* Vol. 3 (1928), 405-411.

The Highland Openfield System, in *Report of the Commission on Types of Rural Settlement*, Union Géographique Internationale 1928, 102-113.

1929 The Eighteenth Century Laird and his Estate Accounts, in *The Scottish Land and Property Federation Notes for Members* No. 14 (August 1929), 14-21.

1930 *The Social and Economic Development of Scotland Before 1603* (Oliver and Boyd, Edinburgh 1930), 594pp.

Reprinted by the Greenwood Press in 1971 and republished in London by Shepheard-Walwyn in 1982.

A wide-ranging work of summary and synthesis with notable contributions of her own to the subject area such as an account of the feuing movement in the sixteenth century (Section II, Chapter 5), an investigation of the economic history of the Highlands including the origins of the clans and an account of the evolution of the tacksman system.

The Highland Exhibition Inverness 4 August to 20 September 1930 (Robert Carruthers and Sons, Inverness 1930), 13pp.

Introductory booklet, illustrated, published in advance of the Highland Exhibition.

The Highland Exhibition 1930 (Catalogue of the Highland Exhibition, Inverness, 4 August to 20 September) Inverness 1930, xxxii, 136pp.

The Early History of the Highlands [*Northern Chronicle*, Inverness], 18pp.

1931 *In the Tracks of Montrose* (Alexander Maclehose, London 1931), 319pp, maps, index.

Everyday Life in Old Scotland (George Allen and Unwin, London), 3 Parts; (1) *Part 1: to 1603*, 1931, 156pp; (2) *Part 2: From 1603 to 1707*, 1931, 291pp; (3) *Part 3: From 1707 to the End of the Nineteenth Century*, 1932, 407pp.

George Allen and Unwin published the three parts in a single volume edition in 1932.

Grande-Bretagne: le déclin des métiers domestiques parmi les femmes de l'Écosse, in *XVe Congrès Internationale d'Agriculture* (Praha 1931), VIIe Section, 1-6.

Paper presented at the 15th International Agricultural Congress in Prague, 5-8 June 1931.

Scotswomen's Work in the Eighteenth Century, in *The Scots Magazine*, New Series Vol. 15:2 (1931), 115-123.

1932 *A Masque of Sir Walter Scott. A Series of Episodes from his Life and Works* (Grant and Murray, Edinburgh 1932), 172pp.

The Scottish People. A Masque of Sir Walter Scott's Characters, Sir Walter Scott Centenary Celebrations 1932, 40pp.

The Kingis Quair, typescript, 24pp.

James I reads his folio, and the incidents which he recalls are acted out.

1933 Old Highland Cottages, in *The Scots Magazine*, New Series Vol. 19:3 (1933), 231-234.

1934 *The Economic History of Scotland* (Longmans Green and Co., London 1934), 295pp.

This work was reprinted by AMS Press, New York in 1976 and by the Greenwood Press, London in 1979.

1935 *The Lordship of the Isles. Wanderings in the Lost Lordship* (The Moray Press, Edinburgh 1935), 514pp.

Facsimile edition published in 1982 by the Mercat Press, 55 South Bridge, Edinburgh. The first significant assessment of the Lordship of the Isles of the fourteenth and fifteenth centuries presented in the framework of travel in the districts associated with successive phases of the Lordship. Dr Grant always regretted that the academic framework of references had been omitted from the book on the advice of the Publishers.

History made Tangible — Culross, in *Scotland*, Vol. 1:6 (1935), 34-36.

This article records the early work of rescue of decaying buildings by the National Trust for Scotland, then newly formed. Dr Grant's turn of phrase contains a personal note of patriotism which provides a rallying-cry as relevant today as it was when written: '. . . here survives the outward setting of the life of old Scotland, in its pride and poverty, and quarrelsomeness and earnest searching after the things of the spirit — the setting of the events that fashioned the national destiny — and the setting of the daily life of the forebears of whom one is sprung'.

1936 *Proposals for the establishment of a Highland Folk Museum*, typescript.

1938 Highland Homestead, in *Scottish Pavilions Official Guide, Empire Exhibition Scotland 1938* (Glasgow 1938), 50-51.

1945 *Am Fasgadh. The Highland Folk Museum at Kingussie: Inverness-shire* (Glasgow [1945]), 7pp., illustrated.
Introduction and guide leaflet for the Highland Folk Museum including some valuable insights into the development of the Museum in its first decade.

1948 Am Fasgadh, the Highland Folk Museum, in *The Scottish Art Review*, Vol. II: 2 (1948), 2-6.

1950 *Let's See Badenoch and Rothiemurchus* (William S. Thomson, 3 Cameron Square, Fort William [1950]), 32pp., 28 black and white photographs.

1951 Life under the Clan System, in *Scotland's Magazine*, Vol. 47:8 (August 1951), 24-28.

1952 *The Clan Donald: A Gaelic Principality as a Focus of Gaelic Culture* (W. and A. K. Johnston, Edinburgh and London 1952), 32pp.
Reprinted in 1958. Second edition published in 1963 and reprinted in 1970 and 1972. Third edition published in 1979 and W. and A. K. Johnston and G. W. Bacon.

1953 *The Clan MacLeod* (W. and A. K. Johnston and G. W. Bacon, Edinburgh and London 1953), 31pp.
Reprinted in 1958. Second edition published in 1966 and reprinted in 1972. Third edition published in 1979.

1955 *The Clan Grant: the development of a clan* (W. and A. K. Johnston and G. W. Bacon, Edinburgh 1953), 30pp.
Dr Grant's third volume in the Johnston Clan Histories series.

1959 *The MacLeods: The History of a Clan, 1200-1956* (Faber and Faber, London 1959), 653pp., illustrated, map.
Dr Grant's clan history of the MacLeods is a notable contribution to this potentially barren type of history in that the lives and characters of the chieftains are not allowed to preclude discussion of the wider fields of the social and economic history of the clan folk as a whole, genealogical references do not clutter a proper historical framework and narrative, illuminating comparisons are made with a wide range of historical material, and the darker sides of clan history are met head on and dealt with honestly; for example Dr

Grant shows that the 22nd Chief was implicated in the infamous plot of *Saoitheach nan Daoine* to sell people kidnapped from Skye and Harris into slavery in North America.
The Macleods was republished in 1981 by Spurbooks, London with an epilogue by John MacLeod of MacLeod.

1961 *Highland Folk Ways* (Routledge and Kegan Paul, London 1961), xiii, 377pp., illustrated.
This invaluable text was published as a companion volume to Prof Estyn Evans' *Irish Folk Ways* (1957). Dr Grant dedicated it to the Friends of *Am Fasgadh*, and the book serves as a penetrating evaluation of Highland rural society and a detailed examination of the collections of the Highland Folk Museum. Few 'Folk Museums' are fortunate in having such a rich guidebook. Unlike other studies of Highland history, much material is drawn from the East Coast and the east central Highlands.

1962 Photographs for Remembrance, in *The Scots Magazine*, New Series Vol. 77:5 (1962), 439-448.
Account of collecting for *Am Fasgadh* in the 1930s, illustrated with photographs from the Robert M. Adam Collection.

1965 *Random Recollections of the Distribution of Local Types of Highland Cottages*, typescript, 17pp.
Deposited with Edinburgh City Libraries as a companion piece to the I. F. Grant Collection of photographs.

1969 *Angus Og of the Isles* (W. and R. Chambers, Edinburgh 1969), xi, 193pp., illustrated, genealogical table, map on lining papers.
Dr Grant wrote this book to explain and analyse the decline and downfall of the Lordship of the Isles in the late fifteenth century. The bare outline of facts is supplemented by improvisation and by imaginative and intuitive insight.

1975 *Highland Folk Ways* (Routledge and Kegan Paul, London, paperback edition).
This was reprinted in paperback in 1977 and 1980.

1978 A Little Town in the Hills, in *The Scotsman*, 1 July 1978.

1980 *Along a Highland Road* (Shepheard-Walwyn, London 1980), 198pp., maps, illustrations.
Survey of the historical background of an area of twelve miles of the modern A9. With her own deep personal attachment to Strathdearn in the centre of this area, Dr Grant writes with great feeling while also maintaining a fair measure of objectivity.

1981 *Everyday Life on an Old Highland Farm, 1769-1782* (Shepheard-Walwyn, London 1981), ix, 191pp.
This new edition of Dr Grant's first book includes a

new Preface, two maps and fifteen black and white illustrations, none of which was in the edition of 1924. The book is handsomely presented by her Publishers, Shepheard-Walwyn, in a book jacket reproduced from a specially woven sample of Mackintosh tartan.

1983 *Random Recollections:* stories from overseas, type-script incomplete, describing life in Malta and India.

Forthcoming:
Periods in Highland History (Shepheard-Walwyn, London).

Typescript:
The Making of Am Fasgadh.

Acknowledgements
I am most grateful to Miss Catherine Dickson for her help and encouragement in the preparation of this article, and I would also like to thank Mr Ross Noble, Curator of the Highland Folk Museum, for his interest and help in the work of putting on record some of Dr Grant's considerable achievements.

References
1. I. F. Grant, *The Highland Exhibition, Inverness, 4 August to 20 September 1930* (Inverness 1930), 7-8.

2. Rev. T. Sinton, *The Poetry of Badenoch* (Inverness 1906), 253.

3. R. Noble, The Changing Role of the Highland Folk Museum, in *Aberdeen University Review* 47 (1977), 142-147.

4. I. F. Grant, *Along a Highland Road* (London 1980), 83.

5. I. F. Grant, *Along a Highland Road*, 27.

6. I. F. Grant, *Highland Folk Ways* (London 1961), 131.

7. I. F. Grant, *Highland Folk Ways*, 118.

Reviews

Hungarian Folk Jewelry, (translated into English by Corvina Kiadó: Kner Printing House, Hungary, 1983: orders to Kultura, Budapest 62, P.O.B. 149, Hungary H-1389), 66pp. 17 colour, 43 b and w illus. Terézia Balogh-Horváth

In her small, well-illustrated book, *Hungarian Folk Jewelry*, Terézia Balogh-Horváth sets out to study the personal ornaments worn by the peasantry of her country in the nineteenth and twentieth centuries. Drawing on her own original researches and the information gathered in questionnaires sent out by the Hungarian Ethnographical Atlas, she provides a far wider survey than her title might suggest, summarising the whole history of jewellery in Hungary, a land where Western European fashions combined with Eastern influences to generate a tradition of intricate and sumptuous decoration.

The author discusses each item of jewellery in turn, analysing its origins, tracing its rise and fall in popularity and examining its varying functions. Finger rings, for example, were always important as status symbols, while earrings began as no more than ornaments but came to be prized for their supposed powers of protection against eye disease. Nor was this merely a stray superstition. The actual piercing of the ear lobe was what mattered, for as the author points out, the base of the ear is an acupuncture point as well as being the place where leeches were placed in order to drain off diseased blood.

There are many other fascinating insights in this splendid study, which not only makes available valuable comparative material for the expert, but provides a stimulating introduction for everyone who is interested in the psychology and evolution of personal adornment.

RKM

Virgins and Viragos. A History of Women in Scotland from 1080 to 1980, (London 1983), 365pp. 10 plates £13.50
Rosalind K Marshall

Dr Marshall's book traces the public role and private experience of women in Scotland from medieval times until the modern day. In the eleventh century women were dependent on the protection of their fathers or husbands, and their precarious lives were defined by their social position in a hierarchical society.

Until the nineteenth century domestic tasks, marriage and childbearing were their only sphere, with few but notable exceptions, mostly among aristocratic women. Gradually, as is well known, literacy, education and enlightenment ideas opened up other opportunities, most rapidly to the middle and upper classes, who increasingly played a part in business and the professions. The changing economy drew working-class women into burgeoning domestic service and work in factories.

The evidence of the early period is scanty, which makes the work anecdotal. The detailed examination of the medieval marriage contract is fascinating and shows that the law offered important protection to women. The gradual widening of the female sphere in the seventeenth and eighteenth centuries seems to be a product of growing prosperity and urbanisation. The development of Edinburgh as a centre of Society generated social mobility among both sexes (p. 182).

The lot of women in rural areas, however, changed very little. Their unrecorded lives were spent in childbearing and domestic work which had hardly changed since medieval times.

This is a most enjoyable book for its wealth of charming detail and variety of sources. Dr Marshall searches for the antecedents of the modern independent women and finds them: Black Agnes who defended the Earl of March's fortress at Dunbar in 1338 or Agnes Campbell, who became the King's Printer in 1716. She shows that in all ages some women achieved more than the private role of wife and mother.

But the lot of Scottish women in general did not change, and could not, until safer childbirth and techniques of birth control were developed. No other factor is so important in the process of change. The opening up of professional and business opportunities came slowly and involved small numbers of people. It is tempting to view the emancipation of women as a gradual process with its roots in earliest times; but this is not really valid. Certainly the urbanisation process expanded opportunities for men and women, but the fact remains that most women, up until 1914, like their medieval forebears, were primarily concerned with the work of the home. Only in the twentieth century have educational and political developments offered genuine choices to women and involved them directly with the process of government. As Dr Marshall reminds us, this means that power previously exercised within the domestic sphere can now, if it chooses, be exercised at work, in business, in the professions and in politics.

Jane Stanley

Muster Roll of Prince Charles Edward Stuart's Army, 1745-6, (Aberdeen 1984), 219pp. £12.50
Alastair Livingstone of Bachuil, Christian W H Aikman and Betty Stuart Hart, eds.

For more than forty years, members of the 1745 Association were anxious to compile a comprehensive Muster Roll of Prince Charles Edward's army, and the results of this lengthy research project have now been published by Aberdeen University Press to mark the opening of the National Trust for Scotland's improved visitor centre at Culloden.

In a brief introduction, Bruce Lenman analyses the military expertise of the Jacobite army and finds that, although sadly lacking in well-trained men, it had good weapons, the soldiers' resourcefulness was impressive, and not only in discipline but in humanity they far outdid their opponents. Had the desired French help arrived and made possible a Jacobite triumph, Mr Lenman believes that Britain would have been the better for their success. Religious tolerance would have been achieved more quickly, he feels, and what he terms the abuse of power by Westminster would have been curbed at the outset.

This is a controversial conclusion, of course, although not unfitting in a work which is in many respects a tribute to the men who fought with Prince Charles Edward. The Muster Roll itself runs to more than two hundred pages of carefully verified detail. Unlike previous lists, this one includes every soldier known to have been with the Jacobite army, not just those who were captured, transported or executed. Their names are conveniently divided into regiments, and each section is introduced by a short, clear history of that regiment's part in the Rising.

The geographical and occupational range of the men is fascinating, from an eighteen-year-old Perthshire pedlar to the Edinburgh wigmaker who became the Prince's personal barber. Genealogical interest apart, valuable studies of the military personnel will surely follow, and this elegantly presented volume should prove an invaluable reference work for all future historians of the period.

R K M

The Fishertown of Nairn, (Nairn Fisheries Museum 1983), 20pp. 25 illus.
Margaret Bochel

Although this publication covers a lot of ground in a short span, the heart of it is the days of the herring boom from the 1880s to the demise of the steam drifters in the 1930s. Miss Bochel has drawn on documentary sources to provide what might be called the statistical framework, but in the main the most interesting material and the inspiration have come from her memory, and that of her family and other descendants of the old fishing community.

As a background to the Nairn Fishertown Museum, the study concentrates on the general milieu rather than continuous detail. As the progressive silting of the harbour from the 1960s has choked off the presence of home-based boats, this recalls something that has reached the end of the line, rather than being an earlier part of a continuing tradition. The result is the sense of first-hand knowledge of a community but conveyed with historical perspective, a clear admiration for the tenor of the old ways which gives an attractive sense of enthusiasm, but does not cloud the clarity of the writing.

There were several balances which gave the community its character which are caught here — people who were 'harshly self disciplined, but kindly and generously disposed towards others', the sobriety and temperance which co-existed with considerable prosperity — important, as the fruits of industry were not wasted. The concrete expression of social and community spirit is covered — the seamen's Hall with its Library, the local choir and societies, the 'harbour parliament', and so on. Although not an economic study, that side is not neglected. The ownership of boats, the allocation of shares is touched on, and the field of ancillary trades is illustrated by the reproduction of eleven letters and invoices from various suppliers and chandlers, the letter-heads of which convey interesting social information as well.

What is evidently childhood memory gives a vivid sense of family life. There are also surprises, for instance that whole families lodged in Fraserburgh during the summer fishing season before the Great War, when a weekend breakfast could consist of steak and eggs. This stands in sharp contrast to the diet of most farm servants, who would not see fresh meat from one year's end to the next, except when the pig was killed or when snared rabbits or a braxy sheep came their way.

There are aspects recorded that perhaps lie beyond immediate memory and outside any printed record, but about which the reader would like to know more. For instance, earlier, during the summer herring fishing, the families would not lodge in Fraserburgh, but the women folk would stay in huts and tents on the shore and cook for the men. The details of such practices take us beyond the horizon of arrangements that we can visualise from our own experience into a much older world of native diet and house-hold arrangement. Again, what preceded the Band of Hope? Although the temperance movement is now itself part of history, it overlaid many social arrangements which were part of an older way of life and did not always have an outcome of thriftlessness and dissipation. These things may be accounted for generally, but in the light of this skilful portrait of a local community, earlier references of a local nature would have been valuable.

Other areas such as the line fishing have been only incidentally touched upon. Although statistically insignificant compared with the herring and even the latter-day seine-netting, it was a tradition that reached back to much older ways of doing, with more localised boat types and gear and organisation of smoke curing and selling through fishwives.

This publication is most attractively laid out, well sub-divided and with a balanced selection of halftone illustrations which complement the text well. Within the nineteen pages of its A4 format, on the whole it provides an excellent introduction to the Nairn Fishertown Museum in particular and to the character of a small Scottish fishing community in general.

G. Sprott

Scottish Studies
Scottish Studies is a Journal of the School of Scottish Studies, University of Edinburgh, and is published once a year. The annual subscription rate is £6.00 (U.S.A. and Canada $14.00); single numbers are £7.00. Orders as well as editorial correspondence should be sent to: The Editor, *Scottish Studies*, School of Scottish Studies, University of Edinburgh, 27 George Square, Edinburgh EH8 9LD.

Scottish Studies reflects the wide interests of the School of Scottish Studies in the social, cultural and intellectual history of Scotland, and many of its articles focus on aspects of oral tradition and material culture. The 'Notes and Comments' section includes reports on field work and research, and review articles and bibliographies are published from time to time. *Tocher*, published twice a year and available from the above address, annual subscription £2.00, concentrates on transcriptions of oral material on a variety of subjects from the sound archive of the School.

Ethnologia Europaea
Ethnologia Europaea is an international journal started in 1967 by a group of leading European ethnologists.

Its aim is to provide material of value for European ethnologists and also anthropologists, social historians and others studying the social and cultural forms of everyday life in recent and historical European societies.

Papers are mostly in English; any contributions in German or French have summaries in English.

There are two issues of about 100 pages each, appearing in June and December of each year.

Subscription rates are: Individuals: Danish crowns 140.00 including postage. Institutions: Dkr. 210.00 including postage.

The amount should be transferred in Dkr. to the postal giro account no. 7 29 98 77 in Denmark.

Subscription address:
Ethnologia Europaea
Hestehaven 3
DK-5260 Odense S
Denmark